GREER

POLICE REFORM IN MEXICO

POLICE REFORM IN MEXICO

Informal Politics and the Challenge of Institutional Change

Daniel M. Sabet

Stanford Politics and Policy
An Imprint of Stanford University Press
Stanford, California

Stanford University Press
Stanford, California

©2012 by the Board of Trustees of the Leland Stanford Junior University.
All rights reserved.

Printed in the United States of America on acid-free, archival-quality paper

Library of Congress Cataloging-in-Publication Data
Sabet, Daniel M., 1976– author.
Police reform in Mexico : informal politics and the challenge of institutional change / Daniel M. Sabet.
pages cm
Includes bibliographical references and index.
ISBN 978-0-8047-7865-7 (cloth : alk. paper)
1. Police administration—Mexico.   2. Police—Mexico.   3. Police professionalization—Mexico.   I. Title.
HV8161.A3S23 2012
363.2068'4—dc23   2011046226

Typeset by Westchester Book Services in 10/14 Minion.

Written in honor of those many police officers
who are fighting for a professional, honest police force.

Contents

Illustrations

Tables

Figures

Acronyms

Acronym	English	Spanish
AFI	Federal Investigations Agency	Agencia Federal de Investigaciones
AFO	Arellano Félix Organization	
CAAP	Sonora University's Police Support and Attention Center	Centro de Atención y Apoyo Policial de la Universidad de Sonora
CALEA	Commission on Accreditation of Law Enforcement Agencies	Comisión de Acreditación para Agencias de Aplicación de la Ley
CANACO	Chamber of Commerce	Cámara de Comercio
CIPOL	Intelligence Police Force	Cuerpo de Inteligencia Policial
CISEN	Intelligence and National Security Center	Centro de Inteligencia y Seguridad Nacional
CNDH	National Human Rights Commission	Comisión Nacional de Derechos Humanos
CONAGO	National Conference of Governors	Conferencia Nacional de Gobernadores
COPARMEX	Mexican Employers' Confederation	Confederación Patronal de la República Mexicana

DARE	Drug Abuse Resistance Education	Educación Preventiva Contra el Consumo de Drogas
DFS	Federal Security Directorate	Dirección Federal de Seguridad
FASP	Public Security Support Fund	Fondo de Aportaciones para la Seguridad Pública
GPS	Geographical Positioning System	
ICAC	Independent Commission Against Corruption	
ICESI	Citizen Institute for Insecurity Studies	Instituto Ciudadano de Estudios sobre la Inseguridad
INEGI	National Institute of Statistic and Geography	Instituto Nacional de Estadística y Geografía
LAPOP	Latin American Public Opinion Project	Proyecto de Opinión Publica de América Latina
MUCD	Mexico United Against Crime	México Unido contra la Delincuencia
NAFTA	North American Free Trade Agreement	Tratado de Libre Comercio de América del Norte
PAN	National Action Party	Partido Acción Nacional
PFP	Federal Preventive Police	Policía Federal Preventiva
PRD	Democratic Revolution Party	Partido de la Revolución Democrática
PRI	Institutionalized Revolutionary Party	Partido Revolucionario Institucional
PRONASOL	National Solidarity Program	Programa Nacional de Solidaridad
SIDEPOL	Comprehensive System for Police Development	Sistema Integral de Desarrollo Policial
SIEDO	Assistant Attorney General for Specialized Organized Crime Investigation	Subprocuraduría de Investigación Especializada en Delincuencia Organizada
SNSP	National Public Security System	Sistema Nacional de Seguridad Pública

| SUBSEMUN | Municipal Public Security Subsidy | Subsidio de Seguridad Pública Municipal |
| SUIC | Unified Criminal Information System | Sistema Único de Información Criminal |

Acknowledgments

THERE ARE MANY PEOPLE WHOSE HELP AND SUPPORT HAVE MADE this book possible. First, I would like to thank Georgetown University's School of Foreign Service for their generous funding and support for this research project.

I owe a great debt to colleagues at the National Strategy Information Center (NSIC), including Jeff Berman, Roy Godson, Jane Grabias, who gave me the opportunity to work with and learn about the challenges confronting Latin American police forces. During my time at NSIC, U.S.-based police officers Jorge Gaytan, Andy Mills, David Contreras, Don Gosselin, Manny Rodriguez, and Dennis Kenney helped provide me with a U.S. perspective on policing. In addition, numerous police and public officials in Mexico, Colombia, and Panamá helped me understand the challenges of institutional change in their respective departments, including José Luis Montoya, Alejandro Lora, Esther Cruz Martínez, Javier Salas Espinoza, Rosario Medrano, Francisco Javier Luna Poyorena, Fabián Galindo, Rafael Buelna Rodríguez, Humberto López Favela, Rafael Ramírez Leyva, Ivan De La Garza Santos, Aroldo Pérez Porras, Wilfredo Miranda, and Fernando Torres.

Several research assistants provided invaluable assistance throughout the course of this project, including Alejandro Hernandez, Diana Murray Watts, Marcos Baez Moreno, Carla Tena Unna, and Louise Ashton. Their many hours spent reviewing newspaper articles and government documentation, following up on information requests, and translating articles are very much appreciated.

There are a number of U.S.-based colleagues who offered valuable advice and food for thought in conversations and writings, and through their comments on drafts, including David Shirk, Andrew Selee, John Bailey, Shanna O'Reilly, Eric Olson, Robert Donnelly, Diana Negroponte, Lazaro Cardeñas, Jaime Arredondo Sánchez, Octavio Rodriguez, Shannon O'Neil, and James Creechan, and anonymous reviewers. The large and growing community of academics in Mexico working on issues of public security was enormously helpful in illuminating the complexities of Mexican policing. In particular, I would like to thank María Eugenia Suárez de Garay and also Elena Azaola, Antia Mendoza, Juan Salgado, Marcos Pablo Moloeznik, Marcelo Bergman, Arturo Arango, Carlos Silva, Marco Antonio Carrillo Maza, Ernesto López Portillo, and José Arturo Yáñez.

Close to two hundred people were interviewed as part of this research, and while I cannot mention each by name, I am grateful that they were willing to share their time and knowledge with me. I never ceased to be amazed by the openness, kindness, and desire to improve policing in Mexico. Several individuals played an invaluable role in facilitating the research, including Luis "El Barbaro Jefe" Manzanera, Fernando Torres, Ángel Briam Gutierrez, Julian Dominguez, Susana Alvarado Lopez, Martha Santana Valenzuela, and José Carlos Vizcarra Lomelí.

I also would very much like to thank the many police chiefs who not only participated in the study but opened the doors of their police departments, organized interviews, and provided documentation, including Lázaro Gaytán Aguirre, Javier Aguayo y Camargo, Juan Manuel Pavón Félix, Ramsés Arce Fierro, Carlos Huerta Robles, Alonso Ulises Méndez Manuell- Gómez, Alberto Capella Ibarra, and Julián Leyzaola Pérez.

Finally, and most importantly, I owe a great debt to Shanna and the rest of my family for their continuous love and support.

POLICE REFORM IN MEXICO

1 Two Realities

José Luis Montoya

In 1995, the National Action Party candidate (PAN—Partido Acción Nacional) won the mayorship of Mexicali, Baja California. It was the first time since Baja California became a state in 1953 that Mexicali would be governed by a party other than the traditionally dominant Institutionalized Revolutionary Party (PRI—Partido Revolucionario Institucional). The new mayor, Eugenio Elorduy Walther, promised to usher in a period of reform, and the local police force was a major focus for the new administration. José Luis Montoya remembers it as an exciting time. In 1996, he graduated from the newly created municipal police academy as part of the first generation of cadets to receive formal police training in Mexicali. He remembers that they felt special: like they were going to be different from the police who had come before them. As the police force purchased new equipment and police cars and invested in training and education, there was a sense that the Mexicali police were on a path toward modernization and professionalism.

After seven years of service, in 2003, José Luis Montoya was promoted to the position of supervisor, roughly the equivalent of a sergeant in many U.S. police forces, and given command over twenty men. He remembers his promotion fondly as his first opportunity to do policing the way that it was supposed to be done: working with citizens and doing honest police work. Recognizing that corruption was commonplace in the department, he told his men of his intentions and requested that anyone who was not in agreement ask to be removed from his command.

Montoya was assigned a dangerous low-income community with a history of drug dealing and consumption problems. Drug sales were technically federal crimes and not within his jurisdiction; however, the federal government did not have the capacity to enforce drug laws at the neighborhood level throughout the country. As a result, this major source of crime and violence went largely unaddressed. Moreover, it was common for municipal police to look the other way about drug dealing and accept a little money from dealers in exchange. Their technical lack of jurisdiction gave such deals political cover. In many respects, things had improved dramatically since Elorduy was elected mayor, but corruption was still a daily part of police work.

Montoya approached his supervisors and proposed attacking the drug dealing directly. He remembers arguing, "The federal and state police are not doing anything. You know that. At the end of the day, the community blames us for not fixing the problem. They don't care who is technically responsible." Today Montoya believes that his supervisors were complicit in the drug trade; at the time, however, they gave him the go-ahead. While wanting to go after local drug dealers seems like it should be part of the basic instincts of a police officer, Montoya's actions were somewhat revolutionary. Attacking drug dealers meant threatening agreements that had been made between the police and criminals. Even those police who shared Montoya's vision of an honest, professional police force were wary of the risks. His commanding officer warned him, "If the state police ever try to pull you over, don't stop. They are complicit and will plant drugs on you."

With at least tacit support, Montoya and his men began going after the several different drug-dealing groups in the community. One of the main gang leaders was a man by the name of Jazzan Manuel Torres García, known as "El Chango." He had connections to powerful drug traffickers and surrounded himself with strongmen. One of El Chango's muscle just happened to be a boyhood friend of Montoya's, and Montoya persuaded him to serve as an informant—another revolutionary break from standard municipal police practice in Mexico.

Using his friend and other informants, Montoya and his men busted several drug-dealing establishments. When the dealers would try to move locations, Montoya and his team, acting on reliable intelligence, were always one step ahead. The work was not easy, however. He caught some of his men accepting bribes, and several attempts were made to threaten and/or bribe him into accepting the status quo. In his own personal account, Montoya recounts one dealer stating, "You don't know for whom I work for. If you arrest me, they are going to kill you. You don't know how many people are behind me; here we have always been '*arreglados*' [colluding with the police] for years, and you are not going to come here and tell us what to do" (Montoya 2005). At one point a corrupt superior officer acting on behalf of the dealers ordered him to desist; however, according to Montoya, the officer was unwilling to put the order in writing, and Montoya persisted.

One day, El Chango came to Montoya's house in search of a deal. Theoretically, El Chango should not have known where Montoya lived, but the dealer informed him that fellow police supervisors had given El Chango the young officer's address. The dealer offered Montoya $2,000 a week, a surprising sum that was more than several months of his official police salary. The money was not just to look the other way. El Chango also promised to provide Montoya with intelligence so that he could arrest rival groups in the community. The deal would benefit everyone: El Chango would obtain a monopoly over selling in the community and Montoya would still get to make arrests. However, the young police supervisor rejected the deal, and two days later at 5 AM his men arrested El Chango.

The persistent Montoya stayed with the suspect for all of the arrest process to make sure that El Chango did not threaten or bribe his way to freedom. Montoya returned to his house later that morning and lay down to sleep. Minutes later his sister rushed into the room in a panic: their house had been set on fire. The flames were extinguished, but this was not the end. At 1 AM, a floral funeral arrangement arrived at his house with another threat. A short time later, his friend and informant was found dead.

Montoya went to the state police, who are responsible for the investigation of crimes, and told them everything he knew. Much to his satisfaction, El Chango was convicted. Had the story ended there, it might have been a success. However, El Chango, with the benefit of one of Mexicali's best lawyers, won on appeal and went free. He returned to running drugs and bragged that he had beaten the system and Montoya, expressing his intention to have the young officer killed.

With a $10,000 to $25,000 price on Montoya's head, the stress was at times too much. Fearing for his life and the lives of his wife and young son, he left the force. With few other options, he went public with his story so that, as he put it, "If tomorrow something happened to me, they [the authorities] couldn't argue they didn't know and with the hope that they would become interested and do something about it." Montoya eventually returned to the force, but he was not a hero in his department. He was viewed as too uncompromising and as a threat. By 2010, he no longer held a leadership position, instead patrolling alongside young officers he once taught in the police academy. He continued to see endemic corruption, even among those former cadets who were his students in a class entitled "A Culture of Lawfulness." Montoya acknowledges that the justice system failed him, but he remains as committed as ever. He stated in an interview:

> If I backslide, then others will as well. I don't feel like I have an alternative and just have to keep moving forward, adding my grain of sand and doing what I can. If I stop what I am doing, I can't expect that others will keep going. My father has scolded me. He calls me stupid and says I should take the easy way out like everyone else. But I tell him that this isn't what he taught me. He taught me to do the right thing and pardon me for believing in something and fighting for it . . . And you know what; my son is going to be worse than me.

This is a book about efforts to reform and professionalize Mexico's municipal police departments. Through a qualitative and comparative case study of four municipal police agencies in Chihuahua City, Hermosillo, Mexicali, and Tijuana, set against a survey of additional departments and supplemented by public opinion and other data, this book explores the challenges confronting police reform in Mexico's municipalities. I offer José Luis Montoya's story as an introduction because it illustrates a couple of important points. Montoya entered the force at a time that appeared to be a watershed moment in policing in Mexicali. There is consensus in the Mexicali law enforcement community that the force began to professionalize in 1995 with the election of an opposition party to power. But this begs the question: why then was Montoya still confronted by such pervasive corruption and ineffectiveness despite years of reform efforts?

The need to professionalize Mexican law enforcement has been widely recognized since the mid-1990s, and numerous political and police leaders have come to office promising to do just that. A host of policies, purges, and programs have been implemented, and police and police leaders point to a number of advances in recent years, including improved training, higher selection standards, better operating procedures, and improvements in technology and equipment. To be sure, the Mexicali police force is in most ways far better off than it was in 1995. Nonetheless a casual review of newspaper reports and public opinion surveys suggests that police corruption and ineffectiveness are worsening rather than improving. It appears as though there are two realities to Mexican policing: one of reform and one of stasis. This book will explore these two realities as it seeks to answer why so many reform policies have failed to produce meaningful institutional change.

Montoya's story is also a helpful introduction because it illustrates the many challenges confronted by those officers who want to change the way policing is done: corruption, jurisdictional conflicts, unsupportive leadership, criminals with the power to carry out reprisals, and a justice system that does not always deliver justice. While corruption is endemic in Mexican police forces, highly committed individuals risk their lives and some lose them for the security of their city and the integrity of their beliefs. Overgeneralizing about the police means ignoring the positive steps that have been taken and diminishing the contributions of those who deserve to be, although are usually not, treated like heroes. A central argument throughout this work is that reform requires incrementally building on the advances that have been made thus far. Police reform involves many challenges, but as this work will reveal, the erroneous perception that everything is wrong with Mexican policing ironically serves as an obstacle to meaningful change.

The Police and Reform in Historical and Comparative Perspective

Policing in Mexico got off to a bad start. Throughout Mexico's early history during the 1800s, the central government had varying degrees of control over the large and diverse country. In the mid-1800s, then-president Benito Juárez founded a federal police force known as the *"Rurales."* Attempting to govern amidst a civil war, the Juárez government was forced to embrace bandits to fill a portion of the ranks of the new police agency. Vanderwood (1992), in his history of Mexican policing, profiles commanding officers like León Ugalde, "an unmitigated and unmerciful bandit" who was bought off to fight the French and later given command of a rural police unit (58). The *Rurales* were founded to fight and dissuade crime, but they had a dual mission of repressing political opposition (López Portillo Vargas 2002). This dual mission would continue throughout much of Mexico's history and as such, the police and their political leaders placed a higher price on loyalty to the government than to the law. Rather than to protect citizens, their job was to protect the state. Writing about the years under the rule of the dictator Porfirio Díaz, López Portillo Vargas notes, "The Mexican state made a deal—impunity and a certain degree of autonomy in exchange for political loyalty" (112), a deal that appeared to continue in the decades of one-party rule (Gómez-Cespedes 1999). For some, law enforcement's historical antecedents appear to have foreshadowed today's crisis.

Of course, a historical perspective on policing tends to reveal an unsavory past in most countries (Vanderwood 1992). Case studies of policing throughout Latin America frequently note that police forces emerged to protect the state and/or elites rather than the citizens (Eaton 2008; Birbeck and Gabaldón 2009). Many contemporary studies of police misconduct recognize the sad irony that those entrusted to enforce the law are the very ones who abuse and violate the law for personal gain. A historical-rational choice, or political-economic approach, flips this argument on its head, however. Mancur Olson (1993) goes so far as to argue in his theoretical piece on the origin of government that predecessors of modern governments were roving bandits who learned that if they settled down as "stationary bandits," they could monopolize and rationalize theft in the form of taxes. In fact, scholars of police deviance note that absent accountability mechanisms, the discretion and secrecy under which police operate make misconduct probable—regardless of the ostensibly noble reason for having a police force (Sherman 1974; Kleinig 1996). From this perspective, police integrity rather than police misconduct is the historical anomaly.

A comparison with U.S. police history is illustrative of the extensive challenge to transitioning away from this norm of corrupt, politicized policing. While there are considerable differences in the two countries' economic and political histories, the United States is one of the few countries in the hemisphere that shares Mexico's highly decentralized police structure. Moreover, U.S. policing has slowly overcome many of the same challenges that Mexico's police currently confront. In many ways, the United States offers a better historical comparison than many Latin American countries, where police reform has focused on overcoming the legacies of relatively recent military dictatorships.

The early days of policing in the United States (1840–1930) was branded the "political era" of policing (Kelling and Moore 1998), a term that could easily be applied to policing in Mexico today. During this time, the police were part of their cities' political machines and took their command as much from political ward or district leaders as they did from their police chief (Fogelson 1977). The lack of organizational control over the police resulted in corruption, abuses of rights, ineffectiveness, and use of the police for political purposes. Warren Sloat (2002) uses court documents and commission reports to profile extensive corruption and abuse in the New York City police in the late 1800s. Although the police were overseen by a Police Board, the board was more of a tool to divide up patronage and ensure political allegiance. Commissioners representing Tammany Hall (the Democratic political machine) would appoint Democratic loyalists to the force and ensure their favored officers were promoted. Republican commissioners would do the same, and both sets of commissioners were able to get rich in the process through the sale of positions.

The extent of police abuses provoked the emergence of a progressive reform movement in many of the nations' major cities, led by groups such as New York's Society for the Prevention of Crime, the New York Chamber of Commerce, the Citizen's Municipal Association of Philadelphia, the Baltimore Reform League, and the Los Angeles Committee of Safety (Fogelson 1977). While their successes were limited, they laid the groundwork for political reformers and police leaders of the early and mid-twentieth century such as August Vollmer, J. Edgar Hoover, and O.W. Wilson, who helped transition the police from corrupt political appendages to autonomous, professional law enforcement agencies. To remove political influence, civil service reforms were introduced, and efforts were made to insulate the police leadership from the political process (Kelling and Moore 1988). Throughout the following decades, reform chiefs throughout the country's major departments introduced knowledge and psychological tests to police selection criteria, stressed officer education and training, expanded car patrols, improved and tracked uniform crime statistics, introduced accountability mechanisms, and began evaluating the police based on measurable indicators such as response times (Kelling and Moore; Grant and Terry 2005). The federal government also played a hand in promoting local reform. In 1964, the Law Enforcement Education Program (LEEP) was created and funded to encourage policing-related training and education throughout the country's academic institutions, and the National Institute of Justice was established in 1960 to promote research and advanced study of criminal justice and law enforcement issues.

While reformers made substantial advances, scandals of corruption and abuses of individual rights persisted. Following race riots in 1967, the 1968

Kerner Commission of the Lyndon Johnson administration (1963–69) found widespread racial injustices and insufficient internal review mechanisms to ensure police accountability. In New York City, the 1972 Knapp Commission, which grew out of the whistleblowing of policeman Frank Serpico, found systematic corruption throughout the department and an ineffective internal affairs unit. Contemporaneous and future commissions, such as the 1974 Pennsylvania Crime Commission, the 1991 Christopher Commission, and the 1994 Mullen Commission would continue to identify problems of police misconduct and insufficient accountability. These commissions gave rise to renewed efforts to improve selection criteria, create better procedures and systems for monitoring agents, raise police salaries, and strengthen internal affairs units, often with citizen oversight.

Police misconduct still occurs in the United States; however, it is no longer believed to be systematic, and professionalism is seen as the norm throughout U.S. departments. Reform was possible in U.S. municipalities; however, it was an extremely long-term process that required an active civil society, reformist police chiefs, separation between politics and public administration, public investigations into police corruption, federal involvement, and considerable economic resources. Reform might have occurred more rapidly in the hemisphere's other success stories, Chile and Colombia; however, institutional change in these two cases involved many of the same elements. Of particular importance to both—with particular relevance for Mexico—was the separation between politics and policing (Dammert 2006; Llorente 2006).

Unfortunately, this complicated professionalization process is only just beginning in Mexico. Arguably a concerted effort to professionalize Mexican law enforcement did not begin until around the time that Eugenio Elorduy Walther took office in Mexicali, which was during the federal administration of Ernesto Zedillo Ponce de León (1994–2000). Upon election in 1994, Zedillo's administration conducted a diagnostic study of the state of the country's police forces (Sandoval Ulloa 2000). The results were not encouraging. Investment in public security was minimal, estimated at .008 percent of the GDP. Despite so many departments, there were only forty-one police academies across the country; these offered, on average, 4.5 months of training, and many police never received any formal training. Of these forty-one academies, only fourteen required education up to the ninth grade. In fact, 56 percent of preventive police had only primary school or no education at all. In response to this reality, Arteaga Botello and López Rivera wrote in 1998,

It should be emphasized that the problems that police in Mexico suffer are not that different than those suffered by their colleagues in the previous century. Emigrated from rural areas, low levels of education, a life noted for violence and illegality, condemned to have to pay a quota to their superiors, as well as to use extortion to collect money: all of this accents the fact that the problems from 100 years ago still have not been resolved. (11)

Their research, a two-year undercover ethnographic study, paints a vivid picture of Mexican policing that at times borders on the unbelievable. They detail how illegality and corruption begin even before future police are admitted to the academy. In a world of low opportunity for Mexico's lower-income citizens, candidates enter the academy fully intending to participate in corruption. Some of the candidates have even committed major crimes in other jurisdictions or been fired from other police forces for serious offenses. The bribing begins immediately, as those conducting the entrance exams in health, knowledge, and psychology offer good marks in exchange for money. Corruption is taken as a given aspect of policing among both the cadets and the academy personnel. The academy director is quoted as telling the class,

> When someone tells about the things that his companions do—that is about the worst thing that can happen because everyone comes out covered in mud, and there can be even killings or jailing. Consequently, it is necessary to value the friendship and solidarity that we have between us, take care of one another, and don't gossip about what we do. (Arteaga Botello and López Rivera 1998, 57)

Corruption is even endorsed in the police ethics class, where cadets are taught to "steal with professionalism," by, for example, not extorting citizens but waiting for them to offer money. While supposedly guarding cars to prevent parts from being stolen during practical policing exercises, cadets accept money to look after specific cars and additional money to ignore thefts from other cars.

Once on the force, the corruption worsens. While not explicitly solicited, it quickly becomes clear that the young police are required to pay a quota to their commanding officer if they wish to obtain "good job assignments," which provide officers the opportunity to extort bribes. Police work, such as responding to crime, still occurs, but in a perverted form. The authors describe officers chasing and catching a burglar, beating him as a form of punishment, and then letting him go after taking all of the stolen possessions for themselves. The stories continue of police shaking down prostitutes, illegally detaining and abusing gang members, and seeking every advantage to make money. The study contains no heroes or villains, but rather a form of doing business that is simply accepted by everyone, from incoming police to police commanders to citizens.

Mexico's Police Forces Today

The Zedillo administration committed itself to changing this status quo, a goal presidents Vicente Fox Quesada and Felipe Calderón Hinojosa continued. The results of their efforts and those of governors, mayors, and police chiefs are mixed. On the one hand, there is plenty of evidence to support the claim that change has still not come to Mexican policing. Simply opening a daily paper in Mexico lays bare the continued problems faced by Mexican police forces. Nonetheless, the headlines obscure real changes that have occurred. The vast majority of police have received academy training, education levels of police are higher, and investment in public security has increased dramatically. Police officials and officers interviewed for this study expressed frustration at the citizenry's failure to recognize these advances. While conducting interviews for this study, I frequently found myself confronting two separate realities: the reality of police corruption, ineffectiveness, and abuse alongside an additional reality of measurable improvements in police professionalization.

Official statistics as of August 2009 placed the number of police in Mexico at 409,536 (See Table 1.1). When population is taken into account, Guillermo Zepeda Lecuona estimates that there are 351 police for every 100,000 people in Mexico and 299 police per every 100,000 people when the Federal District is excluded. Both these numbers are above the United Nations average of 225 and the recommended level of 280 police per 100,000 people, although some individual states fall below this mark (Zepeda 2009).[1]

Law enforcement in Mexico is divided by both geographical jurisdiction and function. Jurisdictionally, the police are organized into municipal, state, and federal police departments, each of which has different responsibilities. For example, the transport of drugs is considered a federal crime, and therefore, it falls under the jurisdiction of the federal police. Functionally, the police are divided into preventive and investigative departments. Preventive

TABLE 1.1. Breakdown of Mexico's police forces (August 2009)

Police force	Number	Percent
Federal police	32,264	7.88
Federal ministerial police and immigration agents	4,347	1.06
State ministerial police	26,329	6.43
State preventive police*	186,862	45.63
Municipal preventive police	159,734	39.00
Total Police	409,536	100

NOTE: *This number includes police from the Federal District, which are at times presented as municipal police and as of June 2007 included 77,132 officers.
SOURCE: Data from the Sistema Nacional de Seguridad Pública. August 30, 2009.

police departments operate at all three levels of government and are typically organized under the auspices of a Secretariat (Secretaría) or Department (Dirección) of Public Security. Their primary job is to conduct patrols, maintain public order, prevent crimes and administrative violations, and be the first responders to crime. The ministerial police, formerly known as judicial police, are organized under the auspice of a public ministry at the state and federal level and are responsible for investigating crimes and carrying out warrants. The transit police, responsible for enforcing traffic laws, are typically considered part of the preventive police; however, in some cases they are organized as a separate police force. In the face of enormous coordination problems among Mexico's over two thousand police agencies, the Calderón administration has sought to consolidate and unify policing. At the federal level, the Federal Police replaced the Federal Preventive Police and was provided investigative authority that had traditionally been reserved for the ministerial police. A handful of states have consolidated their investigative and preventive departments into one agency, and some states are moving ahead with a proposal to collapse municipal police forces into a unified state police.

Regardless of jurisdiction or function, however, there are three major (and related) accusations commonly leveled against Mexico's police forces. These include (1) corruption, or the use of public office for private gain; (2) ineffectiveness, or the failure to address crime problems; and (3) violations of human rights, including arbitrary detentions and physical abuse. Evidence of these three problems has produced a deep- seeded lack of confidence in the police, which perpetuates a vicious cycle: furthering corruption, making the police even less effective, and producing additional abuses.

The most salient aspect of police corruption is collusion with organized criminal groups. In 2010, there were an estimated 715 police killed in Mexico's drug wars (Cruz and Herrera 2011), up from 475 in 2009 (Herrera 2010), 429 in 2008, and 251 in 2007 (Otero 2008). While many are believed to have been killed for their opposition to criminal groups, such as Juan Manuel Pavón, the director of the Sonoran state police force, it is believed that many more died because of their complicity in organized crime. There is no shortage of examples of police found working in the drug trade, participating in kidnapping gangs, or looking the other way to criminal activity. Some of the disturbing events include:

- A USB drive recovered from a police raid on a safe house in Villahermosa, Tabasco, revealed a list of police receiving payments from Los Zetas, at that time the armed enforcers of the Gulf organization. The criminal group was paying over $400,000 a month to municipal, state, and federal police forces (El Universal 2008a). The payments ranged from a low $125 a week to $1,000 a week, this latter amount allegedly to the state police director (Gómez 2008). Similar payroll lists would also be discovered in 2009 in Nuevo León and Hidalgo.

- Two municipal police officers from Torreón, Coahuila, were arrested by federal police when they attempted to prevent the arrest of five individuals on drug charges. In response, according to federal reports, twenty-eight municipal patrol cars blocked the road as federal police were transporting the detainees. A confrontation resulted leaving one municipal police officer dead and two wounded (El Universal 2008b). Federal officials reported that municipal police were being paid between $200 and $1,000 a week to support activities of the Gulf organization (Medellín 2008a).

- The January 2008 arrest of organized crime leader Alfredo Beltrán Leyva was a surprise to the Beltrán Leyva brothers, one of Mexico's powerful criminal groups, because the man responsible for coordinating operations between the federal Attorney General's organized crime investigations agency (Subprocuraduría de Investigación Especializada en Delincuencia Organizada—SIEDO), Fernando Rivera Hernández, was on the organization's payroll for hundreds of thousands of dollars. The subsequent attempts by

Rivera Hernández and other SIEDO officials to free the younger
Beltrán Leyva brother led to their discovery and arrest (Benavides
2008).

These and many other salient stories have shocked the conscience of Mexican society and undermined citizen trust in the police. But corruption manifests itself in ostensibly less pernicious forms as well. The Latin American
Public Opinion Project's AmericasBarometer survey reveals that in 2010, 24.6
percent of Mexican survey respondents reported that a police officer had solicited a bribe from them in the last year, a percentage higher than any other
country in the region.[2] According to Transparencia Mexicana's 2010 survey of
15,326 households, individuals attempting to avoid a traffic violation reported
paying a bribe 68 percent of the time, an increase over previous studies dating
back to 2001, suggesting that the problem might be getting worse rather than
better. Other surveys have offered similar findings. The 2004 Latinobarómetro
found that a stunning 70.9 percent of Mexican survey respondents felt that the
probability of successfully bribing a police officer was either high or quite high,
a percentage far above any other Latin American country in the survey.

The second allegation, ineffectiveness, is highly related in the public's mind
to corruption and can be seen most visibly by the impunity of the drug cartels
and the inability of law enforcement to stop Mexico's increasing violence.
Since a conflict between organized criminal groups in 2005 for control over
the Mexican border city of Nuevo Laredo, there has been an exponential increase in organized crime-related violence that the Mexican state has been
unable to arrest or even slow down. According to government estimates, organized crime-related assassinations rose to 2,826 in 2007, 6,837 in 2008, 9,614 in
2009, and 15,273 in 2010 (Presidencia 2011). Ciudad Juárez offers the most visible example of the state's inability to stem the violence. Despite massive military deployments, federal police deployments, and a new municipal police
force, organized crime-related killings steadily rose from a mere 136 prior to a
conflict for control of the city in 2007, to 1,332 in 2008, 2,230 in 2009, and 2,738
in 2010. Standardizing these numbers by population is complicated because of
uncertainty over Ciudad Juárez's population in the wake a steady out-migration;
however, if we assume one million inhabitants, this would suggest a rate of 274
organized crime-related killings per 100,000 people. By comparison, New
Orleans had the highest murder rate in the United States, a much broader
category of killings, with an estimated 52.3 homicides per 100,000.[3] Fernando

Escalante Gonzalbo's (2011) analysis shows that state efforts to reduce violence throughout the country have been at best unsuccessful. In fact, he shows that violence has increased even in areas of concentrated state response.

Other high-impact crimes, such as kidnappings and extortion, also increased dramatically in certain cities as criminal organizations diversified their activities in response to competition and shifts in the drug market.[4] Nationwide, reported kidnappings had been down in the early 2000s from the 1990s; however, they rose from a low of 323 in 2004 to 1,163 in 2009 (SNSP 2010b). These statistics probably reflect an underestimation of the problem, as the majority of such crimes are not reported because of lack of confidence in the police and receipt of direct instructions from kidnapping gangs. As one study participant in civil society said, "The very police tell you that it is too dangerous to report kidnappings." Criminals and criminal groups have also diversified into extortion of businesses and protection rackets. Victimization surveys conducted under the auspices of the civil society group Instituto Ciudadano de Estudios sobre la Inseguridad (Citizen Institute for Insecurity Studies—ICESI) traditionally excluded extortion as a separate category of crime simply because it was not a common phenomenon. In 2008, however, their survey of over forty-five thousand respondents found that reported extortion was as widespread as the growing problem of car theft, affecting an estimated .87 percent of the adult population (ICESI 2009).

Table 1.2 presents three indicators over time and across Mexico's thirty-one states and the Federal District. Even though estimated victimization does not change from 2004 to 2008, the data show the dramatic increase in organized crime-related killings between 2007 and 2010 and a corresponding increase in perceived insecurity. It is important to note that Mexico's security crisis does not affect the entire country. Querétaro, for example, only witnessed a small number of organized crime-related killings (thirty-seven over four years), and only a small minority of the population felt insecure in their municipality (26 percent). In many states, however, most notably Chihuahua, an increasing majority feels insecure. It is safe to assume that this sentiment rose further in 2009 and 2010, and, in fact, in a national survey from October 2010 (MUCD 2010) found that 83 percent of those surveyed felt that insecurity had increased over the previous year.

To address this problem, the federal government has relied on the military to shore up the deficiencies of the police. Use of the military to complement or

TABLE 1.2. State-by-state comparison of crime

State	Percent victims of crime 2004	Percent victims of crime 2008	Total estimated organized crime-related killings 2007	Total estimated organized crime-related killings 2010	Total estimated organized crime-related killings 2007–10	Percent who feel insecure in their municipality 2004	Percent who feel insecure in their municipality 2008
Aguascalientes	13	16	37	46	152	24	63
Baja California	20	15	209	540	2,011	55	59
B.C. Sur	11	12	6	10	19	31	29
Campeche	6	11	8	10	31	33	33
Chiapas	3	5	57	77	304	40	33
Chihuahua	11	14	244	4,427	10,134	52	73
Coahuila	9	15	18	384	659	29	45
Colima	7	13	2	101	148	19	27
Distrito Federal	19	19	182	191	652	62	66
Durango	9	7	108	834	1,892	26	63
Guanajuato	8	11	51	152	516	34	50
Guerrero	8	7	299	1,137	2,727	32	52
Hidalgo	7	8	43	52	167	32	43
Jalisco	14	13	70	593	1,072	38	41
México	15	15	111	623	1,538	54	59
Michoacán	9	13	328	520	1,727	30	47
Morelos	12	10	38	335	538	47	55
Nayarit	6	11	11	377	453	19	27
Nuevo León	9	11	130	620	967	29	52
Oaxaca	8	5	62	167	438	26	32
Puebla	12	8	6	51	107	32	41
Querétaro	7	12	5	13	37	28	26
Quintana Roo	14	12	26	64	151	48	54
San Luis Potosí	6	9	10	135	187	24	39
Sinaloa	14	8	426	1,815	4,384	49	54
Sonora	14	15	141	495	1,253	39	39
Tabasco	.	.	27	73	200	.	.
Tamaulipas	.	.	80	1,209	1,475	.	.
Tlaxcala	7	6	0	4	13	25	36
Veracruz	4	4	75	179	452	30	36
Yucatán	14	6	4	2	25	23	27
Zacatecas	5	6	18	37	130	22	51
National	11	11	2,832	15,273	34,550	40	49

NOTE: While victimization data was available for 2009, ICESI publically stated their lack of confidence in the results. Data is not available from Tamaulipas and Tabasco because of surveying problems in those two states. Perception of insecurity in the state tends to be even higher than insecurity in the municipality.

SOURCE: Data from the Sexta Encuesta Nacional sobre Inseguridad, 2009, Instituto Ciudadano de Estudios sobre la Inseguridad A.C. Data on organized crime-related killings is from the Base de datos de estados y municipios sobres homicidios presuntamente relacionados a la delincuencia organizada en el periodo diciembre 2006 a diciembre 2010 made available by the Presidencia de la República.

supplement the police in law enforcement duties is not a new strategy. The military has long had a strong presence in the rural areas of the country, at times even serving as a de facto rural police force. It has also intervened in the urban areas, including the takeover of the police in Culiacán, Sinaloa, in 1977 (Riding 1980) and in Mexico's Federal District in 1996 (Lopez-Montiel 2000). The Mexican Supreme Court ruled in 1996 that the use of the military was constitutional in situations that threatened national security, but its role has always been controversial. While both Fox and Calderón offered their commitment to strengthening the police and returning the military to its barracks, they increasingly relied on the military as the primary vehicle to respond to organized crime-related violence. In the first few months of his administration, Calderón ordered massive military deployments of thousands of troops accompanied by smaller numbers of federal police and criminal justice officials to the country's various hot spots, including Michoacán, Baja California, Guerrero, Sinaloa, Tamaulipas, and Nuevo León. Throughout his administration, these operations would be reinforced and new operations initiated, including the most visible-yet-ineffective Operation Together Chihuahua (Operación Conjunto Chihuahua), which at its peak included some fourteen thousand military personnel.[5] In its 2009 annual report, the Mexican military stated that it had an average of 48,750 soldiers involved in combating organized crime (SEDENA 2009).

Use of the military has several practical advantages. It offers a large, well-disciplined force that can reassure insecure populations with its mere size. Its deployment also signals the public that political leaders are taking security threats seriously. In addition, while certainly not immune from corruption (as illustrated by a number of well-documented cases), the military is believed to be less susceptible than the police.[6] But the military is nonetheless a blunt instrument not meant for policing functions, particularly in urban areas. In Tijuana, for example, when the military replaced the municipal police force in the eastern half of the city in late 2008, it quickly became clear that the military lacked the local knowledge necessary to carry out police functions. Criminal groups responded with strategies as simple as removing street signs to confuse military personnel.

In addition, the extensive use of the military has led to a number of legal and constitutional controversies and the violation of individual rights. The military regularly searches private homes without warrants, circumventing criminal justice procedures. The human rights organization Centro Miguel

Agustín Pro Juárez Derechos Humanos found "at least fifty cases or generalized situations of human rights violations by the military," mostly in states
with a heavy military presence such as Chihuahua, Sinaloa, and Tamaulipas
(Brewer 2008, 12). These include fifteen reported cases where soldiers erroneously fired on civilians, such as the June 1, 2007 killing of five family members
in a car that failed to stop for a military checkpoint. In early 2009, Human
Rights Watch issued a report detailing seventeen "egregious" crimes committed by military personnel and condemning the military's de facto jurisdiction
over the investigation of crimes committed by its personnel (Human Rights
Watch 2009).[7]

Of course, the police also violate human rights, and, in fact, this is the third
accusation leveled against the police. The type of human rights abuse often
depends on the type of police department (Naval 2006). Allegations of torture
are more likely to be directed at ministerial police, while allegations of arbitrary
detention are more likely to be aimed at preventive police. Many abuses have
become national-level scandals, including several incidents of police abuse in
response to civil and uncivil protest activity. In 2004 in Guadalajara, police
repression of antiglobalization protestors resulted in, according to the National Human Rights Commission (Comisión Nacional de Derechos Humanos), nineteen cases of torture; seventy-three illegal detentions; and fifty-five
cases of cruel, inhumane, or degrading treatment (CNDH 2004). In 2006,
police from the State of Mexico clashed with protestors in San Salvador Atenco resulting in numerous alleged violations including arbitrary detentions,
torture, and even rape (CNDH 2006).

While these cases captured national attention, state and national human
rights commissions have documented violations and issued recommendations
for a variety of more day-to-day offenses. As such, there are numerous documented cases of police making arrests on private property without a warrant
(PDHBC 2007), stealing from alleged criminals (PDHBC 2006), inappropri-
ately using force resulting in death (PDHBC 2008), improperly treating minors
(CEDHSON 2007a), improperly transporting a detainee resulting in death
(CEDHSON 2007b), and many other violations.

Sadly, many violations occur precisely because of the distrust that exists
between the police and citizens. While police expect their commands to be
respected and often (for their own safety) view potentially innocent citizens as
suspects, citizens fear the police will abuse their authority. To offer one example given by an interviewee at the state human rights commission in Baja

California, when the police search a suspect with his or her hands up against a car or a wall, it is common practice to take the person's wallet to obtain identification. While the detainee has been ordered to face forward, the individual, distrustful of the police, will instinctively want to watch what the officer is doing with the wallet. The police on the other hand will tend to view the movement of the suspect as either a potential threat or a failure to respect orders, laying the foundation for the use of force. State human rights commissions have documented a number of similar occurrences (PDHBC 2004, CEDHSON 2005).[8]

In summary, this discussion illustrates that there have been rather serious and widespread incidences of corruption, ineffectiveness, and abuse. These have collectively produced a severe lack of confidence in the police. Perhaps the best indicator of this is the large amount of crime that goes unreported. ICESI's (2010) comparisons of crime reported through their victimization survey and official crime rates suggest that 78 percent of crime in 2008 went unreported. Public opinion polling also reveals a lack of confidence in the police. Only 25 percent of those surveyed by ICESI (2010) had some or a lot of confidence in the local police. While there was more confidence in the federal police (37 percent), there was much greater confidence in the military (55 percent). Similar findings can be found in variety of other studies. In the federal government-conducted 2007 National Survey on Political Culture and Citizen Practices (Encuesta Nacional sobre Cultura Política y Prácticas Ciudadanas) respondents rated the police on average a 5.55 on a scale from 1–10, below every other group besides political parties (5.3) (SEGOB 2005). Respondents to the academic AmericasBarometer survey rated the police dead last, 3.3 on a scale of 1–7 (or the equivalent of 4.7 on a scale of 1–10) (Parás and Coleman 2006). This resulting public distrust furthers a vicious cycle whereby citizens fail to report crime, provide the police with information, serve as witnesses, or work together with the police to address crime problems, factors that have been shown to be essential in addressing security problems and solving crimes (Cosgrove and Wycoff 1997; Bieck and Oettmeier 1998).

Despite the frustrating and disturbing evidence and arguments presented here, the story of Mexican policing is not entirely negative, and police and police leaders offer counterarguments to popular perception. Even in locations with such historic challenges as Tijuana, many police ardently defend their record. One interviewed line-level officer commented,

The police has changed dramatically. The Tijuana police is a police department with good technology and good tactics. I was in Sinaloa just 15 days ago giving a course and I can assure you that Tijuana has credibility and is known for best practices that are recognized in a number of states. Despite the problems, we have good quality police.

Tijuana's assistant chief across three municipal administrations, Julián Domínguez, also argues against this first reality of corruption, ineffectiveness, and abuse, contending that his personal story is testament to the quality of the police. He has risen up through the police ranks, has a law degree, and has been a member of an international policing association since 1982. He recognizes the perception of corruption, but from his point of view, he is living proof that popular perception is not always correct.

Police and police leaders also point to numerous changes within their departments. Education levels have risen dramatically. According to Zedillo's diagnostic study only 13.7 percent of police had a high school education in 1996 (Sandoval Ulloa 2000), but by 2010, this percentage had risen to 37.8 percent (SESNSP 2010). Over a mere three-year period from 2007 to 2009, public security spending in Mexico grew from 5.9 percent to 6.4 percent of public expenditures, and from 1.2 percent to 1.7 percent of GDP (Mendoza Mora 2009).

Government officials contend that there are now a host of tools to ensure the integrity of officers, including citizen attention offices, internal affairs agencies, state and national human rights commissions, intensive vetting programs, and Honor and Justice Commissions (Comisión de Honor y Justicia) to receive complaints, conduct investigations of misconduct, and hold officers to account. A number of departments and local governments have experimented with rather innovative policies. For example, when a 2007 investigative journalistic report discovered corruption in traffic stops established to detect drunk driving in Monterrey, Nuevo León, representatives from the state human rights commission were posted at the stop areas to monitor police behavior. In Tuxtla Gutiérrez, Chiapas, the municipal department replaced its traffic police with a well-trained entirely female force, which it was hoped would be less inclined toward corruption (Gutiérrez 2008). In Mexico State, Nezahualcóyotl's police force received a great deal of media attention for mandating weekly literature-reading programs to develop more well-rounded police (Gutiérrez 2006). In Guadalajara, police commanders were replaced by civilian commanders who had been selected from a public competition and specially trained. In Hermosillo, veteran police were removed from one sector of the city and policing services were provided entirely by cadets recently graduated from the department's new police academy.

Police leaders also claim that they are far more effective than commonly perceived. While they recognize the increasing organized crime-related violence, they argue that such crimes are outside of their jurisdiction. In the areas where they have full jurisdiction, local police contend that they are actually quite effective. Despite the increase in certain violent crimes and the rising sense of insecurity, police leaders point to crime statistics that show that overall crime rates have not changed much in Mexico in recent years (Escalante Gonzalbo 2009). While this surprising finding could be attributable to problems of data collection and biases in failing to include unreported crime, even homicides with the intent to kill, a more reliable official statistic, steadily decreased from 17.6 per 100,000 inhabitants in 1997 to 9.7 in 2007 until more recent increases from 2008 onward. More important, the ICESI victimization study, a civil society-led initiative, found approximately the same level of victimization in 2008 as they did in 2004 before the drug wars started (ICESI 2009).

In addition to the creation of the National Human Rights Commission (Comisión Nacional de Derechos Humanos – CNDH) in 1990, which was later made independent, given constitutional status, and replicated across the Mexican states, police leaders laud a variety of means to prevent abuses. Medical doctors examine arrestees, detention facilities are video monitored, police receive human rights training, officers are required to pass psychological evaluations to carry a weapon, rules restrict police from firing their weapons unless shot at, and Mexico does not have the problems of killings by police that have plagued other countries in the region, like Brazil and Venezuela. In interviews and surveys police commonly argue that practices that were acceptable even ten years ago are relatively rare today (Uildriks 2010).

How can one make sense of these rebuttals juxtaposed with the widespread evidence of police corruption, ineffectiveness, and abuse: these two realities? Have the police changed? As this research will show, the answer to this latter question is yes and no; the police have improved in measureable ways, but nonetheless, the police have still not realized meaningful "institutional change." In other words, even as education levels, training, and salaries have improved, the rules of the game governing Mexican policing remain largely the same. Throughout the course of this work, I will explore numerous policy developments and improvements; however, I find that reform has struggled under policy design, implementation, and institutionalization challenges, and that two areas of policing remain largely unaffected by reform: (1) patronage politics within the police promotion process, and (2) the absence of effective accountability mechanisms combined with continued tolerance of police corruption. It is not that policies have not been created to address these two problems, but as reformers have discovered, and as I will explore here, there is a wide gap between creating a formal policy and seeing it effectively institutionalized.

Reducing Corruption, Ineffectiveness, and Abuse

Given a situation where corruption, ineffectiveness, and abuse continue despite reform efforts to address these problems begs the question: why has meaningful institutional change not occurred in Mexican policing despite numerous reform efforts? This is the central research inquiry of this book. To begin to answer this question it is helpful to think about the factors that would encourage an individual officer to engage in actions related to corruption, ineffectiveness, and abuse, which I will broadly refer to as police misconduct, and factors that would incentivize an officer to engage in actions that are honest, effective, and protective of rights, which I will refer to as police professionalism.[9] Of course, this choice is probably not a dichotomous one, and there are varying degrees of misconduct and of professionalism, and shades of grey between the two. As such, individual behavior might fall along a continuum from extreme misconduct to extreme professionalism.[10] Following Sanja Kutnjak Ivkovic (2005), Table 1.3 divides the explanations for the choice between misconduct and professionalism into (1) individual, (2) organizational, and (3) external or society-wide factors. Each of these broad categories can be

TABLE 1.3. Factors affecting police professionalization

Individual-level factors	Organizational factors	External factors
(1) basic demographics, (2) psychological factors, (3) professional development	(1) selection and recruitment, (2) training, (3) salaries and benefits, (4) procedures, (5) resources, (6) opportunities for advancement, (7) accountability mechanisms	(1) local political system (2) organized crime, (3) citizens and civil society (4) higher levels of government, (5) the military and larger criminal justice system

broken down into component parts that can either negatively or positively impact professionalism.

Individual-Level Factors

In their study of criminality, Wilson and Herrnstein (1985) present the decision to engage in criminal behavior as the result of a cost-benefit analysis comparing the net rewards of the crime to the net rewords of non-crime. Acts of corruption by public officials have been portrayed in a similar light (Rose-Ackerman 1999).[11] Building on this approach yet recognizing that not all individuals respond exactly the same way to similar situations and similar information, Klitgaard (1988) argues that the decision to engage in corruption is also a function of the moral cost of corruption multiplied by an individual's professional level of development. In other words, those who are ideologically or normatively constrained from misconduct will be less likely to engage in such behavior regardless of the potential benefit.

Other authors have dug further, opening the black box of the individual and exploring why some individuals are more resilient to the temptations of corruption and abuse than others. They have found a variety of demographic and life history factors that might correspond with either misconduct or professional action. Research in the United States has shown that education levels, peer associations, income level, prior criminal behavior, prior military experience, and motivations for joining the police all might have an impact on propensity for misconduct or professionalism (Kutnjak Ivkovic 2005). Still others have moved beyond demographics and probed into different psychological factors that might explain variation in conduct. For example, some individuals are more risk averse than others (Brockhaus 1980). Kohlberg (1981) argues that individuals operate at different levels of moral reasoning, ranging from those who follow rules to avoid punishment to those who act out of personal conviction.

While these studies provide insight, and while individual-level explanations for misconduct or professionalism are compelling, they are potentially misleading in a context where misconduct predominates. Historically, police chiefs have favored individual-level explanations for police corruption, ineffectiveness, and abuse. Known commonly as the "rotten-apple theory," a focus on individual-level factors suggests that incidences of misconduct are isolated, deviant behavior, and the product of a few rotten apples. This perspective obscures the reality that perfectly good "apples" often become rotten because they are inside a "rotten barrel" (Sherman 1974). Itself confronted with a rotten barrel, the Knapp Commission (1972) concluded in its report that, "The rotten-apple doctrine has in many ways been a basic obstacle to meaningful reform" (6–7).

To illustrate, individuals with a propensity toward misconduct should be weeded out by selection criteria long before they are ever put on the street. If we return to the Arteaga Botello and López Rivera (1998) study discussed above, we see that even a shallow investigation of the incoming cadets would have revealed numerous red flags. In their research on police corruption in Miami, Burns and Sechrest (1992) conclude that about three quarters of the eighty officers dismissed or suspended following a scandal in the 1980s were brought on to the force during a period of relaxed selection standards. In New York City, the Mollen Commission (1994) found that 20 percent of those officers fired in the proceeding six years never should have been allowed onto the force. In other words, what appears to be attributable to individual factors could often be prevented by organizational rules.

Organizational Factors: The Institutional Rules of Policing

Given that systematic problems of corruption, ineffectiveness, and abuse exist, there is clearly a need to focus attention on the broader institutional rules that can encourage professionalism. Institutions are often misunderstood as the *formal* governing structures, laws, and rules, but scholars of institutional analysis define them far more broadly. Douglass North (1990) defines institutions as the "rules of the game in a society or, more formally, the human devised constraints that shape human interaction" (3).[12] These rules can be formal or informal, and together they serve to "reduce uncertainty by establishing a stable (but not necessarily efficient) structure to human interaction" (North, 6). While obviously much harder to study than formal policies, informal rules can be equally or even more important.

Formal rules can change rapidly, particularly in a response to a crisis. Weyland (2008) notes how crisis leaves policy makers casting around for solutions. In his specific examples, perceived successes of economic liberalization and social security privatization in some countries produced a demonstration effect that led to rapid adoption in a number of other countries. Similarly, policy makers in Mexico have been casting about for solutions in response to the country's security crisis, which has resulted in rapid policy changes, such as militarization, consolidation of existing police forces, and creation of new forces. Nonetheless, the success of these sometimes-dramatic formal policy changes depends on the informal rules of Mexican policing and politics. North (1990) notes that:

Although formal rules may change overnight as the result of political or judicial decisions, informal constraints embodied in customs, traditions, and codes of conduct are much more impervious to deliberate policies. These cultural constraints not only connect the past with the present and future, but provide us with a key to explaining the path of historical change. (6)

A great deal has been written on the informal rules within the police and police culture (Sherman 1974; Drummond 1976; Azaola Garrido and Ruíz Torres 2009; Suárez de Garay 2009; Uildriks 2010). Uildriks (204) writes, "The absence of a rule of law culture and the presence of more or less hidden informal networks and decision-making structures outweigh the importance of formal bureaucratic rules and structures." Formally, promotion is based on merits, but informally, it depends on political connections and personal trust. While accepting bribes is against the rules, informally, mid-level police commanders might require their subordinates to pay them quotas.

Informal rules emerge through a process of learning. Mantzavinos, North, and Shariq's (2004) "pragmatic mental model" posits that people learn what actions produce positive outcomes and which do not, and they adjust their beliefs accordingly, creating "cognitive path dependency," which guides individuals' future actions. When a critical mass of people arrives at the same conclusions, informal rules about the way things are done consolidate and reproduce, yielding "institutional path dependency," which creates incentives for others' future actions. Police quickly learn if corruption is punished, tolerated, or encouraged and if professional policing or developing the right connections offers the best ways to rise up through the police ranks. After decades, corruption tolerance and clientelism have become a consolidated part of Mexican policing.

The example of weak accountability mechanisms in Mexican policing is illustrative of the primacy of informal rules. Most Mexican police departments have a formally established Honor and Justice Committee that is responsible for sanctioning police misconduct; however, in practice, these committees and other agencies responsible for investigating the police are often unable or unwilling to carry out their mandate. Accountability mechanisms might have considerable authority on paper and very well-laid out rules governing their operations; however, these might be undermined by informal rules and practices tolerant of corruption. In Mexicali, as in many police departments, it is formally established by law that police are to report any act of misconduct by a colleague. On paper, failure to do so requires dismissal from the force. And yet, the city's internal affairs agency reported receiving no corruption complaints from police officers despite the recognized pervasiveness of corruption. The infamous informal "code of silence" cannot be easily superseded by formal legislation.

As such, Mexico's numerous formal mechanisms to detect and sanction police abuses in Mexican law enforcement, such as Honor and Justice Commissions, citizen attention offices, internal affairs sections, and human rights commissions, exist alongside pervasive misconduct and have failed to result in institutional change. This problem is not unique to Mexico. There is evidence that accountability mechanisms have been either underfunded, co-opted, or designed to fail in a variety of countries in the hemisphere, including Argentina (Meagher 2004); El Salvador (PDDH 2007), Guatemala (Arias and Zúñiga 2008), and Brazil (Macaulay 2002), to offer a few examples.

While formal policies can seek to alter this status quo, as Elster (1986) explains, individuals' actions are highly interdependent on one another: the *rewards* an individual receives for her actions depends on the choices and actions of others, and therefore, her *choices* depend on those of others. Those who would benefit from change will only receive the rewards of change if others adopt the new rules as well. To continue the example, if the informal rules tolerate corruption and dictate that promotion is based on connections rather than merit, a young officer in the force who forgoes the benefits of corruption gains little beyond moral satisfaction in return. Her corrupt colleagues are not likely to get caught, and she will not be promoted or rewarded as a result of her honest policing. While some officers may have a sufficiently strong moral compass to avoid misconduct in this institutional environment, others will not. The result is a self-enforcing vicious cycle.

Beyond this generalized collective action problem, reform faces an even more serious challenge from those actors with a strong stake in the current system. Reform could mean a dramatic decrease in illegitimate income, loss of rank within the department, firing, and even prosecution. For these actors, reform represents a zero-sum game. In his study of police reform in Latin America, Ungar (2011) summarizes this problem by quoting Bachrach and Baratz (1970, 58):"While advocates of change must win at all stages of the political process—issue recognition, decision, and implementation of policy—the defender of existing policy must win at only one stage in the process."

As regards the implementation challenges confronted by police reform initiatives, authors such as Pressman and Wildavsky (1979) long ago noted that the development of a policy does not ensure its implementation or its success. The former chief of police in Tijuana, Júlian Leyzaola Pérez, related how he was contracted by the mayor-elect of another Baja California municipality to review the public security plan of his predecessor and to help create a new plan for the incoming administration. Leyzaola reviewed the old plan and returned to the mayor-elect, handed him the original document, and stated, "Here is your plan." According to Leyzaola, the mayor-elect looked at the plan and replied, "But you didn't change anything." Leyzaola responded, "Yes, all you have to do is implement it."

As a result, this research is concerned with not just the formal rules but the informal rules, and not just policy design but actual implementation. Throughout the course of this research I will explore a number of important aspects of police reform, including (1) recruitment and selection criteria, (2) training, (3) salaries and benefits, (4) operational and administrative procedures, (5) resources and equipment available to officers, (6) opportunities for advancement, and (7) accountability mechanisms. There is general consensus on the importance of these elements of police reform, and the theory linking them to professionalism is fairly self-evident. Good organizational practices in these seven areas will allow departments to (1) recruit and select the best candidates; (2) train them in the tactics of policing as well as inculcate professional norms; (3) offer salaries and benefits that permit officers to meet their needs, raise a family, and live with dignity without resorting to corruption; (4) provide clear guidelines on proper and improper behavior; (5) offer sufficient tools to meet police objectives; (6) provide opportunities for advancement that reward honesty, effectiveness, and protection of individual rights; and (7) identify and remove officers who do not live up to the standards of professional policing.

Chapter 2 and subsequent parts of this volume will explore several of these aspects of reform and discuss the implementation challenges reformers have confronted. Surprisingly, even once reform efforts have overcome policy design and implementation challenges, they still risk being overturned by subsequent administrations. In other words, implementation does not ensure institutionalization. It is one of the unfortunate aspects of politics in Mexico that each administration seeks to clearly distinguish itself from its predecessor, even when the predecessor is from the same party (Guillén Lopez 1996;

Merino 2006b). New administrations typically reappoint all top- and middle-management positions throughout the bureaucracy, and at times do not honor agreements made by previous governments. This is particularly problematic at the municipal level where administrations only last three years, resulting in constant turnover and policy change. It is not uncommon to hear members of civil society quip that municipal officials spend one year learning the job, one year working, and one year preparing for what they will do at the end of the administration. This brings the discussion to the importance of factors external to the police department.

External Factors: The Policy Subsystem

Just as officers operate within a police agency, police agencies function within a broader context, or what Paul Sabatier (1993) calls a "policy subsystem." Policies enacted by a police chief can impact the internal incentives within the police department, but they do not necessarily address the incentives created by the political system, criminal justice system, or the wider society. In fact, the institutional rules governing police departments are embedded within formal and informal rules governing public administration and local politics. Beatriz Martínez Murguía (1999) writes, "Without a doubt, the professionalization of the police is indispensable. Nevertheless, it is not sufficient. The complexity of the problem, as we have explained it, requires structural transformation." (168). In other words, the problems are so entrenched and so diverse in their manifestations that they go far beyond the areas of influence of individual officers, commanders, or police chiefs. It is not just the police barrel that is rotten.

According to Sabatier (1993), policy subsystems include a diversity of relevant actors operating within institutional and resource constraints. This research systematically explores incentives created by five aspects of the external environment: local politics (Chapter 3), organized crime (Chapter 4), day-to-day interactions with citizens (Chapter 5), organized civil society (Chapter 6), and the federal government (Chapter 7). Additional external actors, such as other police departments, the courts, the penitentiaries, the state legislators, and the military, also impact the police and police effectiveness; however, they do not receive systematic treatment here.

In the context of municipal public security in Mexico, the most important of these external actors is the mayor. In Chapter 3, I argue that the limits to police professionalization are the product of several interrelated institutional rules that affect not just the police, but many aspects of municipal public administration. The end result is a municipal government that is guided by the discretion of individual leaders rather than strong institutions. This personalization of politics prevents policy continuity between constantly changing administrations and results in a tendency to continually reinvent the wheel, a problem that is further exacerbated by the informal rules of patronage, which ensure frequent turnover of police commanders and appointments based on loyalty rather than merit. Despite a popular perception that the failure of police reform is primarily the result of organized crime and a lack of leadership, I argue that shortcomings are principally the product of the rules of Mexican politics and *too much* leadership. This conclusion is supported by evidence of an unusually successful police reform effort in Chihuahua during a time of relative insulation from politics.

Although organized crime is not the primary obstacle to police reform, it is by far the most visible negative external factor. Mexico has become home to a number of organized criminal groups, who have diversified from drug trafficking into a wide variety of criminal activities requiring a compliant or corrupt police force. Many journalistic accounts have boiled down the calculus of police corruption to the simple formula "the bullet or the bribe"; officers either accept money from organized crime or they will be killed. Chapter 4 will examine in detail the negative impact of organized crime on the police and the challenges to creating accountability mechanisms to detect organized crime infiltration.

In theory, citizens could provide a counterbalance to the threat posed by organized crime. Effective citizen oversight could reduce the opportunities for misconduct, increase the probability of being caught, and ensure sanctions. As residents, citizens have a wealth of information about criminal activity in their communities that could help law enforcement wage a more effective battle against crime. As taxpayers, citizens can support increases in public security budgets and pay for officers. Unfortunately however, because of deep-seeded mistrust between citizens and their police, residents rarely play these important roles. On the contrary, citizens are often willing participants in police corruption. Nonetheless, an active civil society that on the one hand uses and expands political opportunities to monitor and hold public officials accountable, and on the other hand supports and works with the police, represents perhaps the best hope for meaningful change. Chapters 5 and 6 explore the ambivalent relationships between citizens and civil society and their police.

The final empirical chapter, Chapter 7, examines the role of the federal government in promoting reform. Recognizing the limitations of local efforts, the federal government under the Calderón administration has taken unprecedented steps to create incentives for municipal police professionalization. As public security is a municipal responsibility, there are limits to what the federal government can obligate municipalities to do; however, the federal government has successfully used the power of the purse to incentivize reform. In order to receive the Municipal Public Security Subsidy (Subsidio de Seguridad Pública Municipal—SUBSEMUN), municipalities must match a certain percentage, submit their officers to "integrity control tests," and implement new administrative and operational procedures. The program is well designed, but like other reform efforts, it confronts considerable implementation and institutionalization challenges.

Chapter 8 lays out the conclusions of the research project. By examining the implementation and institutionalization challenges, the informal rules of municipal governance, the threat posed by organized crime, the ambivalent relationship with citizens, and the inadequate vertical accountability mechanisms, this research is able to provide a fairly clear answer to the question: why has reform fallen short of meaningful institutional change? Given the current situation of insecurity, corruption, and violence, it is hard to be optimistic about Mexico's municipal police forces, and, in fact, pessimism is endemic throughout Mexican society and even within police departments. Under such challenging conditions, maintenance of the status quo becomes a self-fulfilling prophecy. In light of these failings, Mexico is considering removing policing authority from its municipalities and subsuming the municipal police into state forces. Despite the good intentions of this proposal, the findings presented in this book suggest that restructuring the police will amount to yet another change in the formal rules that falls victim to persistent informal practices of patronage, corruption tolerance, and constant policy and personnel change. Nonetheless, this research suggests that an active civil society, willingness to identify and "reform" specific informal rules, and effective federal incentives offer a path to meaningful change.

Three outcomes are possible as Mexico progresses through the current security crisis. First, it is possible that political leaders will continue to introduce new policies, new reforms, and new efforts to professionalize the police that will fail to rewrite the informal rules of Mexican policing or alter the status quo of corruption, ineffectiveness, and abuse. As scholars such as Thelen (1999) note, however, path dependency need not be deterministic. Committed long-term "muddling through" might move Mexican police departments and society slowly along the continuum toward professionalism. While perhaps the most likely, under this second scenario (as occurred in the United States) progress will likely be measured in decades rather than years. Third, it is possible that Mexico is in a period of what Baumgartner and Jones (1993) called "punctuated equilibrium," whereby continued scandals will have mobilized and motivated civil society, political parties, and the police to produce meaningful institutional change. This last option, while perhaps the most naively optimistic, is not outside of the realm of possibility. Civil society mobilization is at a historic high, the justice system is transitioning to an accusatorial system with oral trials, and there are renewed efforts to professionalize the police at both the local and federal levels. While it is hard to be too optimistic given the reality of the drug war, police corruption, ineffectiveness and abuse, change is possible.

Methods and Research Sites

To understand the challenges of municipal police reform in Mexico, this book employs a variety of research methods. At its core, this research is a comparative study of four municipal police departments, including the Chihuahua Municipal Public Security Department (Dirección de Seguridad Pública Municipal de Chihuahua) in Chihuahua City, Chihuahua; the Mexicali Municipal Public Security Department (Dirección de Seguridad Pública Municipal de Mexicali) in Mexicali, Baja California; the Tijuana Public Security Secretariat (Secretaría de Seguridad Pública de Tijuana) of Tijuana, Baja California, and the Hermosillo General Public Security Department (Dirección General de Seguridad Pública de Hermosillo) of Hermosillo, Sonora. Data from these cases are complemented by a survey of a broader selection of some of the country's major municipal departments, including Monterrey, Nuevo León; Guadalajara and Zapopan, Jalisco; San Luis Potosí, San Luis Potosí; Mérida, Yucután; Mexico D.F.; Ahome (Los Mochis), Sinaloa; Cuernavaca, Morelos; and Torreón, Coahuila.

The four research sites were selected to control for cultural, economic, and political factors. Several studies have noted cultural and attitudinal differences among South, Central, and Northern Mexico (González, Minushkin, and Shapiro 2004), and focusing on Northern Mexico controls for potential cultural variations. Three of the cities are about the same size, with 2010 populations of 819,543 in Chihuahua, 784,342 in Hermosillo, and 936,826 in Mexicali, while Tijuana is larger with a 2010 population of 1,599,683. The states of Baja California, Sonora, and Chihuahua all have among the strongest economies in Mexico. Using indicators such as state-level gross domestic product, investment, and employment, Campos Serna et al. (2004) rank Baja California, Chihuahua, and Sonora second, third, and sixth (respectively) in economic performance of the thirty-one Mexican states and the Federal District. Finally, all four cities have had competitive political elections for at least a decade and a half, and all three states were on the cusp of Mexico's political transition. Chihuahua elected its first opposition mayor in 1983, Hermosillo in 1982, Tijuana in 1989, and Mexicali a short time later in 1995 (Arreola Ayala 1985). As such, the case selection controls for important cultural, economic, and political factors. In addition, the four cities offer an environment that should in theory be more favorable to reform than other parts of the country. This allows the analysis to rule out overly deterministic alternative explanations for the failure of reform. For example, insufficient economic resources are constantly put forward as the overarching obstacle to reform. While economic factors are unquestionably important, the four research sites contain more wealth per capita than most Mexican localities and far more wealth than many lower-income countries, suggesting that the obstacles to reform are much greater than simple economics.

Each of the four departments is considered a "preventive" police force. As such, their responsibilities are to maintain order, enforce municipal regulations, prevent crime, and be the first responders to crime. The departments in Mexicali, Hermosillo, and Tijuana also include traffic police, who are responsible for enforcing traffic laws and responding to traffic accidents. In Chihuahua, however, this service is provided by the state police. Chihuahua, Hermosillo, and Mexicali all have forces of just over one thousand men and women, and Tijuana has a force of over two thousand. None of the departments is responsible for investigating crimes, a task that falls to the ministerial police organized under the offices of the state and federal attorneys general.

At the time this research was initiated in 2007, the selected cases varied on what could be considered the dependent variable: successfully implemented and institutionalized police reform. Chihuahua City, while not without challenges, had achieved a certain degree of professionalization absent in almost all other Mexican police departments. In 2007, the Altus Global Alliance gave the city's police stations its highest marks out of a large sample of stations selected from throughout the developing world, and in 2004, the department received an award from then- president Vicente Fox Quesada. The department's most salient distinction, however, is as the first police department in Mexico to be accredited by the U.S.-based Commission on Accreditation of Law Enforcement Agencies (CALEA). CALEA is a Section 501(c)(3) nonprofit organization founded in 1979 as a joint effort by several prominent U.S. law enforcement executive associations. It certifies police agencies for maintaining a body of standards covering many aspects of policing and is accepted by public security practitioners and experts. Obtaining accreditation is rigorous, time-consuming, and expensive, and requires that departments comply with up to four hundred standards. As a result, however, Chihuahua has distinguished itself in a number of ways, including requiring a high school degree for admission onto the force and for promotion, mandating annual in-service training for all officers, developing a rigorous set of operational procedures, creating a merit-based promotion process involving citizen participation, working with an active citizen public security council, and maintaining a high rate of sustained financial investment in police equipment and resources. By contrasting Chihuahua with the other three cases in Chapter 3, I am able to show how the relative insulation of the Chihuahuan police from the informal rules of Mexican politics allowed for continuity in personnel and policies and subsequent advances in reform not experienced in the other three research sites.

On the other extreme, Tijuana has suffered from a number of setbacks to reform. For example, during the 2004–07 administration of Jorge Hank Rhon the department relaxed rather than strengthened selection criteria and training standards in an effort to put more police on the street. There is evidence that criminal elements took advantage of these relaxed standards to infiltrate the police, exacerbating long-standing problems in Tijuana's force. While the department's subsequent leadership has worked to purge the agency of corrupt elements, new revelations of police corruption constantly emerge. Tijuana's police owe their underdevelopment to the strong presence of the Arellano Félix organization, and in Chapter 4 I focus on Tijuana to explore the deleterious impact of organized crime on the police. In just the first half of 2008, the following stories captured the headlines of the local paper:

- An attempted robbery of an armored car, which was frustrated by police, resulted in the killing of one of the suspects who turned out to be a municipal officer with one year on the force.
- After a youth who claimed to have "connections" was detained, a municipal officer with a historically clean record arrived at the station

and made threats in an attempt to obtain the youth's release (Andrade 2008a).

- A major shoot-out took place between two rival groups within the Arellano Félix organization (AFO). Sixteen people were killed in the incident including a municipal police officer fighting on the side of one of the rival groups (Frontera 2008b). The weekly newspaper *Zeta* (2008) alleged that ten other municipal police participated in the fighting.
- Three police officers were detained along with fifty-five others in a police raid of what would become known as the "narcobautizo," a baptism for the child of a member of the AFO (Andrade 2008b).
- Mexicali police detained a band of kidnappers, two of whom were Tijuana municipal police (Murillo 2008).

In 2007, Mexicali was moving in the direction of Chihuahua. The city was not without its scandals: former police chief in the 1990s Antonio Carmona Añorve had been arrested and sentenced for ties to the Arellano Félix criminal organization. Nonetheless, Mexicali's police was one of the first departments to require that its incoming cadets have a high school degree, and it too would eventually obtain CALEA accreditation in 2010. Hermosillo got off to a late start and did not even begin systematically training police cadets until 2001. As of 2011, only 65 percent of its officers have been through formal academy training. Nonetheless, Hermosillo has also been home to innovation and was one of the first departments to track its police vehicles using geographical positioning systems (GPS).

There is a risk in developing a research design in a constantly changing policy arena, and many things changed in the research sites over the four years of this research project, which was conducted between 2007 and 2011. A protracted organized-crime conflict in Chihuahua state beginning in 2008 and skyrocketing crime rates undermined the credibility of the Chihuahua force, resulted in the replacement of its reformist police chief with a retired military general, and produced backtracking on some of the department's reform policies. Rather than detract from the conclusions of this analysis, however, this unexpected change only reaffirmed the challenge of institutionalization and the primacy of the informal rules of Mexican politics. Changes in Chihuahua do, however, highlight an important limitation of this research. Although this study focuses on the *process* of police reform, it is impossible for reformers in the real world to ignore policing outcomes. Reform is unlikely to lead to immediate reductions in crime, and yet, at the end of the day,

Chihuahua's reform project depended on positive outcomes. Conversely, in Tijuana, a drop in organized crime-related violence and the successful efforts of a hard-nosed police chief dramatically improved the reputation of the Tijuana department.

Across the four research sites a number of activities were conducted, including a total of over 150 structured interviews with police, police leaders, and members of civil society during initial visits to the research sites in 2008, and follow-up visits in 2009 and 2010. These interviews were supported by an analysis of thousands of newspaper articles concerning the police and public security in each of the research sites, including *La Frontera* and *Zeta* in Tijuana, *La Crónica* in Mexicali, *El Imparcial* in Hermosillo, and *El Diario* and *El Heraldo* in Chihuahua. Finally, a study of municipal government annual reports and development plans published over a period of ten to twelve years, and a review of human rights recommendations by state commissions as well as other primary and secondary source documents offered additional historical perspective.

To place these four cases within the national context, a detailed survey was developed and sent to the forty largest municipalities in the country. In addition to Chihuahua, ten departments responded to the survey, including: Monterrey, Nuevo León; Guadalajara, Jalisco; San Luis Potosí, San Luis Potosí; Mérida, Yucutan; Ahome (Los Mochis), Sinaloa; Cuernavaca, Morelos; Puebla, Puebla; Torreón, Coahuila; Zapopan, Jalisco; and Mexico's Federal District. Given the likelihood of response bias, it is safe to assume that the responding municipalities are more advanced in the policy areas of concern than their peers who did not respond to the survey. As such, the data is not intended and should not be interpreted as representative of the rest of Mexico's large municipalities; however, it does offer a snapshot of the state of many of the country's most important departments.

An additional forty interviews were conducted with police, public officials, and members of civil society from throughout the country, including interviews with federal officials in Mexico City about federal efforts to incentivize reform. Furthermore, Chapter 5 uses survey data collected by the Citizen Institute for Insecurity Studies (Instituto Ciudadano de Estudios sobre la Inseguridad, A.C. – ICESI), a survey with over forty-five thousand respondents over multiple years intended to offer representative samples of fourteen Mexican municipalities, including three of the research sites, and comparative survey data from the Latin American Public Opinion Project's AmericasBarometer.

It should also be mentioned that the research benefits indirectly from the author's ten years of research experience in Northern Mexico and three years of experience working with Mexican police departments from throughout the country on police education projects for the U.S.-based National Strategy Information Center's Culture of Lawfulness Project. During this latter time period, I had the opportunity to work with, instruct, conduct focus groups, and interview hundreds of police from throughout the country and from other Latin American countries. While information from this work does not appear here, the experience inevitably shaped and facilitated this analysis.

2 Troubled Reforms

Emerging from the Limited-Discretion Paradigm:
Benign Implementation Challenges

The question that this research seeks to answer is why reform efforts in Mexico have not led to more professional police departments. As discussed in Chapter 1, reform could fail because of the officers themselves, because of the police institution, or because of factors outside of the police force. While this book concludes that the primarily obstacles to reform come from outside the department, this chapter focuses on the challenges within the police agency itself.

Police departments are often presented as quasi-military organizations that function hierarchically, whereby orders are given by the chief and then trickle down through the chain of command to line-level officers. From this perspective, the failure of reform is a failure of police and mayoral leadership, which itself could be a product of inexperience, inability, or (the most commonly feared) corruption. This explanation has considerable resonance among citizens and police alike, who often lament the lack of effective leadership.

There is certainly some evidence to support this perspective. In Ciudad Juárez, the police director Saulo Reyes Gamboa during the 2004–07 administration of Héctor Murguía Lardizábal was arrested and convicted by U.S. authorities in 2008 on drug trafficking charges. Clearly one cannot expect meaningful police reform under the direction of a police chief or mayor involved with drug trafficking. Although we cannot rule out the possibility of failed leadership and corruption at the top of the agency and city government (a topic that will be revisited in Chapter 4), this can only be part of the problem. Given that there are over two thousand police forces in the country, surely more successful models would emerge if it were just a matter of individual leadership. And in fact, one can point to cases of honest mayors and police chiefs who came into office with well-developed plans and good intentions to improve the integrity of their departments only to leave three years later at the end of the administration with little noticeable change. In many ways, a failure of leadership would be the most optimistic scenario, as solving the problem of the police would imply simply finding the right political and police leaders.

A variation of the failed-leadership explanation views failed reform as a problem of *the policies* selected and designed by police and mayoral leaders. In other words, past leaders were not necessarily corrupt or dishonest; they simply failed to develop appropriate policies. In fact, there have been problems of policy design in the recent past. While there has been general agreement that reform is urgently needed, there has been disagreement about what that reform should look like. The response to the problem of police misconduct in Mexico during the 1990s and much of the 2000s was based on what I refer to as the "limited-discretion model." In 1988, the well-regarded anti-corruption specialist Robert Klitgaard (1988) wrote that *monopoly* plus *discretion* minus *accountability* equals *corruption*. Deeming accountability too challenging, many police, municipal leaders, and legislators instead acted to reduce police discretion as a means to prevent corruption and human rights abuses. The hallmarks of what can be termed the limited-discretion model include constant rotation of personnel (to prevent police from developing unhealthy commitments), deployment in large groups (to make it harder to arrange corrupt deals), restricted access to information (to prevent leaks), and reductions in authority (to prevent abuses of authority). Legislators and police leaders guided by the limited-discretion model sent preventive police to patrol in a district of which they have no knowledge, did not allow officers to make arrests unless a criminal was caught red handed, and prohibited preventive police from handling evidence or interviewing witnesses. The same approach was applied to the investigative police as well. They were tasked with carrying out warrants on cases they knew nothing about, asked to chauffeur witnesses to the public ministers rather than conduct interviews themselves, and buried under paperwork.

Ironically, these policies have not only failed to reduce corruption and abuse, but they have had the unfortunate impact of turning the police into ineffective and reactive security guards. Elena Azaola and Marco Antonio Ruíz Torres (2009) argue that rather than create accountable police, reporting requirements for investigative police have created what they call "investigadores de papel," or "paper investigators." Guillermo Zepeda (2009) sums the problem up well when he writes, "Generally speaking, both society as a whole and the authorities themselves mistrust the police, but instead of taking steps to improve the police, the police have seen their functions stripped away piece by piece." Because officers lack the legal faculties much less the training to actively prevent or effectively respond to crime, their primary role under the limited-discretion model is to dissuade crime from occurring through their sheer presence. Rather than implement intelligence-based, problem-oriented, or community policing models that rely on professional officers, the predominant crime-fighting strategy under the limited-discretion paradigm is simply to increase the number of police on the streets.

There continues to be disagreement about the best direction for police reform in Mexico. Those more concerned with police abuse tend to advocate for continuing to limit police discretion, and those concerned with police ineffectiveness tend to push for expanded police authority (Ungar 2002). Increasingly, many political leaders and citizens have embraced variants of the limited-discretion approach in "centralization" and "militarization." It is hoped that concentrating authority under ostensibly more trustworthy former military generals and strengthening the hierarchy within the police through military discipline will both overcome the potential for poor leadership and increase control over the police bureaucracy. As of 2011, seventeen of Mexico's thirty-one states and the Federal District had current or formal military leaders in their top public-security positions and many municipalities had followed suit, including three of the four research sites (Gálan 2011). It is too early to determine if such an approach will be effective, but there are several reasons militarization is potentially problematic. In addition to having been tried before (López-Montiel 2000) and to undermining democracy when applied elsewhere (Zaverucha 2000), police work is simply not the same as military work. At the end of the day, militarization, like other variations of the limited-discretion approach, assumes that rank-and-file officers on the street do not need the authority, discretion, and professionalism to effectively prevent and respond to crime. While militarization offers an appealing solution to the problems of the police, there is likely to be no shortcut to professionalization.

As such, other reformers have sought to develop police forces deserving of the authority and discretion necessary to be effective. At least rhetorically, there is general agreement on the desired nature of the reform initiatives laid out in the previous chapter: (1) Departments require policies to ensure effective recruitment and selection of potential future officers. (2) Those recruits need to be well trained, and officers need to have regular in-service training throughout their career to review important elements of policing and to learn new techniques, tactics, and approaches. (3) Officers require a dignified salary, benefits, and pension characteristic of a "profession" rather than an ordinary job. (4) A professional department will ensure that the officers who rise up through its ranks do so because of their abilities and merits rather than their connections and political considerations. (5) Departments should develop clear operational procedures, make them available to officers in procedure manuals, and train police in their details and application. (6) Like any profession, officers require the tools and resources to do their jobs effectively; this includes proper uniforms, firearms, vehicles, and the latest technology. (7) Finally, police should be held accountable for their actions. They should be rewarded for work well done and sanctioned for violating procedure and the law.

If the problem of reform amounted to one of leadership, then given acceptance of the desirability of these policies by police leaders, policy implementation would follow smoothly from policy design. Rather than as a hierarchy where orders are implemented down the chain of command as intended by the leadership, however, the police are better viewed as a bureaucracy subject to what Gary Miller (1993) calls "managerial dilemmas." A given police chief lacks sufficient "time and place information" (Hayek 1948) to make good decisions about very-localized crime problems, and therefore some form of decentralized decision making is required in a large organization like a police department. Consequently, reform efforts do not depend just on police chiefs, but their assistant chiefs, operational commanders, and district commanders. Lipsky (1980) goes a step further and demonstrates how reform also depends on the actions and responses of numerous line level officers, or what he calls "street-level bureaucrats." The challenge is that subordinates have their own interests and might not act in the interests of their chiefs, the police department, or the public, a feature of bureaucratic politics known as the principal-agent problem (Klitgaard 1988; Miller).

In theory, good reform policies are designed to align the street-level bu-reaucrat's interest with the public interest, and yet such formal policies do not occur in a vacuum but within a dense network of preexisting institutional rules, including persistent informal rules that, as discussed at length in the previous chapter, might contradict reform efforts. As such, the lack of effective reform might be the product of ineffective leadership and poor policies, or it might be due to the failure of implementation and an inability to overcome principal-agent, collective action, and zero-sum opposition problems. Fur-thermore, this discussion has been limited to factors within the police agency itself, and has excluded external factors of municipal governance, organized crime, and police-citizen relations, which will be explored in later chapters.

Inevitably, analysts and researchers tend to focus on either leadership, bureaucratic, or external explanations for failed or successful reform. On the one hand, if we assume the primacy of one of these three explanations, we risk identifying only partial solutions to the complex problems facing the police. On the other hand, broad-based approaches focused on the full range of actors might obfuscate responsibility. Placing the blame for failed police reform on everyone from citizens to judges allows ineffective mayors and police chiefs to divert responsibility away from their failings. The solution to this problem of causality is to recognize that police reform is made up of a basket of diverse reform policies, some of which confront challenges primarily within the area of influence of police chiefs and city leaders, others the police bureaucracy, and still others the larger external environment.

To illustrate, improved selection criteria, cadet and in-service training, salaries, benefits, pensions, and equipment all primarily confront leadership challenges. While not necessarily easy to implement, these are in many ways the low-hanging fruit of police reform. Generally speaking, they are accepted and even desired by police officers, who would generally prefer better recruits, opportunities to learn and improve their craft, better salaries and benefits, and adequate equipment. Provided expected support exists from the rank and file, police and mayoral leaders looking to improve these aspects of reform only confront what might be considered "benign implementation" hurdles from within the department.

Admittedly, all of these efforts require additional economic resources, and mayors and police leaders might depend on constituents, the city council, and the federal government for such resources. Nonetheless, obtaining major in-creases in public-security budgets first and foremost requires overcoming the limited-discretion paradigm among police and mayoral leaders. If the primary function of police is merely to offer a physical presence to dissuade crime, then there is no need for specially selected, well-trained, and well-equipped officers. On the contrary, as the limited-discretion approach requires a strong physical presence, strict selection criteria and long training times limit the pool of potential officers who could be on the street at a given time.

In contrast to policy reforms primarily dependent on leadership and economic resources, merit-based promotion reforms and many operational and administrative procedures confront collective action problems in addition to benign implementation challenges. Such reforms require the cooperation of police commanders inside the police bureaucracy; however, these same actors achieved their positions through the old system and often benefit from the absence of clearly defined procedures. While reforms to merit-based policing encounter challenges within the department, they confront greater challenges from political leadership. As we will see in Chapter 3, police leaders and their political overseers benefit from the power to distribute positions within the department, to determine who gets access to policing services, and to permit exemption from the law. Ironically, in the long run, officers, mid-level commanders, and police and political leaders would stand to benefit from strong institutional rules governing police operations, administration, and promotion. Police and political leaders would have a more reliable bureaucracy better able to address crime concerns, and police would operate in a more certain and less arbitrary institutional environment. Making this transition, however, faces the above mentioned collective action problem, whereby individuals must forego the benefits of the old system (e.g., the ability to dispense patronage) without garnering the benefits of a professional bureaucracy in an environment where others continue to play by the old rules of the game.

Attempts to combat corruption and to implement operational procedures that might reduce opportunities for corruption likely confront zero-sum opposition in addition to collective action and benign implementation challenges. Attempting to reduce the opportunities for corruption or to confront corruption directly risks conflict with rank and file officers who rely on corruption to supplement their salaries. The extent of opposition might even go up the entire chain of command in departments where higher-level officers collect a quota of bribe money from their subordinates. Perhaps more important, organized crime requires police corruption to operate effectively, and can also be expected to resist anticorruption probes. Illustrative of the extent of zero-sum opposition, numerous police leaders have been killed by organized crime and even by their own officers as a result of anticorruption initiatives.[1] If improving training is the low-hanging fruit of reform, addressing corruption is the fruit at the highest and most dangerous part of the tree.

In summary, police reform includes diverse elements that provoke different implementation challenges and draw opposition or support from different actors in what Paul Sabatier (1993) refers to as the "policy subsystem." Some problems confront only benign implementation and resource obstacles, while others face collective action problems, and still others involve zero-sum conflicts. In addition, recognizing the diverse sources of opposition to reform is important to avoid the current tendency among many individuals active in the policy arena to shirk responsibility and place the problem elsewhere. Police leaders interviewed contend that their hands are tied by the politicians above them and the large bureaucracy below them; officers allege that they are powerless; and politicians condemn the police as corrupt, abusive, and ineffective. Recognizing the diverse challenges and specific actors central to reform will allow for improved lines of responsibility.

In the chapters that follow, this book will explore all of these implementation challenges in thorough detail. This chapter begins with the low-hanging fruit of reform and explores the "benign" implementation challenges confronted by police departments in improving selection criteria, cadet and in-service training, salaries and benefits, and equipment, prior to and/or excluding federal intervention. The chapter provides qualitative examples from the four research sites, supplemented by data from the eleven departments that responded to the 2009 Police Professionalization Survey. I will revisit these issues in Chapter 7, which will explore in detail efforts by the Calderón administration beginning in 2008 to promote municipal police professionalization. As such, this chapter will focus on municipal initiatives, mostly prior to 2008. Unfortunately, I find that although these reforms do not confront the collective action and zero-sum problems of developing merit-based promotion and combating corruption, they nonetheless have often eluded local reformers. Of the three departments, only Chihuahua achieved clear, recognized successes. While the other departments have made significant advances since the mid-1990s, their advance is best described as one of two steps forward and one step back. The following discussion explores the obstacles that they have confronted.

The Benign Implementation Challenges to Police
Reform in Mexico's Municipalities

As noted above, policing in general and policing at the municipal level in particular has traditionally been a highly neglected policy arena governed by the limited-discretion paradigm. As a result, one does not have to go back very far to see overwhelming deficiencies in municipal police forces. Hermosillo and Mexicali offer similar histories. As crime began to rise in the mid-1990s, opposition parties saw public security as a winning policy concern. As such, initial efforts at police reform began with the arrival of *panista* administrations in 1995 in Mexicali and in 1998 in Hermosillo. In his municipal development plan, the newly elected *panista* mayor of Hermosillo Jorge Valencia Juillerat (1998–2000) offers a highly critical diagnosis of the department's problems:

> At the beginning of our administration . . . the police force suffered the effects of incorrect personnel selection, few or zero opportunities for promotion for officers, an inadequate work environment, low salaries, insufficient incentives, poor or bad equipment, little or no training and more than anything a lack of leadership . . . The patrol cars were (and continue to be) insufficient, guns were scarce; all the equipment had serious mechanical problems. The command posts were in a deteriorated state after years and years of abandonment and neglect (Valencia Juillerat 1998).

While incoming politicians have strong incentives to make such claims about predecessors from an opposing party, Valencia's concerns appear to be valid. To begin, the city was highly dependent on the state government to solve the problems of local policing. Its police chief was actually appointed by the governor, and the city depended on the state academy for police training. State law made such training optional, and as a result, 85 percent of the force had no formal police preparation (Valencia Juillerat 1998).

In response, and despite a serious fiscal problem, Valencia increased the public-security budget by 70 percent and raised salaries by an equal amount. His administration established an internal affairs unit within the municipal government and began instituting drug testing of officers (Valencia Juillerat 1999; 2000). The city government also passed regulations to create something akin to a police civil service, and Valencia's successor founded the city's police academy (Búrquez 2001).[2]

Eugenio Elorduy confronted analogous problems in Mexicali, with a similar percentage of police lacking formal training. He also increased investments in public security and more than doubled police salaries. His administration initiated infrastructure projects and founded a municipal academy. By the end of the term, around four hundred cadets had graduated from the academy's six-month training program, raising the size of the force to around 1,100 and dropping the percent of officers without training to 44.5 percent (Elorduy Walther 1998).

As these two examples illustrate, municipal policing had been neglected prior to the mid-to-late 1990s. Interviews reveal that at the time there was considerable optimism about the ability of new reformist administrations to transform the police forces. However, consistent with North's discussion of persistent informal rules and path dependency, radical change did not come to these municipal police forces. Rather than usher in a period of reform, these administrations initiated a process of change best described as two steps forward – one step back.

Selection Criteria and Recruitment

Good police work is a challenging job that requires a diverse set of skills. August Vollmer, one of the preeminent reformers in U.S. policing, ironically contended that:

> The citizen expects police officers to have the wisdom of Solomon, the courage of David, the strength of Samson, the patience of Job, the leadership of Moses, the kindness of the Good Samaritan, the strategic training of Alexander, the faith of Daniel, the diplomacy of Lincoln, the tolerance of the Carpenter of Nazareth, and finally, an intimate knowledge of every branch of the natural biological, and social sciences. If he had all these, he might be a good policeman![3]

Such a combination of abilities is of course impossible to find, but it nonetheless suggests the diverse qualities that good policing requires. Not just anyone should become a police officer, and the first step to ensuring outstanding officers is ensuring quality cadets. It is not surprising, therefore, that independent investigation commissions in the United States have typically included in their recommendations improving selection criteria (Knapp Commission 1972). In Mexico, however, the quality of police recruits has traditionally been a secondary concern, and police departments have failed to draw qualified applicants. Interview respondents frequently made statements like this one from a police training administrator:

> In the old days they would ask, "Do you want to be a police officer?" "Then come on in; we need police." Or, "You can't find work, join the police." And they didn't come for the salary. The salary was just the tip. What you can get on the street was much more.

This reality and the August Vollmer quote stand in stark contrast. The latter statement suggests that police forces have not only failed to attract sufficiently qualified applicants, but in some cases, they have actually drawn individuals predisposed toward corruption and abuse.

Changing this status quo is not an insignificant undertaking, and without a doubt there are considerable implementation challenges. Due to a variety of factors including a negative reputation, high risks, and low pay, Mexican police agencies report considerable difficulties in attracting a sufficient number of *quality* applicants to be highly selective. Godoy's study of the Hermosillo police department in 2004, after efforts had been made to improve selection criteria and training, highlights these challenges. In collaboration with the municipal police department, Sonora University's Police Support and Attention Center (Centro de Atención y Apoyo Policial de la Universidad de Sonora—CAAP) conducted a study of 135 active police officers who had graduated from the police academy in the previous two years. Of the sample, 44 percent had finished high school, and all had completed academy training. The selected officers were given IQ and psychological tests with the hope that they would score better than an earlier group of older police officers, many of whom had failed previous psychological testing and not been trained. While there were differences between the younger recruits and the older veterans, they were not substantial, and the study's author Fernando Godoy concludes, "In some respects, the results of the younger police were more worrisome than their predecessors." According to the results, 44.5 percent had a less-than-average IQ test result, which is contrary to national criteria that police have *at least* an average IQ. Moreover, 12.6 percent of the total had a "deficient" IQ. Most disturbing, however, was CAAP's conclusion that almost all had "some pathological traits." The study concluded that 30 percent had a tendency toward substance abuse; 28 percent showed signs of paranoid tendencies; 15 percent showed signs of slower brain function, perhaps due to injury; 64 percent showed signs of being sociopaths and 12 percent of being psychopaths;

and 15 percent had suicidal tendencies (Godoy 2007). While other psychologists might arrive at other conclusions using different criteria, the results nonetheless raise considerable cause for concern and outline a profile that does not match citizen's expectations for the police officers as summed up by Vollmer. The findings suggest that a high school degree and training are not by themselves adequate criteria for predicting good police officers and that there is no silver bullet for improving the quality of incoming police.

Instead, a combination of psychological and drug tests, minimum high school education requirements, background checks, interview processes, and lie detector tests conducted by qualified professionals have the combined ability to ensure only the best candidates are admitted to the force. Psychological and drug testing was, in fact, used in all four of the research sites prior to 2008. In Mexicali and Chihuahua, a high school degree was required. In Hermosillo, background checks that included visits to the aspirants' homes were conducted of all incoming cadets. The federal government's efforts to create a national database with information about all current and past police officers throughout the country (Registro Nacional de Personal de Seguridad Pública) made it possible to verify that applicants did not have criminal records and had not been fired from another police agency. Table 2.1 illustrates that four of the surveyed municipal departments had recently made a high school degree a requirement and some cities, such as Chihuahua and San Luis Potosí, were able to accept only the best applicants, as reflected by their lower acceptance rates, 15.67 percent and 12.82 percent respectively.

Nonetheless, the majority of the surveyed departments still required education only through the ninth grade. Moreover, as of the time of the survey, only a handful of departments used labor-intensive background checks and lie detector tests to screen candidates, suggesting there were still considerable advances yet to be made.[4] Although there was widespread recognition and rhetoric about the need to improve selection criteria, in practice, the limited-discretion paradigm, which focused on the quantity of police rather than their quality, predominated. As the table illustrates, the relatively low numbers of qualified applicants mean that low acceptance percentages depend on small cadet classes. When departments wanted to rapidly increase the number of police on the force, new selection criteria frequently were relaxed in order to ensure a sufficient number of incoming cadets. A worst case scenario can be found in Tijuana, where, as mentioned in Chapter 1, the Jorge Hank Rhon administration (2004–07) wanted to expand the size of the force dra-

TABLE 2.1. Cadet selection and education levels

City	Minimum education requirement	Year high school is made a requirement	No. of qualified applicants to the last cadet class	Percent of qualified applicants accepted	Percent of officers with at least a high school degree
Guadalajara	Secondary	n/a	94	26.6%	34.2%
Monterrey	Secondary	n/a	44	65.9%	34.0%
Mérida	Secondary	n/a	.	.	28.4%
Ahome	High School	2008	50	54.0%	55.2%
México DF°	Secondary	n/a	563	22.0%	40.0%
S.L. Potosí	High School	2007	390	12.8%	35.3%
Torreón	Secondary	n/a	71	45.1%	.
Chihuahua	High School	2006	134	15.7%	59.6%
Cuernavaca	High School*	2005	.	.	55.8%
Zapopan	Secondary	n/a	124	32.3%	34.5%

*High school was only a requirement for transit police
° Data does not include the Auxiliary Police, which number an additional forty thousand.
NOTE: Secondary school is grades 7–9, and high school is grades 10–12. Puebla did not provide responses to these questions and is excluded. Ahome is in Sinaloa and contains the city of Los Mochis.
SOURCE: Information provided by police departments in response to the Police Professionalism Survey administered in early 2009.

matically to respond to the city's crime wave. Under his leadership, the department grew from around 1,500 to almost 2,400 in just three years. During the expansion, selection and training filters were quickly overwhelmed by the need to put more police on the street. One former instructor at the academy commented that they knew they had a problem on their hands when cadets started showing up with expensive brand-new cars. Despite relatively high salaries in Tijuana, police are not at the top of the income ladder, and the prospect of a new car is out of reach of many police even after years of service. In fact, several police officers found to be collaborating with organized criminal groups in subsequent years entered the force during this recruitment drive.

Even Chihuahua has not been immune from such challenges. In 2004, the former mayor of Chihuahua, José Reyes Baeza, was elected state governor. He brought with him the municipal police chief, Raúl Grajeda Domínguez, to lead the state police, which formed a new elite unit called the Intelligence Police Force (Cuerpo de Inteligencia Policial—CIPOL). To fill its ranks, CIPOL pulled heavily from the police department that Grajeda formally commanded, drawing over two hundred police away from the municipal force and leaving the city with a deficit of police that it had to fill in the short term. Although

Chihuahua is currently turning away a higher percentage of applicants, at that time, attracting a sufficient number of new police to the department required relaxing acceptance criteria in the short term. Not surprisingly, several police interviewed complained about the quality and the integrity of these now-junior police agents. The ironic undermining of police professionalism to ostensibly better combat rising security concerns occurs nationwide and even at the federal level.[5] The Federal Preventive Police (now Federal Police) was unable to attract college graduates to fill an announced eight thousand positions in its intelligence units (Gandaría 2007b). As a partial result of its recruiting challenges, the Federal Preventive Police had by mid-2007 filled more than half of its ranks with sixteen thousand transferred military personnel (Gandaría).

Although important advances were made in improving selection criteria, as of 2008 very few departments used the full range of selection criteria. In recognition of this problem, changes in federal legislation and federal funding beginning in 2008 have attempted to raise the bar for selection criteria. State governments are now required to establish Integrity Control Centers (Centros de Control de Confianza), which have responsibility for vetting incoming officers using nationally approved standards. The effects of and challenges confronted by these more recent reforms will be considered in Chapter 7.

Even if departments were able to improve the quality of a given cadet class, doing so would not address the problems with existing police. Even in locations like Mexicali that started to require a high school degree in 2005, high school graduates still made up less than half of the force. As shown in Table 2.1, only three departments, including Chihuahua, had forces with a majority of high school graduates. On the one hand this is a major improvement from the 1996 diagnostic study that found that over 50 percent of police had only a primary level of education. On the other hand, however, several departments, even departments that had made great strides in professionalization in recent years like Guadalajara, still had a substantial number of police with only a primary and secondary school level of education (19.8 percent).

This raises a concern that is essential for understanding the limited results of existing reform efforts and the two realities discussed in the previous chapter. Addressing one individual aspect of police reform, while perhaps necessary, is insufficient to bring about a more professional department. As a result, departments require complementary strategies targeting other aspects of reform. In Chihuahua the department did not stop at making high school a requirement for cadets. Instead, it signed agreements with local academic institutions to offer existing officers opportunities to earn high school, college, and even master's degrees, and it made a high school degree a requirement to obtain a leadership post in the force.

Training

High-quality training is clearly an important part of fostering policing professionals, and, like improving selection criteria, it has been a central reform recommendation.[6] Like any group of professionals, police require specialized skills, and while many skills are honed through the practice of day-to-day policing, they nonetheless require formal instruction. Training can be divided into basic cadet training and in-service training for already existing officers, both categories of which have suffered from the same pressures as selection criteria. If the objective of police leaders operating under the limited-discretion model is to increase the *quantity* of police rather than the *quality* of police, and if the preventive police are *not* gathering intelligence, analyzing crime data, applying crime prevention techniques, interviewing witnesses, etc., then it is easy to de-prioritize education and training. New incoming administrations that want to increase the size of the force are unwilling to wait for months and potentially over a year to see new recruits on the streets. When Tijuana's mayor Hank Rhon determined to practically double the size of the police force during his three-year administration, he reduced the training time down to a mere two months. As a result, hundreds of police currently working in the municipal department graduated with only minimal formal training. In 2005, the incoming Samuel Ramos administration in Mexicali also reduced training time from six months to three intensive months.

The need to get cadets out onto the street can also be clearly seen in the use of practical training exercises. In theory, field training should occur under the strict supervision of field training officers and seek to show cadets how the theories, laws, and tactics taught in the academy are applied in practice. Unfortunately, interviewees suggest that practical trainings often devolved into simply using cadets to make up for manpower shortages. The use of cadets to patrol commercial areas or tourist areas during holidays was frequently considered "practical training," even though these uses were not pedagogical exercises. Few departments had figured out how to use practical training effectively, and in the pre-2009 period, none of the four research sites used "field training officers," or specially trained officers who work one-on-one with cadets or new police to continue the learning process during practical day-to-day policing.

If police leaders operating based on the limited-discretion paradigm were hesitant to offer extended training periods for cadets, then they were even more resistant to pull police off the street for in-service training. While most departments have always offered some in-service courses, such opportunities were typically reserved for police leaders and specialized groups. It was not uncommon to hear of rank-and-file officers who had gone for years if not decades without taking a single course. Even when training was offered, officers might have had to come in early or stay late rather than see the course cut into their work shift. Even elements of policing as basic as firearms training were neglected.[7] Until very recently, Tijuana, Mexicali, and Hermosillo did not provide their police with regular training on the use of firearms. A formal, department-wide program in Tijuana to train and retrain police in shooting, which followed the assassination of a number of police in 2008, caused one instructor to remark that he had not seen such a systematic attempt at training in over twenty years.

There is evidence that the under-prioritization of training is beginning to change; however, given the operational priorities some degree of skepticism is still warranted. Under the Calderón administration, Mexico has moved toward certifying police academies and police academy trainers and constraining the ability of police leaders to arbitrarily cut training times. Mexico's National Academy led an initiative to certify academy instructors in seven key areas of policing. In Baja California and Sonora, the state governments are also playing a more active role. After the failure of Tijuana's academy to adequately screen or train applicants, the academy was closed down, and future Tijuana police were ordered trained at the state police academy. Mexicali was required by the state to bring its training time back up to six full months, and it too was eventually folded into the state police academy. Chihuahua's academy went a step further than the other departments and in 2009 became certified by both the National Public Security System and the state secretariat of education. As a result, graduates of the academy receive a recognized technical degree. In addition to improving the quality of instruction, certification means that the police leaders cannot arbitrarily alter the curriculum or the instruction time. As will be discussed in Chapter 7, the federal government is using the power of the purse to encourage states and municipalities to move in Chihuahua's direction.

Despite the challenges, there has clearly been a major improvement from 1996 when many major departments did not require academy training, and average training times for those few officers who were trained was only 4.5 months (Sandoval Ulloa 2000). Chihuahua has had a police academy since 1965, Mexicali since 1996, and Hermosillo since 2001. The length of training has also increased over the 1996 national average of 4.5 months. While not a representative sample, with the exception of Mérida, the surveyed departments all reported a longer instruction time. Training ranged from three months in Mérida to twelve months in Ahome, Sinaloa for an average of 7.2 months if practical training is included and 5.3 months if it is excluded. Several departments responding to the survey in 2009 reported that 100 percent of incoming police receive basic cadet training, and, in the last few years seven of the departments made annual in-service training a requirement.

Chihuahua has an ideal structure for offering in-service courses. One week out of the year, officers rotate out of duty and spend a week at in-service training. During that week they take forty-hours hours of classes in weapons training, physical conditioning, law, use of force, community policing, treatment of suspects, driving, and searches. When a small sample of officers interviewed in Chihuahua were asked to what factors or policies they most attributed improvements in police professionalization in their department, the most common response was improved training. Hermosillo also instituted a systematic in-service training program under the Ernesto Gándara Camou administration (2007–09), which claimed in its Municipal Development Plan that there has not been a similar effort since 1999. Given that many officers in Hermosillo never had basic academy training, in-service courses were for some groups up to three weeks long. In its bid for CALEA recognition, Mexicali developed a permanent in-service training program for its officers in 2008.

As mentioned above, Chihuahua went an additional step and worked to promote general education among officers. Those with only a middle school education were encouraged to attend continuing-education high school classes, and a high school degree became a requirement for promotion to a supervisory position. Many of those participating in these programs were high-level officers, including the city's then-operational commander, who was pursuing a master's degree. While the developments in Chihuahua were positive, the police chief acknowledged that allowing officers the scheduling flexibility to attend and excel in school required enormous institutional commitment to education. Although the general trend in training is very positive, it is important to recognize that this has not been the first time that police leaders have prioritized training. As exemplified in Tijuana and Mexicali, subsequent administrations, influenced by the limited-discretion model, can undermine training programs to keep more officers on the street.

Salary and Benefits

Traditionally in Mexico, police have not been afforded a reasonable pay or benefits packages. In the worst case scenarios, police in departments, such as Mérida's municipal police and Sinaloa's state police, worked twenty-four-hour shifts with only twenty-four hours off for a monthly salary of just over $400.[8] Unfortunately, many departments pay low wages, offer no pension, and provide no health benefits beyond the standard national social security system. To add insult to injury, given the danger inherent in their work, police officers have traditionally been unable to obtain credit to build a home or make large purchases, despite relative job stability.

Improvements to salaries and benefits are perhaps the most visible and often-cited reforms needed to professionalize Mexican policing. It is argued that if police cannot meet their basic needs from their official salary, then they will make up for monetary shortfalls through bribes and extortion. Moreover, if policing is to be viewed as a profession and attract higher-quality applicants, then it has to offer incentives accordingly.[9] Important national- and local-level agreements have reflected this recognition. In Monterrey in late 2008, municipal leaders in the metropolitan area announced an agreement to uniformly raise base police salaries to over $800 a month (El Norte 2008).[10] Table 2.2 shows police base salaries across the studied municipalities, most of which reflect significant increases above more traditional salaries of around $400 a month. Tijuana's salary increase is perhaps the most impressive. During the three-year administration of Jorge Hank Rhon (2004–07) in Tijuana, the salaries of police were doubled. A low-level police officer went from earning around $660 per month to earning around $1,200 per month. While the cost of living is admittedly much higher in Tijuana than in other Mexican cities, Tijuana police made far more than the other municipalities examined here.

Salaries are only some of the carrots that can encourage professionalism. While police departments provide their employees basic social security, some such as Hermosillo offered a fully salaried police pension after a set number of years of service. All of the cities provide some life insurance benefits, and many were working to facilitate housing credits. In Mexicali, Chihuahua, and Tijuana, the department and/or municipality served as an intermediary between lending institutions and qualified officers. Monthly payments were de-

TABLE 2.2. Salaries, select benefits, and budgetary information

	Basic monthly salary	Possible additional bonus	Access to housing credit	Scholarships for children	2007 Spending per police officer	Salaries as a percent of the budget (2007)
Guadalajara	$658	$212	Yes	No	$10,066	–
Monterrey	$602	$187	No	Yes	$21,681	70.00
Mérida	$388	$86	Yes	No	$12,213	78.32
Ahome	$521	$31	No	No	–	–
México DF	$680	$105	Yes	Yes	$15,101	–
S.L.Potosí	$540	–	Yes	No	–	–
Torreón	$550	$668	Yes	Yes	–	–
Chihuahua	$727	$87	Yes	Yes	$19,954	62.68
Puebla	$600	$50	No	No	–	–
Cuernavaca	$494	$83	No	Yes	$15,325	69.10
Zapopan	$752	$212	Yes	No	$10,066	–

NOTE: Pesos converted to dollars at a four-year average of 12.04 pesos to the dollar.
SOURCE: Information provided by police departments in response to the Police Professionalism Survey administered in early 2009.

ducted from paychecks, and the department acted as something of a guarantor as long as the officer stayed on the force. During the Gándara Camou administration (2007–09), Hermosillo's force issued its police small monthly cash transfers to help support their children's education. Private citizens and the business chambers have also stepped in to provide benefits to the police, offering discounts in stores and restaurants. Many departments, such as Chihuahua's, offer "Police of the Month" and "Police of the Year" awards with monetary rewards for the winners.

Nonetheless, improvement of salary and benefits suffers from serious implementation problems. Recognizing that the police should be better paid is one thing; actually raising salaries is something else entirely. While only partial data is available, the surveyed municipalities of Chihuahua, Cuernavaca, Mérida, and Monterrey already pay out between 60–80 percent of their overall budgets in police salaries, leaving little room for investments in capital and equipment and constraining their ability to raise salaries without changes in overall municipal funding priorities (See Table 2.2). Creating pensions suffers from a similar challenge. While attractive in the short term, the offer of good benefits can place a serious onus on future municipal financial obligations. In the U.S. experience, pension benefits that allowed for full salaries after twenty-five years of service meant "many cities were now supporting two police forces, one made up of active officers and another, which was growing rapidly, made up of retired officers. Quite a few citizens wondered if they could afford both forces." (Fogelson 1977, 280).

While Tijuana's pay increase was heralded as essential for improving the force, when asked how the municipality could find the resources to double police salaries, a police administrator countered, "There are no resources. They [the previous administration] did it irresponsibly. Now the municipality has huge financial problems." In fact, Tijuana's municipal government was approximately $50 million in debt at the close of the Hank Rhon administration. Many police chiefs, constrained by municipal budgets, do not even see themselves as being in a position to raise salaries. One interviewed chief resigned to the low salaries in his particularly poor-paying force stated that he considered police wages to be a form of "slavery" but argued that he could do little about the problem.

Although Hermosillo in theory offers a full pension system, it has circumvented this commitment by creating loopholes to reduce the size of an officer's promised benefits. Prior to changes in 2010, official police salaries, upon which pensions were based, were very low, amounting to only $239 a month, far below any of the other cities' salaries presented in Table 2.2. However, Hermosillo offered additional compensations that could raise police monthly salaries to more respectable wages.[11] This system allows the department to pay the police-acceptable salaries without committing itself to future pensions. In addition, the city recently extended the number of years of service to be eligible for pension benefits from thirty to thirty-two years, above the typical twenty-five years in most U.S. departments and many national Latin American police forces.

These experiences illustrate the challenges to substantially raising benefits. While these substantial cost increases might be worthwhile in the long run, they require either tax increases or a reordering of spending priorities, confronting what Vivienne Foster (1996) calls a financing dilemma. On the one hand, if a municipality's citizens want better police officers, they should have to pay them more. On the other hand, why should taxpayers pay more for service today that is clearly substandard?

It should also be mentioned that there is a risk of overstating the benefits of improving salaries. In interviews, many police officers present salary increases as a silver bullet solution and place low wages as the underlying cause of all police ills. While increases are necessary, like other areas of reform, they are insufficient to bring about change on their own. In fact, there is no clear empirical relationship between salary increases and declines in corruption

(Klitgaard 1988; Rose-Ackerman 1999; Treisman 2000; Asch, Burger, and Fu 2011). This is most clearly illustrated in the Tijuana case. While police salaries were practically doubled, the raise did not coincide with other reform efforts, such as improving training, strengthening Tijuana's weak accountability mechanisms, or tightening selection criteria. In fact, the salary increase occurred while corruption was perhaps worsening.

Even given substantial raises, it is hard to imagine police who have partaken in corrupt activities for all of their careers suddenly ceasing to engage in corruption as a result of a pay increase alone. If the probability of being caught and punished for corruption remains extremely low, then a salary increase does not fundamentally alter the equation. As one police officer in Hermosillo stated, "I thought that the more the police were paid the less corrupt they would be, but the more they have, the more they want." Much-needed salary increases must therefore be accompanied by additional reform initiatives, including improved accountability mechanisms.

Equipment

Citizens and experts alike might be inclined to believe that improved accountability mechanisms, selection criteria, and oversight are the essential factors to professionalizing the police; however, when many police were asked, they tended to point toward investments in technology, arms, and equipment. They argued that these factors allow them to better perform their day-to-day work, producing a greater sense of pride and feelings of professionalism. As professionalism is at its core a perception and attitude, this sentiment cannot be easily dismissed.

Although interview respondents perceived a continued need for more equipment, as illustrated in Table 2.3, police departments have invested heavily in technology. Chihuahua has a modern dispatching system, a high-tech mobile command unit with a retractable camera able to read a license plate a mile away, twenty-eight cameras throughout the city, a high-tech video monitoring room, several specialized units such as an immediate reaction team and a K-9 unit, laptops in supervisors' cars, recorders and GPS systems in patrol cars, and a helicopter. Perhaps most important, however, police are assigned their own cars and carry designated guns, a rarity in Mexican policing where most vehicles and guns trade owners and "work" multiple shifts. As a result, Chihuahua has a much higher number of vehicles per officer than the other departments in the survey. Most importantly, all of these investments occurred

TABLE 2.3. Police equipment and technology

	Trucks and patrol cars	Motor-cycles	Vehicles per to police	Mobile command unit	Video cameras in public places	Video cameras in patrol cars	GPS in patrol cars	Helicopter	SWAT like team	K-9 unit
Guadalajara	538	178	2.3	✓	✓	✓	✓	✓	✓	✓
Monterrey	160	44	2.5	No	✓	No	✓	No	✓	✓
Mérida	47	31	2.5	✓	✓	No	No	No	✓	No
Ahome	120	13	1.3	✓	No	No	No	No	✓	No
México DF	4,186	2,234	1.8	✓	✓	No	✓	✓	✓	✓
S.L. Potosí	169	75	2.2	No	✓	No	No	No	✓	✓
Torreón	353	107	4.6	✓	✓	No	✓	✓	✓	No
Chihuahua	560	217	6.8	✓	✓	✓	✓	✓	✓	✓
Puebla	351	189	3.8	No	No	No	✓	No	No	No
Cuernavaca	177	51	2.6	No	✓	No	✓	No	✓	No
Zapopan	236	84	1.9	✓	✓	No	✓	✓	✓	✓

NOTE: Some of these purchases might have been made with federal subsidies initiated in 2008.
SOURCE: Information provided by police departments in response to the Police Professionalism Survey administered in early 2009.

prior to the federal subsidy program. As can be seen in Table 2.2, there is considerable variability in police budgets per police officer, and Chihuahua has made a considerably higher investment than the other forces (with the possible exception of Monterrey).

Other departments are quickly trying to catch up. During the Hank Rhon administration, Tijuana invested heavily in surveillance cameras, placing 128 throughout the city and constructing a state-of-the-art facility to monitor the images. The Ramos administration (2007–10) purchased top-of-the-line vehicles equipped with video and audio recording equipment for both the interior and exterior of the car (a potentially important monitoring tool). Since 2001, Hermosillo has invested in GPS units for its police cars, allowing them to be tracked throughout the city. In fact, Table 2.3 reveals that big-ticket items (such as video cameras, GPS systems, mobile command units, helicopters) and elite specialized units (such as immediate reaction teams and K-9 units) are common across the surveyed sites.[12]

Major purchases have also been made in what might be considered more basic police equipment such as vehicles, firearms, bulletproof vests and uniforms. Shortfalls in these areas have traditionally been a major handicap for Mexican police forces. Departments had grown accustomed to a shortage of vehicles and firearms and to exploiting existing equipment to its maximum; however, the security crisis laid bare the neglect in police equipment. To illustrate, in 2007, the traditionally low-crime community of Hermosillo saw seven of its police officers killed by organized crime over a short period. Lacking bulletproof vests, being armed only with revolvers, and driving weak-engine Nissan Tsurus, the police were highly vulnerable to attack. As a result, government officials in Hermosillo and around the country have scrambled to make up for the lack of past investment. Many departments' officers now patrol with AR-15 (assault rifles), wear bulletproof vests, and carry a 9mm handgun.

In many respects, the purchase of equipment is one of the easiest elements of reform. Despite economic challenges, it is far simpler to spend money than to overcome the political obstacles to creating accountability mechanisms. Nonetheless, even in relatively flush financial times, the purchase of supplies and equipment also faces considerable challenges. In some cases, the rush to make purchases in the face of the security crises has not led to the best decisions. Although Hermosillo responded to the police killings by providing officers with new bulletproof vests, officers complained that the vests were outdated equipment, too heavy for police work. Replacement vests were ordered; however, these did not meet minimum specifications.

Ostrom, Schroeder, and Wynne (1993), in their analysis of infrastructure development policy, find that the challenge faced by policy implementers is not so much investing in infrastructure, but ensuring that there are resources to *maintain* that infrastructure. In several of the cases profiled in the Ostrom et al. study, large investments were entirely lost because very simple maintenance was not performed. The same lack of basic maintenance has affected Mexican policing and threatens the big-scale purchases currently being made with federal subsidy money.

Municipal administrations have, not unexpectedly, flaunted their big-ticket purchases and pronounced them as major accomplishments in their annual reports. The Hank Rhon administration (2004–07) in Tijuana lauded its purchases of cameras for the city, and the Francisco Búrquez administration in Hermosillo (2001–03) highlighted its new GPS technology. But purchasing these tools makes better news headlines than maintaining them. During site visits in Hermosillo, the GPS system was not working, and in Tijuana, many of the cameras were out of order and others had never actually functioned. In some cases, no electricity line had ever been run to the cameras' posts. Furthermore, the Hank Rhon administration entered into a maintenance contract with the provider that the following administration deemed to be far too expensive to continue. Unable to use a rival provider by contract and unwilling to pay the fee, the city let the cameras fall into disuse.

Patrol car maintenance has also been a major concern. From the point of view of police chiefs, who are all but guaranteed to be replaced at the end of an administration, patrol cars have to last the three years of their charge, and then, the quality of the vehicles is the problem of the subsequent mayor and chief. To illustrate the extent of the problem, Grindle (2007) profiles one incoming municipal administration in the state of Sinaloa that organized a parade of the city's poorly maintained vehicles, demonstrating to citizens that it would not be able to provide efficient service because of the state of the equipment inherited from the previous administration.

In Tijuana, during the Jorge Ramos administration (2007–10) the police chief contended in an interview that of the six hundred patrol cars left by the previous administration, only around eighty were in proper condition. Six months into his administration, he only had 320 police vehicles for a city of over 1.5 million and a police force of over two thousand. The chief made vehicle maintenance a priority, but some officers opted to take advantage of the situation. A newspaper investigation found that mechanics were charging the municipality up to three times the normal cost of repairs and paying police kickbacks to bring their cars in for maintenance (Frontera 2008a). In summary, while Mexican police forces have made major strides in improving police equipment, even this aspect of police reform confronts a variety of implementation challenges.

CALEA

A particularly positive development among municipal police departments is recognition and accreditation by the U.S.-based Commission on Law Enforcement Accreditation, Inc. (CALEA). As mentioned above, CALEA recognizes and certifies police agencies for maintaining a body of standards covering many aspects of policing and police administration. To date, around 870 police agencies have been accredited by CALEA, almost all of them in the United States. Chihuahua's police force, which obtained recognition in March 2004 and accreditation in May 2007, was the first police force in Mexico to be accredited by the commission. Several other departments have followed Chihuahua's path, including Mexicali, which obtained accreditation in 2010, and Guadalajara, Zapopan, and Monterrey, which were also recognized.

The CALEA process has helped consolidate substantial changes in policing in Chihuahua. It has corresponded with what several officers referred to as a transition away from *policías empíricos*, or basing one's decisions on one's own personal experience, to *policías científicos,* working based on best accepted practices. Improved selection criteria, cadet and in-service training, and equipment are among the various aspects of police administration and operations affected by CALEA. CALEA accreditation requires a high school education for entrance into the force, all officers must receive annual in-service training, and equipment and infrastructure must comply with international standards. As a result, in the department's internal survey in 2006, 77 percent of the respondents felt that complying with CALEA procedures would improve police effectiveness (Nájera Ruíz 2006).

Departments interested in CALEA recognition and accreditation must adopt and (more important) implement administrative and operational procedures consistent with CALEA standards. Once departments are confident that the new procedures are successfully implemented department-wide, CALEA sends an auditing team to the soliciting city to verify compliance. The process is not foolproof. Officers report cases of plastering over cracks in the wall the day before auditors arrive, and one can only assume that other failings are covered up as well. Moreover, CALEA standards are insufficient to ensure a robust accountability regime or meet many of the specific challenges confronted by Mexican departments. Nonetheless, accreditation does offer an important tool to ensure advances in selection criteria, training, and equipment, along with other operational and administrative procedures. The presence of an external audit and a formal accreditation that police and city leaders can show off to the public helps incentivize leaders to overcome the benign implementation challenges to the professionalization reforms discussed in this chapter. Unlike other promising reforms that have been promoted by the federal government, CALEA certification in Chihuahua and Mexicali, as elsewhere, was the result of local initiative.

Conclusion

The good news is that even prior to the introduction of federal incentives, departments had made important advances in improving selection criteria, cadet and in-service training, remuneration and incentives, and equipment. Unlike just a decade-and- a-half ago, all cadets are receiving training, many officers are participating in annual in-service courses, and investments have been made in cutting-edge technology. CALEA accreditation in Chihuahua, and subsequently Mexicali, suggests that police and city leaders can overcome at least some of the implementation challenges to reform.

While it is important to recognize these improvements, it is also necessary to admit that they have not resulted in the dramatic transformation that many might have hoped for when reformers like Elorduy and Valencia were elected to office in the 1990s. Despite the fact that these reforms were well received by officers and did not confront collective action problems or zero-sum opposition, they still confronted benign implementation challenges. Although Chihuahua was able to find the resources to make major investments in policing, other departments were slower to do the same. Departments struggled to attract the best quality applicants and to develop more robust selection protocols. Developing educational capacity required time, well-trained instructors, facilities, and a willingness to take officers out of service. Equipment did not just require funding but proper administration and maintenance. A summary of design and implementation challenges across the different sub-policy arenas can be found in Appendix A.

In addition, advances in one of these areas alone are insufficient to produce an improvement in policing overall. The Tijuana case suggests that salary increases are insufficient if selection criteria are slack. Good selection criteria and cadet training are inadequate if existing officers are not well vetted and trained or if salaries and benefits cannot attract good candidates. Technology is not useful unless it is used by well-trained officers.

Moreover, as of yet, I have only considered the low-hanging fruit of reform. The obstacles to police reform become even more complicated once merit-based promotion criteria (Chapter 3) and accountability mechanisms (Chapter 4) are taken into account. It is worth remembering that Klitgaard's formula was "monopoly plus discretion minus *accountability* equals corruption." Absent accountability mechanisms or a trustworthy hierarchy, improvements in selection criteria, training, salaries, and equipment will probably not produce substantial benefits. A well-vetted high school graduate, with ten months of training, a good salary, and all the needed equipment to do her job might still engage in corruption if the probability of being caught is low and/or if doing so is encouraged by the institution.

While this chapter has discussed policy design and implementation challenges, there exists an even more fundamental challenge to reform: institutionalization. Reforms in all of these areas will not bear fruit unless they are continued by the following administration. This is the topic of the following chapter. Just as a well-designed policy does not ensure effective implementation, a well-implemented policy does not ensure institutionalization. As the following chapter will make clear, the inability to institutionalize reform initiatives has been the primary obstacle to real reform in Mexico's municipalities.

3 A Problem of Municipal Governance

We have had good programs, but the administration changed, they brought with them new ideas, and they got rid of the old ones. You lose continuity and we need continuity. We cut the tree before the fruits are produced.
—*Hermosillo police officer*

Here in Mexico we have this custom that a new one comes in and what was there before isn't valid. We are reborn every three years. There is no continuity.
—*Member of Tijuana civil society*

The problem here in Mexico is that everyone believes that they are going to change the course of the country. No. Those that come in have to respect what is already there.
—*Tijuana municipal official*

Rethinking Failed Leadership[1]

In his famous book *Controlling Corruption*, Robert Klitgaard (1988) profiles the herculean efforts of Justice Efren Plana to root out corruption in the Philippine tax collection agency during the dictatorship of Ferdinand Marcos. Klitgaard portrays a dramatic success story entailing well-designed and implemented reform initiatives that reduced corruption and increased tax revenues. Almost as a postscript at the end of the chapter, however, the reader learns that upon Justice Plana's departure from the agency, things largely returned to the way that they had been prior to the reforms. Justice Plana's experience suggests that design and implementation are also dependent on a third factor: institutionalization. The inability to institutionalize reforms represents one of the clearest explanations for why numerous reform efforts in Mexico have not been more successful.

In interviews, public officials repeatedly stated that the problem of the police was a product of failed leadership, and expressed their intention to usher in a new period of reform. Nonetheless, a review of past government reports and municipal development plans suggests that this air of optimism was renewed every three years at the beginning of a new municipal administration. The front cover of Tijuana mayor Jorge Ramos's municipal development plan (2008–10) showed a pair of hands cupped around a small seeding growing forth from a fresh pile of dirt. The message was clear: his administration was going to plant the seeds for the future. This symbolism finds itself intertwined in the rhetoric of officials across the research sites. The presumption is that what was done in the past is not working, and there needs to be a fresh start. However, as the above quotes indicate, government officials run the risk of "throwing the proverbial baby out with the bathwater." If the next administration cuts down Jorge Ramos's seedling, then, as one Hermosillo municipal official commented, no one will get to enjoy its fruits.

This chapter argues that the problem of the police is first and foremost a problem of politics. In later chapters, I will explore additional external factors that have hindered police development; however, this research suggests that the primary problem is a political one. In answer to the question why reform initiatives have not produced institutional change, this chapter finds that political leaders have failed to give continuity to reform efforts. The lack of continuity in both personnel and policy is a direct product of the institutional incentives of municipal governance specifically and Mexican governance more generally. Using previous scholarship and a 2004 survey of municipalities, this chapter will explore some of the weaknesses in both the formal constitutional-choice rules and the informal rules of municipal governance. I contend that these rules result in (1) a lack of horizontal accountability between the municipal president and the city council, and (2) a lack of reform continuity across administrations. In turn, these two factors generate systematic obstacles to institutional change. The chapter then delves into the four case studies and provides evidence of these two problems in three of the four research sites. In Chihuahua, however, I find an impressive degree of reform continuity between administrations, which I argue was one of the fundamental causes of its relative success. The chapter identifies a change-continuity paradox, whereby the lack of continuity in reform initiatives and constant changes in policy and leadership allow the informal rules of patronage and corruption tolerance to continue.

A Lack of Continuity and the Politicization of the Police

Although woefully understudied, the challenge of institutionalization has hindered reform efforts throughout the region. At a 2010 conference on police and public security, Ecuadorian academic Fernando Carrión stated emphatically that "Latin America is a cemetery of success stories." Perhaps the most striking example of discontinuity can be found in Argentina's Buenos Aires. Following several scandals, including the involvement of the police in the 1997 assassination of a journalist, then-governor Eduardo Duhalde, along with his newly appointed minister of justice and security León Arslanián, used emergency powers to dismiss over three hundred high ranking officers and over four thousand rank-and-file police, divide the force into distinct agencies, decentralize operations, and establish community groups to oversee the police and participate in public security (Ward 2006; Fuentes 2006; Eaton 2008).

While popular among some constituents, the reforms were resisted by a pro-order coalition of actors, including mayors, police, and citizens who favored a more punitive approach to the province's rising crime problems (Fuentes 2006). Much of the opposition came from within Duhalde's own Peronist party and, upon coming into office in 1999, his successor Carlos Ruckauf reversed course. He appointed a former military officer as justice and security minister, replaced many of Duhalde's civilian appointees, rehired most of the fired officers, recentralized operations, and granted the police greater discretion and authority. Five years later under a new governor, León Arslanián was reappointed as justice and security minister; he reinitiated the community forums, re-decentralized the police, and continued the earlier reforms despite continued opposition from pro-order groups (Ward 2006).

While less dramatic, similar problems can be found throughout the region. In Brazil in the late 1990s, President Fernando Henrique Cardoso's ambitious National Plan for Public Security failed partially because of constant leadership turnover: in just eight years, Brazil had nine different justice ministers (Dellasoppa and Saint'Clair Branco 2006). In Venezuela, in the run-up to the 2006 presidential elections and following several scandals of police misconduct, the National Commission for Police Reform undertook a fairly detailed diagnostic study of the police and offered recommendations for reform; however, the commission lost momentum once the commission's leader was replaced (Birbeck and Gabaldón 2009).

By contrast, Moncada (2009) attributes the success of reforms in Bogotá, Colombia, to reform continuity across several municipal administrations. Colombia's 1991 constitution prohibited the immediate reelection of mayors, thus creating similar political incentives to Mexico. Brought into office in 1995, Antanas Mockus initiated a variety of innovated reforms to involve citizens in public security and oversight of the police. Mockus borrowed much of his approach from the previous mayor of Cali, Rodrigo Guerrero Velasco (Mockus, n.d). Nonetheless, Guerrero's efforts died with the change in administration and Mockus's were continued by his successor, Enrique Peñalosa, and during Mockus's second term beginning in 2001.

It is tempting to attribute the failure of police reform to a lack of leadership, and, of course, leadership is absolutely crucial to any reform initiative, but I argue that in the long run the problem of police reform in Mexico is *too much* leadership. Lacking strong institutions, the Buenos Aires police were entirely subject to the prerogatives of constantly changing elected officials and their appointees. Paradoxically, in each of the three successful cases of police reform in the hemisphere (the United States, Colombia, and Chile), police professionalization occurred during a period of insulation from politics. In the United States, civil service reforms in the early twentieth century ended what Kelling and Moore (1988) call the "political era of policing" and wrested control of the police from the political machine. They write, "In their [reformers'] view, politics and political involvement was the *problem* in American policing," and conclude that, "Political influence of any kind on the police department came to be seen as not merely a failure of police leadership but as corruption in policing" (5). As a result, it was autonomous police leaders like August Vollmer, O. W. Wilson, and J. Edgar Hoover—not elected officials—who oversaw the professionalization of the police.

In Colombia, reform also came from within. Civilian efforts to clean up Colombia's organized crime-infiltrated and corrupted police force in the early 1990s, including the establishment of an external accountability agency, were actively resisted by the National Police. Real change did not occur until the mid-1990s, when police director General Rosso José Serrano initiated a "cultural transformation" of the police force and oversaw a major purging of approximately 11 percent of the agency (Llorente 2006). In Chile, the Carabineros also resisted civilian efforts at control following the country's transition to democracy and in response to the police agency's participation in human rights abuses during the military dictatorship (1973–90). Police leaders contended that removing the police from the defense ministry and subsuming it into the interior ministry would politicize the agency (Dammert 2006). Recognizing their insulation from the citizenry and history of human rights abuses, however, police leaders initiated their own reforms, including the Plan Cuadrante (Quadrant Plan), a Chilean version of community policing (Dammert).

It is important to mention that independence from politics is very much a double-edged sword—after all, in a representative democracy, public administration should be accountable to elected officials. In fact, prior to concerted civil society and political pressure, "independence" from politics led to corruption and human rights abuses in Colombia and Chile. Even in the United States, the insulation of the Los Angeles Police Department helped create an organizational culture that permitted the Rodney King beating and the Rampart corruption scandal in the 1990s (Kutnjak Ivkovic 2005). Clearly, police autonomy is no panacea by itself. Police in all three countries already had robust civil service regimes, and all three faced considerable pressure from an active citizenry. So as not to confront another pendulum like the human rights/pro-order pendulum in Buenos Aires, the appropriate question is: do political and police leaders in Mexico's municipalities have incentives to institutionalize police reform and promote meaningful institutional change?

Institutional Incentives in Mexico's Municipalities

In the previous two chapters, the concept of institutions, or the formal and informal "rules of the game," was introduced. Ostrom, Gardner, and Walker (1994) further divide these rules into three embedded categories, including operational, collective-choice, and constitutional-choice rules. Operational rules are those that affect the incentives and day-to-day decision making of police, including police regulations and policies. Collective-choice rules determine how and who gets to lay out the operational rules; these include the various laws and regulations that govern policing in Mexico. The final set of rules, the constitutional-choice rules, determines who gets to set the *collective-choice* rules and determine their parameters.

Scholars have clearly established a link between constitutional-choice rules and the nature and quality of democracy and governance. For example, proportional representation voting systems, which send candidates to the legislature based on the proportion of votes their party receives, permit the viability of smaller political parties (Duverger 1954). Closed-list systems, where the parties—rather than voters—determine which nominees will have priority on proportional representation lists, helps strengthen party coherence (Mainwaring 1999). The mix of constitutional-choice rules sometimes creates surprising incentives for political actors. Mainwaring, for example, finds that the mix of federalism, open-list proportional representation, and presidentialism combine to produce a weak legislative branch and fractionalized party system.

This analysis is particularly interested in the interaction of formal constitutional-choice rules and the informal rules of Mexican politics. Scholars of Mexican politics have long recognized the importance of the informal rules in municipal governance. Mauricio Merino (2006a) for example, argues that a framework for studying municipal governance should not focus on the formal rules but on what he refers to as the "routines," or day-to-day decisions and actions of public servants. Selee's (2010) exploration of "informal power" in Mexico's municipalities focuses on the informal hierarchical power relations of patronage and intermediation. David Arellano Gault and Juan Guerrero Amparán (2003) contend that informal practices such as corruption, fraud, bureaucratic patrimonialism, clientelism, opportunism, and inefficiency have become part of the governing institutions within Mexican public administration. These examples are representative of a literature that has found that formal policies and legislation are often ineffective and at times meaningless if they are contradicted by the informal rules.

To best understand the incentives operating at the municipal level, it is necessary to explore the history of the Mexican municipality. Municipal government has existed in Mexico since Spanish colonization. The basis of government in Spain was the Free Municipality (*Municipio Libre*), whose government was known as the *ayuntamiento,* which consisted of a local council, or *cabildo.*[2] The *cabildos* were replicated in Mexico; however, their power was subordinated to the Spanish viceroy. After Mexico's independence, the fate of municipal and state governments was brought into question as conservative centrists and liberal federalists vied for control. The federalists eventually won out, and the states and the *ayuntamientos* were preserved in the 1824 and 1857 Constitutions. Municipalities were able to collect a local tariff on goods passing through their jurisdiction, and citizens voted annually on councilmen, or *regidores,* who selected a municipal leader from within their ranks. Even during this period, however, the local governments were held in check by state governments and federal prefects, or *prefectos.* Local power was further reduced during the centralizing dictatorship of Porfirio Díaz (1876–1911), who placed greater emphasis on the prefect system.

After the Mexican Revolution (1910–20), the relative importance of the municipalities continued to decline (Selee 2010). The 1917 Constitution maintained the *ayuntamientos*, but it was unclear about their responsibilities. Municipalities were regulated by state law and became, in effect, administrative units of the state. More important, however, the relevance of both municipal and state governments was eroded by the de facto concentration of power in the office of the president and the PRI corporatist system, which set up a parallel—and more relevant—system of representation based on the sectors of farmers, workers, and what was ambiguously referred to as "the popular sector" (Rodriguez 1997; Ward and Rodriguez 1999; Weldon 1999).

In other words, for most of the twentieth century, municipal governments were very weak institutions with limited responsibility. This situation began to change in 1983, with the passage of constitutional reforms that gave municipalities the right to collect property taxes, full ownership over municipal property, the right to regulate themselves, and primary responsibility for providing several public goods and services, including public security. Decentralization was embraced by then-president Miguel de la Madrid Hurtado (1982–88) both for economic reasons (to reduce the size of the state) and political reasons (to bolster the PRI regime's legitimacy) (Ward and Rodriguez 1999). Opposition parties were also pushing for decentralization as they had won several important municipal elections in the early 1980s, including in Chihuahua City and Ciudad Juárez (Martínez Assad 1985), and saw the municipalities as a vehicle to contest the PRI's monopoly.

In 1997, during the Zedillo administration, the municipalities became beneficiaries of the federal fiscal system, whereby the federal government collects the vast majority of public revenues and redistributes them among the states and now the municipalities (Merino 2006b). The position of the municipality was further bolstered by a 1999 constitutional reform that recognized the municipalities as their own entity within the federal system (Merino; Valencia Carmona 2002). The municipality's legal rights as an independent level of government not subordinated to the states were upheld in a 2005 Supreme Court ruling (Avilés 2005). To illustrate these changes, Rodolfo García del Castillo (2006) focuses on the size of the municipal workforce, which went from an estimated 337,035 in 1995 to 548,610 in 2002, a 61.4 percent increase in just seven years.[3]

Despite a history that can be traced back to the colonial period, meaningful municipal governance is a relatively new phenomenon. Today, Mexico's municipalities confront a number of obstacles to meaningful reform. First, municipalities have only limited fiscal capacity. Second, the electoral system enshrined in the Constitution creates perverse incentives for political leaders. Third, a system of informal rules and routines support and perpetuate the problems created by the formal constitutional rules. The result is an overly strong municipal president with enormous discretion, a weak city council, a system that privileges the informal rules over the former rules and fails to insulate public administration from partisanship and patronage, and constant turnover in personnel and policy.

As of 2006, there were a total of 2,438 municipalities in Mexico, most of which (2022) had their own police force.[4] In some states, there are literally hundreds of small municipalities, such as Oaxaca with 570, while other states have few large municipalities, such as Baja California with five. In fact, the vast majority of the municipalities (1,867) are rather small, with a population of less than fifteen thousand (Merino 2006b). The remaining 276 municipalities account for over two thirds of the country's population, and obviously these jurisdictions have far greater administrative capacity. While this research is focused on Mexico's larger cities, it is important to note that the problems identified by this research tend to be far worse in the smaller municipalities (Grindle 2007).

Despite relatively large operations, municipal governments function on comparatively small budgets. The importance of revenue-generating capacity is highlighted by former Bogotá mayor Antanas Mockus, who argues that it was the essential first step to the city's dramatic security improvements (Mockus, n.d). Although the municipalities are able to levy property taxes, these taxes remain extremely low and municipalities remain highly dependent on transfers from the federal government to cover their expenses. On average, Mexico's municipalities derive 71.8 percent of their revenue from the federal government (See Table 3.1). Larger municipalities have greater revenue-generating capacity and rely on federal funding for a much smaller average of 58.2 percent of their income (Merino 2006b). While the difference is substantial, the latter municipalities still depend on the federal government for over half their revenues. Table 3.1 provides information on revenues for the four research cases. The percent of revenues from the federal government in 2007 ranged from 47.5 percent in Hermosillo to 57 percent in Tijuana.

TABLE 3.1. 2007 Municipal revenues with percent local sources versus federal and state (in thousands of U.S. dollars)

	Total	Local revenues	Federal and state revenues	Available from previous period plus financing
Tijuana	$244,687	$105,329	$139,358	0
	100%	43.0%	57.0%	.
Mexicali	$171,544	$70,123	$90,017	$11,403
	100%	43.8%	56.2%	.
Chihuahua	$122,424	$53,433	$68,991	0
	100%	43.6%	56.4%	.
Hermosillo	$130,751	$68,695	$62,056	0
	100%	52.5%	47.5%	.
Total municipalities	$15,981,251	$4,105,983	$10,471,723	$1,403,545
	100%	28.2%	71.8%	.

NOTE: For Mexicali and Total municipalities, the amount available from the previous period plus financing is subtracted from the total to ensure that the percentages are comparable. Pesos converted to dollars at a four-year average of 12.04 pesos to the dollar.
SOURCE: Data from the *Ingresos y el Gasto Público en México* 2009. INEGI.

While part of the problem at the municipal level is the administrative capacity to levy and collect taxes, there is a general unwillingness to enact needed tax increases. From the perspective of local governments, it is far easier to solicit additional transfers from the federal government than tax local constituents. This is precisely what has happened with the Municipal Public Security Subsidy (SUBSEMUN) mentioned in Chapter 1. Prior to this new federal subsidy in 2008, there had been woefully insufficient economic resources to improve the quality of public security, raise salaries, purchase sufficient equipment, or properly maintain existing equipment. Even training was affected, as police deployments did not traditionally provide sufficient flexibility to temporarily remove officers from service for ongoing training.[5]

Despite these financial challenges, the problems of municipal governance are more political than economic. Like all elected officials in Mexico, municipal presidents and city councilmen and women are unable to run for reelection. "No re-election" was one of the central tenants of the revolution against Porfirio Díaz. While in theory this constitutional restriction limits an unhealthy concentration of power, it has resulted in several unintended consequences. First, the restriction creates a short-term approach to governance. Second, elected officials have to maintain an eye on their next career move after the end of their term. As a result, governing officials have strong incentives to use their posts to earn the confidence and good graces of higher-level party leaders, who have considerable sway over future nomination processes and appointments. While a strong party system is generally viewed as desirable (Diamond and Gunther 2001), Tonatiuh Guillén López (2006) argues that in the Mexican political system, municipal officials act in the interest of the party over that of their constituents. Third, as I will argue below, no-reelection has combined with the informal rules of Mexican politics to produce a system of constant turnover in personnel and policy.

The party-list voting system also produces unintended consequences. Rather than vote directly for city councilmen and councilwomen, the electorate votes for a municipal president accompanied by a party list of candidates for city council. Interestingly, during the campaigns, election propaganda is typically limited to the presidential candidate, and relatively few potential voters even know who the council candidates are. While the nomination process for the slate differs across geography and time, in most cases voters do not determine who is on the list.[6] Guillén López (2006) argues that the PRI and PAN generally pursue different approaches. The PRI, he contends, typically determines list selection based on the old corporatist system, including representatives from the PRI's different sectoral organizations. The PAN used to hold internal votes; however, in many cases a mayoral candidate assembles his or her own slate prior to the nomination process as a means to develop momentum into the nomination process. As a result of this system, councils are generally very loyal to the municipal president, to whom they owe their job. Given the previous rule of no-reelection, continued loyalty to the president and the party are often important keys to future career opportunities. As a corollary, council members are poor representatives of the citizens who only indirectly elected them. As Guillén López argues, "A figure that is unknown (or almost unknown) by municipal society, cannot, in principle, define him or herself as a representative of that society" (148).

A third problematic formal rule is the mechanism for determining who from the different party lists will actually have seats on the council. In 1983, constitutional reforms dictated that the council seats would be determined by proportional representation as a means to ensure some opposition-party representation. However, with the exception of five states, the PRI-dominated state legislatures created a two-tiered system, whereby the winning slate wins a certain predetermined number of seats and the remaining seats are divided up based on proportional representation (in which the winning slate is again included).[7] The result has been that municipal presidents are almost guaranteed loyal supermajorities on the council, thus impeding horizontal accountability between the president and the council.[8]

Provided strong institutions exist, these formal rules by themselves would not necessarily be problematic; however, their ensuing negative incentives are compounded by the informal rules of Mexican politics. Arellano Gault and Guerrero Amparán (2003) argue that one cannot understand governance in Mexico without recognizing that public administration has been highly affected by the informal rules of corporatism and presidentialism. They contend that during the one-party system of government, it was the bureaucracy not the legislature that was the fundamental means of channeling resources to key social sectors. As the president was head of the bureaucracy, power was centered in his office. While the transition to democracy has strengthened the position of the legislature and the judiciary vis-à-vis the executive at the federal level, no such shift has occurred at the municipal level. As such, the presidentialism that characterized Mexico for decades is still the predominant paradigm in Mexico's municipalities.

The second informal rule, or "routine" in Merino's language, is patronage appointments. The municipal president has almost complete discretion in making appointments to head the various government agencies. Typically, only the secretary and treasurer of the city government require approval by the *cabildo*, and given the weakness of the council, this is typically not a major check on presidential prerogative. Guillén López (2006) writes, "Behind this presidential power can be found one of the most harmful practices in municipal administration. The reoccurring pattern is that the president uses administrative posts as an object of political negotiation" (151).

The practice does not just apply to the upper levels of public administration, but reaches down to the middle levels of the bureaucracy, as newly appointed officials also have the discretion to replace existing personnel. Municipal employees are generally divided into two categories: base employees, who are typically unionized and fill the lower-level positions within the bureaucracy, and employees *de confianza*, literally "trust" employees, who serve at the behest of the president. While the former group stays on at the end of an administration, the latter group is subject to change. For the 782 municipalities that provided personnel information in the National Survey of Municipal Governments in 2004, 52.7 percent of personnel were base employees and 47.3

percent were *de confianza*.[9] These percentages are very similar for the thirty-two municipalities with a population of over two hundred thousand that responded to the question: 48.7 percent were base employees and 51.2 percent were trust employees.

Arellano Gault and Guerrero Amparán (2003) further divide trust employees into high- and medium-level positions. They contend that high-level trust employees will generally move with their boss at the end of a new administration, while mid-level (usually technical) employees will generally find a position in a different agency and/or branch of government doing similar work. The product of this rule (combined with no-reelection) is the politicization of the bureaucracy and constant purging of high- and mid-level staff members. Extrapolating from data from 2002, Merino (2006a) estimates that 173,000 municipal employees (31.5 percent) are rotated every year.

Appointments allow new executives to reward supporters, build alliances (particularly if a newly elected mayor has ambitions for the governor's seat), and ensure that his or her subordinates are loyal and trustworthy. Barbara Geddes (1996) identifies a collective action in changing such practices. Because other officials continue to rely on the patronage system, one executive defection does little to undermine the system. Moreover, a defecting official would be surrendering the benefits of patronage without the corresponding gains in a more professional government. With high costs and few benefits, Geddes argues that the dominant strategy of politicians is to play by the patronage game.

While such discretionary appointment power is rational from the executive's point of view, it has negative side effects on public administration. First, when trust and loyalty are valued more than experience, institutional knowledge, and ability, bureaucracies are left with less-than-adequate human resources to overcome all the "benign" implementation challenges discussed in Chapter 2. Merino (2006b) writes, "Principal government officials are recruited based on their party affiliation and ties to the municipal presidents much more so than for reasons of professional capacity or experience in the post they occupy" (63). Beyond the costs of patronage, there is also an opportunity cost. In the case of the police, non-merit-based appointments remove a potential "carrot" for honest, effective police work. As one police administrator argued, "if we don't provide them with the dream that they can rise up the ranks through their merits, then they are not going to invest in becoming better police officers." This is perhaps the largest obstacle to developing a professional police force with its own institutional identity.

Second, it is difficult to imagine continuity in reform efforts when much of the top half of the agency hierarchy is replaced along with the institutional knowledge of the previous three years. As García del Castillo (2006) writes, "Absent organizations that learn and accumulate knowledge, one cannot imagine overcoming all of the shortcomings present in the functioning of our institutions" (149). In fact, newly appointed leaders often spend a significant portion of their time in office just learning the job.

Third, the rotation creates perverse incentives to act contrary to the public interest. As stated above, faced with uncertainty in their posts, officials have to spend their time laying the groundwork for obtaining their next job. In the worst-case scenario, they will seek to obtain as much personal benefit as possible before their tenure expires.[10] Moreover, as appointees owe their job to a patron, there are incentives to act in the interest of the patron rather than the interest of the public (López Alvarado 2009). García del Castillo (2006) sums up these problems well when he writes,

> It is worrying to think that every three years new actors arrive in the municipal governments and that, in the process of learning, they will consume a good part of their tenure and will be able to do very little in the remaining time. This is even more serious if you consider that at the end of the three year period they are primarily thinking how to protect themselves politically (49).

These rules—formal and informal—combine to produce a lack of horizontal accountability and a lack of continuity in reform efforts across administrations, two factors that have systematically undermined reform. As Merino (2006b) notes in the introduction to his book on municipal reform, "In the course of this work we will see that in reality there still is not one complete experience of municipal professionalization that has achieved outlasting the period of government in which it was conceived" (38).

The following section explores the impact of the formal and informal rules of local governance in the four research sites. The discussion limits itself to the years prior to 2009 and new institutional incentives created by the federal government, which will be explored in Chapter 7. The data is drawn primarily from interviews at the research sites and an analysis of documentation from previous municipal administrations. The analysis begins by exploring the continued practice of patronage appointments and the inability to develop something akin to a police civil service despite legal reforms intended to do so. I find that not only is there a lack of continuity in personnel, but dramatic

changes in policies from administration to administration that create an uncertain and erratic reform path. The importance of institutionalization is
clearly demonstrated by the case of Chihuahua, which made unparalleled
(although imperfect) strides in professionalization largely because of a degree
of reform continuity not afforded in the other three sites. In theory, the city
council members could provide oversight and ensure the continuity of effective programs; however, the case studies reveal their relative weakness and
partisan nature. The ironic result of these constitutional and informal rules is
that while there is a constant flow of fresh blood and new (sometimes innovative) policies, the old ways of doing things persevere.

Patronage Appointments

While the lack of reform continuity manifests itself in a number of ways, it
begins with the constant turnover in personnel and the failure to develop an
effective mid-level command staff. An incomplete census of municipalities
conducted in 2004 revealed that the median tenure of directors and secretar-
ies of public security at the time of the survey was a mere two years. Two years
was also the median tenure in large municipalities of over two hundred thousand inhabitants.[11] Table 3.2 shows the average tenure of the four previous
police chiefs in each of the eleven surveyed sites. It ranges from just .73 years

TABLE 3.2. Average tenure of police chiefs

	Average tenure of the previous four police chiefs (years)
Guadalajara	3.00
Monterrey	1.65
Mérida	2.25
Ahome	2.00
México DF	2.65
S. L. Potosí	1.83
Torreón	2.96
Chihuahua	4.67
Puebla	0.73
Cuernavaca	2.44
Zapopan	1.93
Average	2.37

SOURCE: Information provided by police departments
in response to the Police Professionalism Survey
administered in early 2009.

in Puebla to 4.67 in Chihuahua. Of forty-four police chiefs, the average lasted 2.47 years.

Provided strong institutions exist, turnover of the police chief alone would not necessarily undermine a reformist agenda; however, personnel changes also dip down into the upper and middle sections of the police agency. During the 2006–09 administration, the Hermosillo police department published a directory of thirty-five high- level positions within the agency, including fifteen operational positions and twenty nonoperational and administrative positions. The following administration published a similar list with all of the same positions including a few more (for a total of forty-five). Of the previous administration's staff, 9 of 15 (or 60 percent) of the operational staff and 11 of 20 (or 55 percent) of the administrative staff had left or were replaced. The changes were not 100 percent, but they were the majority.

In interviews, midlevel commanders in Mexicali complained at length about the promotion criteria in their city. Of the seven commanders interviewed, all had moved up and down the ranks of the department, holding high posts in one administration and lower posts in another; none had followed a steady trek upward. When asked what percent of the hundred-plus commanders in the Mexicali police had moved up and down in the agency, the consensus was 100 percent. Tijuana police confront a similar reality. For example, one officer interviewed reported holding the rank of sergeant (*subjefe*) in one administration, dropping to agent in the next administration, being promoted to lieutenant (*jefe*) in the next, and having fallen again to agent. Another had been operational commander for the whole city but now only held the rank of agent. The first commented, "Promotion has always been based on one's personal connections. It has always been that way and it continues that way." Hermosillo officers confirmed similar problems, and even in Chihuahua, a 2006 survey of 250 officers found skepticism toward the promotion process. In response to the question, "do you think that the process for determining promotions is clear and fair?," 39.14 percent agreed, 25.68 percent neither agreed nor disagreed, and 35.15 percent disagreed (Nájera Ruíz 2006). A small minority of study participants in Tijuana and Hermosillo even alleged that the sale of leadership positions went on; this is a long-standing practice, but one that police leaders contended was a thing of the past.

While on the whole interview respondents felt that the mechanisms for determining promotion were woefully inadequate, some showed general acceptance of the status quo, and a small minority even defended it. There are two main advantages to executive discretion in appointments of upper- and mid-level management. First, if there is a commander who is ineffective or believed to be engaged in corruption, he or she can be removed from the post without confronting inflexible civil service rules. Second, given the amount of corruption and organized crime infiltration within many police forces, it is argued that the executive needs to be able to appoint people that he or she can trust.

Although the current system of director discretion offers flexibility, the costs far outweigh the benefits. As discussed above, leadership roles are not necessarily filled by the best-qualified people, institutional memory is lost, and there are *disincentives* for up-and-coming officers to excel. One officer complained, "I have no incentive to better myself. I have a college degree, but that doesn't really matter here. I could get assigned to be one of the guys flipping the switch to make the traffic lights turn color." He added jokingly that at least people would refer to him as "*licenciado* light switcher" (*licenciado* being the formal title and term of respect for someone with a college degree). Although meant to be humorous, the comment is illustrative of how a non-merit-based promotion system fails to create incentives for professional, effective, and honest police work protective of individual rights. If professional behavior is not rewarded, then it would be unlikely for professionalism to emerge within the department. If a promotion system favors loyalty over ability, then the police force will be more loyal than capable. And, in the worst case scenario, if leadership positions can be bought, then corruption will invade all other aspects of policing.

The arbitrary nature of current promotion criteria creates additional incentives for corruption. In Mexicali, for example, a city that pays its officers well compared to other departments, a shift supervisor (equivalent of a lieutenant) earns a salary of $1,692 a month. A demotion at the end of the administration back down to agent implies a 40 percent cut in salary to $1,032, Commanding officers might be hesitant to crack down on day-to-day bribe payments if they know that they will see their salary slashed in the not-so-distant future. Moreover, officers will be hesitant to make the unpopular decision of punishing misconduct among their subordinates if they know that their rank is temporary.

The alleged benefits of the status quo also assume that the executive will use his or her power in the best interest of the community and the department; however, as discussed above, political leaders face considerable pressure to use their appointment power in a way that balances the need for effective public administration and their future political careers. Consider the trajectories of the mayors in the four research sites from the administration proceeding the study period. In Mexicali, Samuel Ramos went on to be the head of the PRI party in Baja California, and then made a run for congress. In Tijuana, Jorge Hank Rhon left office in a losing bid for the governorship of Baja California under the PRI ticket. In Hermosillo, María Dolores del Río Sánchez ran for the nomination of the PAN for the governorship of Sonora. In Chihuahua, Juan Alberto Blanco Zaldívar was in the process of running for congress and he was a favored candidate for his party's nomination for governor when his campaign was derailed by bribery charges. His successor, Carlos Borruel Baquera, took an early leave from his mayoral responsibilities to run for governor. Given the need for political support to obtain these nominations and a long history of patronage in Mexican politics, it is problematic to assume that mayors with full discretion in political appointments will act in the public interest.

The need for flexibility is of course important, and therefore continuity of personnel should not be a goal in and of itself. Much like independence from politics, continuity is also a double-edged sword. Maintaining leaders that achieved their positions through an unreliable promotion process is not necessarily desirable. Elena Azaola (2009), for example, offers testimonials by police in Mexico City complaining of a "brotherhood" among high-level officers that controls the promotions process to its advantage. In Tijuana, one assistant chief who held on to his position after the change in administration ended up being arrested by federal authorities and brought up on drug charges (Frontera 2008c). Instead, the goal should be to create a merit-based promotion process to ensure that those who arrive at positions of leadership are honest, professional, effective, and protective of individual rights.

Achieving such a goal, however, transcends a three-year administration, and an incoming mayor needs commanders right away. Incoming officials could opt to invest in a system that will provide their successor with such information, but the successor might simply choose to skirt the new system and appoint personnel based on the informal rules of patronage. Consistent with Geddes's collective problem, the reformer would have borne the costs of forgoing patronage without any benefits.

In theory, the solution to this continuity problem should be a legislative one; however, a number legal reforms and policy initiatives designed to create something akin to a police civil service have failed to do so. In Mexicali as early as 1982, municipal regulations were passed creating a formal promotion procedure. More recently, the 2001–04 administration of Jaime Díaz established three classes of police: A, B, and C agents, with criteria for moving between the different levels. The legislation was a step forward because commanding officers could only be drawn from among the A agents, effectively restricting the pool from which commanders could be selected. Nonetheless, the reforms still allowed the police leadership discretion in choosing its commanding officers from among this group, and, in fact, the following administration announced that it would select an entirely new team of commanders. Officials in the Samuel Ramos administration (2004–07) contended that this was a sincere effort at a deliberate and competitive process. Detractors, however, noted that the Ramos administration was the first PRI administration in nine years, and alleged that the "reform" was really an effort to select commanders loyal to the new government and the new chief. The Ramos administration did, however, continue to perfect the existing legislation, calling for all police to be evaluated annually, the creation of a Manual for Re-categorization and Promotions, and the formation of a nine member Committee for Promotions and Recognition, which was to meet monthly and include a member of the city council and the president of the Citizen Public Security Council. Unfortunately, however, despite being written into municipal regulations, these efforts were never fully implemented.

When the next administration came into office, the top operational leaders were brought in from the outside. In addition, the new administration announced in its first annual report that it too had "renovated the leadership ranks," continuing the process of demoting some commanders and bringing up others. Twenty-eight years of failed formal rules suggests the primacy of the informal rule accepting discretionary promotion over formal initiatives that have sought to create a flexible, merit-based system. Many Mexicali officers were resigned to this fact. As one officer stated, "At the end of the day we are all agents . . . we serve in the leadership at the will of the director." This sentiment was expressed by a number of interview respondents throughout the different police agencies and is both a product and evidence of an informal rule deferring to police leadership and granting priority to personal trust.

Tijuana has experienced a similar problem. Its 2004 legislation details the creation of a special promotion commission, which is to oversee a formal evaluation, examination, and selection process to determine leadership posts within the department (Ayuntamiento de Tijuana 2004). The examination is to include a psychological exam, a knowledge exam, a practical policing exam, and an exam on command and control. In practice, however, interviews make clear that this formal process was avoided and selection for leadership posts remained at the discretion of the secretary, the director of public security, and the mayor.

Hermosillo has also experimented with creating a merit-based process. In 1999, the reform-oriented administration of Jorge Valencia Juillerat (1999) bragged that, "We have given to the police the chance for promotion, not based on favoritisms, but based on a competition." The statement is partially true. Because of reforms initiated during Valencia Juillerat's tenure, rank, once given, cannot be taken away in Hermosillo. Nonetheless, police leaders have preserved their discretion to appoint commanders by simply divorcing leadership from rank. It is common, therefore, for an officer to hold the rank of unit commander (*comandante de unidad*) or first officer (*oficial primero*), but have no actual command. Rank became meaningless. Nonetheless, an increase in rank did come with a corresponding pay raise, and critics, both inside and outside the police, contended that it was little more than a means to financially reward loyalists. As such, most officers interviewed felt that operational command positions were more likely to be based on merit than rank. The reform had the opposite of its intended effect.

As in the other locations, there is general acceptance of this arrangement. One administrator argued that talented young police officers should not have to slowly work their way up the bureaucracy. Another discussed the virtues of constant rotation of commanders. He contended that commanders should be rotated every six months to avoid corruption and to give other officers the chance to prove themselves. While a promotion system does require flexibility to ensure that well-qualified up-and-coming officers are being promoted and poorly performing leaders are not protected in their leadership roles, the de facto system has had the reverse effect: allowing unqualified officers to be promoted and capable leaders to lose their leadership roles.

A Lack of Continuity in Reform Policy

The constant turnover in high and mid-level management corresponds with continuous changes in reform policy. Much like personnel, bad policies should not be maintained for their own sake. In theory, policies should be evaluated and continued or cut based on their merits, but instead, policies come and go arbitrarily with the changes of personnel. As discussed in Chapter 2, one administration might work to strengthen the police academy, while the next might shorten training times to graduate more cadets faster. Another administration might build in-service training capacity, while the next will cancel such programs to keep more police on the street.

Operational procedures offer an illustrative example. There is currently a strong push for municipal police agencies to be certified by the U.S.-based Commission on Accreditation of Law Enforcement Agencies (CALEA); however, in the late 1990s and early 2000s there were political incentives for certification by the International Standards Organization, ISO-9000. While not geared toward policing like CALEA, ISO certification also implies developing and implementing a series of clearly laid out policies and procedures. Both Mexicali and Hermosillo sought and obtained ISO certification: Mexicali in 1999 and Hermosillo in 2002. As in Chihuahua today, Mexicali officials bragged that theirs was the first police department in Mexico to obtain ISO certification. However, what looked like a clear step forward for police reform was quickly reversed with the change of administration. The subsequent municipal administration of Jamie Díaz (of the same PAN political party) failed to give the procedures priority, sought to implement an alternative approach, and allowed the certification to lapse.[12] The next administration of Samuel Ramos (PRI) dusted off the old procedure manuals and updated them; however, application was weak and they were not externally certified. The following administration updated the existing procedures, initiated a strong enforcement effort, and successfully obtained CALEA recognition and accreditation. As Table 3.3 illustrates, each administration had its own police chief and its own policy toward procedures.

TABLE 3.3. Lack of continuity across administrations in Mexicali

Timeline	1998–2001	2001–04	2004–07	2007–10
Party in Power	PAN		PRI	PAN
Mayor	Hermosillo Celada	Díaz Ochoa	Ramos Flores	Valdez Gutiérrez
Police chief		Fernando Díaz / Efraín Guevara	Javier Salas	Ulises Méndez
Policy	ISO-9001	Citizen Evaluation of Public Security institutions and Policies	Internal	CALEA

Not surprisingly, a similar fate befell ISO certification in Hermosillo, which lapsed under the del Río administration (2004–06) and was not reinitiated under the Gándara administration (2007–09). What should have been a strong foundation to further build on in both these cities turned out to be a passing fad.

The lack of continuity and partisan politics interact to produce an almost comical and yet pernicious impact on equipment purchases. PAN administrations argue that police the world over wear blue uniforms and therefore issue uniforms and vehicles in blue. However, blue happens to be the color of the PAN party, and PRI governments have tried to emphasize other colors. When *priísta* Hank Rhon came to office in Tijuana in 2004 after fifteen years of PAN rule, he gave the police new black uniforms, repainted the police cruisers black, and created a new emblem for the police. Hank Rhon sold the action as symbolic of a new police force that was making a break from the past and reinventing itself, but the partisan undertone was unmistakable. When the PAN returned to office in 2007, they reversed the previous administration's changes, issued new blue uniforms, painted the patrol cars blue, and returned to the old police emblem. Mexicali's PAN administration repainted the city's black-and-white cruisers blue when it came into office in 2007. Hermosillo's new PRI government, on the other hand, chose to paint the formerly blue police cars orange, a color they argued is the color of Hermosillo and not of any political party. The painting and repainting of vehicles and buildings and changing of uniforms is, for many, an apt metaphor of the many new policies, programs, and reforms that never seem to go beneath the surface.

Other examples of a lack of continuity abound:

- Operations: In Mexicali, each of the last four administrations announced a *"resectorización"* or realignment of police sectors and redistribution of police patrols. In addition, each created its own special operations units. Groups with names such as Tourist Police, Special Anti-Robbery Unit, Cobra Tactical Group, and the Bank Protection Tactical Group have all come and gone. The same is true in Tijuana. The González Reyes and Hank Rhon administrations worked to decentralize the police, creating small police command posts throughout the city and abandoning an incomplete centralized command center initiated by their predecessors. The following administration, however, centralized the police, abandoned the smaller stations, began construction on new modern stations, and finalized construction on the abandoned central command. Hermosillo has also seen changes in its operation. One administration created an equivalent to a SWAT team, another disbanded it, and a third reinitiated it. The Dolores del Río (2004–06) administration initiated the Secure Neighborhood (*Colonia Segura*) program, which entailed intensified operations in conflictive communities and was profiled in the book *Municipio y Buen Gobierno* (*Municipality and Good Government*) as a successful municipal innovation (Guillén López, Fernández, and Calzada 2006). It required human and financial resources, however, and the following administration discontinued the program.

- Equipment: The Hank Rhon administration bet and invested heavily on video surveillance equipment and installed over two hundred cameras throughout the city. However, the administration negotiated an expensive maintenance contract favorable to the provider, and the indebted subsequent administration deemed it too expensive to continue. As a result, many of the cameras fell into disuse.

- Citizen outreach: Community policing and community outreach efforts also come and go. In Hermosillo, one administration built small police outposts, trained officers in community policing, and ensured that the officers were not rotated; however, the program was discontinued. In Mexicali and Tijuana, administrations have helped organize public security neighborhood associations only to see their successors replace them with new associations.

- Police benefits: Under the Búrquez administration (2002–04), Hermosillo contracted with the University of Sonora to provide psychological services to the police. Psychologists and clinicians at the university conducted psychological screenings, led trainings, and offered counseling services to the officers. The initiative's founders contend that their services were greatly needed by a population that not only confronts traumatic events but is socially stigmatized. The initiative lasted three years, and although it survived one administration change, it was cut when a new director came to office and never reinstated.

- Access to information: Mexican municipalities often have better websites than many U.S. cities; however, like police vehicles, city websites are completely redesigned with the change of administration. While this can mean more information is provided to the public, it can also mean less. In Tijuana, for example, there was considerable information on the city's website about public security during the Hank Rhon administration; however, most of this was immediately removed with the administration change and never replaced. In fact, it is very difficult to obtain even basic information about previous administrations.

Of course, not every program and policy is discontinued. For example, the Domestic Violence Units have outlived administrations in Mexicali and Tijuana, and the youth educational and outreach program DARE (Drug Abuse Resistance Education) has survived numerous administration changes in all four municipalities. Continuity is possible and does occur; however, there is a disconcerting amount of policy change with the arrival of a new administration.

Chihuahua and the Importance of Continuity

Absent from the preceding discussion were many examples from Chihuahua. This was not an accidental omission; Chihuahua has witnessed a degree of continuity not present in the other three locations (and much of the rest of the country), which I argue is the primary reason for its relative success. When asked when Chihuahua began to professionalize, several senior police officers interviewed pointed back to 1992. According to one high-level officer with twenty-one years on the force, "Since 1992 we have experienced a complete turnabout. We have better technology; we are more professional; we have paid more attention to our human resources, and CALEA has been the icing on the cake."

In 1992, Patricio Martínez García was elected mayor, and he appointed Steven Slater, a former U.S. police officer from New Mexico, to head Chihuahua City's police academy. Slater brought with him the perspective of U.S. policing, and police leaders interviewed credited him with making several small changes that have had long-term effects. Of particular importance was his focus on standardization. He initiated a process of standardizing police procedures and police training, including regular in-service training. Finally, he helped the department create specialized police units, such as the K-9 and special tactics units that continue to this day. As is the custom in Mexican politics, Slater left with the change in administration, but his efforts had a long-term impact. Here is where Chihuahua parts ways with other Mexican departments. Good leadership is not uncommon in Mexican policing. There have been a number of visionaries who have developed and implemented good programs and policies. The challenge is making those initiatives last the administration change.

In Chihuahua, rather than replace these policies, the department built upon them. In fact, the agency has experienced an unprecedented degree of continuity. To illustrate, mayor José Reyes Baeza, who came to office in 1998, appointed Raúl Grajeda Domínguez to head the municipal police force. Grajeda's tenure lasted six years and expanded over the terms of three city mayors from the Institutional Revolutionary Party (PRI), an unusual feat in Mexican local politics, even given the continuity of the party in power. Grajeda left the agency after the National Action Party (PAN) won the municipal government in 2004, and the new mayor, Juan Alberto Blanco Zaldívar, appointed Lázaro Gaytán Aguirre to head the organization. Gaytán also managed to outlast an administration change and remained municipal director under the PAN administration of Carlos Borruel Baquera until Gaytán's replacement in 2009. It would be surprising to find another major municipal police agency that has been led by only two men over an eleven-year period. Certainly, it stands in stark contrast to the statistics provided above.

Continuity has also occurred within the ranks of the police itself. Since legal reforms in 1993, every operational commander has come from within the department, ensuring that operations benefit from both institutional memory and local knowledge. As with the police chief, there were only two operational directors over the same course of eleven years. In addition, at the time of the initial research visit, all of the police senior leadership at the rank of captain (*coordinador*) had served in the department for over twenty years.[13]

There is even continuity in police-citizen interactions. Consistent with the limited-discretion model of policing, in most Mexican police agencies, officers are rotated regularly and never patrol for long in the same area. Ostensibly, this is an anticorruption mechanism, designed to prevent police from extorting businesses for protection or developing commitments to criminal elements. In Mexicali, for example, the Díaz Ochoa administration (2004) bragged that it had made five thousand rotations during its tenure. In Chihuahua, by contrast, the municipal police have always maintained their patrols in the same communities.

Finally and most importantl, there has been continuity in policy. To illustrate, the process for CALEA recognition actually began during a PRI government, while Raúl Grajeda Domínguez was chief of police. Even though the

TABLE 3.4. Continuity across administrations in Chihuahua City

Timeline	1998–2001	2001–02	2002–04	2004–07	2007–09
Party in power	Institutional Revolutionary Party (PRI)			National Action Party (PAN)	
Mayor	Reyes Baeza	Barousse Moreno	Cano Ricaud	Blanco Zaldívar	Borruel Baquera
Police chief	Raúl Grajeda Domínguez			Lázaro Gaytán Aguirre	
Policy	CALEA Recognition and Accreditation				

NOTE: Borruel Baquera would push Gaytán out of office in 2009 and replace him with a retired military officer.

accreditation process began under a different chief, a different mayor, and a different political party, the incoming chief Gaytán Aguirre continued the program of his predecessor and obtained both recognition and accreditation. This is not insignificant. As mentioned above, both Mexicali and Hermosillo administrations had allowed ISO-9001 certifications to lapse and their procedures to fall into disuse. Tables 3.3 and 3.4 offer a comparison of Mexicali and Chihuahua. Over the course of four administrations, Mexicali had five police chiefs and four different policies toward procedures. Over the same time period, Chihuahua only had two police chiefs and one policy toward procedures. It is because of this degree of continuity that operational leaders can point as far back as 1992 to mark the beginning of the department's professionalization. It is for this reason that the advances made by an academy director seventeen years in the past are still viewed as important for the department's current development. In summary, the continuity of two reformist police chiefs and continuity of policy allowed for incremental but significant change in Chihuahua—change that has not been allowed to occur at the other research sites.

Horizontal Accountability: Can the Councils Provide Continuity?

To some extent the amount of personnel and policy change at three of the research sites is surprising. In theory, incoming executives should be more constrained by the law, and council members should ensure continuity by passing municipal regulations and overseeing their application. By formal and informal design, however, the city council does not provide a sufficient check on the authority of the executive or oversight of public administration. Council members also rotate every three years, and, as discussed above, they have strong incentives to be loyal to the municipal president.

Tijuana, during the Ramos administration (2007–10), offers a clear example of this problem. The council member heading the public security commission on Tijuana's city council was a trusted colleague of the mayor who had joined the mayor's ticket prior to the mayor's nomination by the party. With only a short time on the council and many committee assignments, the council member was not familiar with the city's regulations regarding merit-based promotion in the police force. When asked why the regulations were not being followed and if it was his job to oversee their application, he contended simply that the rules did not need to be adhered to. Repeating an often-heard refrain, the council member contended that the mayor and the police chief needed the discretion to appoint the people that they trusted to lead operations. Given the danger that police leaders face, and given the urgent need to meet Mexico's security threats, following a formal process to determine promotions, would, in his view, do little more than encumber the leadership with "bureaucratic inflexibility." While the desirability of the existing regulations could be debated, the council member's remarks suggest a lack of respect for the council's own regulations and reveal the limitations of horizontal accountability.

There are other examples of the informal rules overruling formal legislation in the absence of horizontal accountability. The state of Baja California is unique in that it passed a law in 1998 requiring all police to have at minimum a high school education. The language of the law was later amended to allow departments to hire officers with a secondary level of education (through grade nine) so long as they pursued a high school degree. As of 1998, 90 percent of Tijuana's police force did not meet the requirement, including over an estimated 1,400 police who had joined the department since the law was passed. Prior to 2005 when Mexicali began to require a high school degree, that force too was in violation of the law.

Opposition lawmakers, who have an incentive to point out such violations, contend that they are locked out of the process. Despite the fact that public security was the main policy issue in 2008 and 2009, the Tijuana council's public security commission met only a handful of times over the course of these two years. PRI opposition council members argued that because the PAN and its coalition had three of the five seats, they could prevent the commission from meeting, effectively locking the opposition party out of public security policy making and police oversight.

In Hermosillo the tables were turned. During the Gándara Camou administration (2006–09), the PRI was the government in office and the PAN was in opposition. The highly partisan PAN opposition councilman on the public security commission alleged that he also was locked out of the process. Although he was guaranteed a seat on the police's Honor and Justice Council that oversees disciplinary cases, he contended that cases never made it to the council because the PRI administration did not want a PAN council member to have access to the files. In April 2008, the council member was arrested by an officer who allegedly smelled alcohol and marijuana in his car. The councilman tested negative to alcohol or drug use and insisted that the arrest was a reprisal from the PRI administration to discredit him (Imparcial 2008b).

Chihuahua also lacked horizontal accountability. In Chihuahua, the PRI opposition presided over the public security commission during a PAN administration (2007–10), but the result was very similar. In an interview, the council member argued that with the exception of the budget, he had no real oversight authority. For example, although the police department was required to provide him with information solicited, his requests were frequently denied. The administration acknowledged the illegal denial of information, but argued that the council member sought the information only for partisan purposes.

Interestingly, in interviews with journalists and members of civil society, there was very little sympathy expressed for the opposition council members in these cities. Absent real divided government, interviewees argue that opposition leaders frequently use their very limited authority to position their party for the next election. In fact, the city council members are often dismissed as irrelevant, overly partisan actors.

It is, however, possible for the council to play a stronger oversight role. In Mexicali during the Valdéz administration (2007–10) the public security commission met regularly; it received a monthly report from the police department on crime statistics, and it frequently requested that the director come before it to answer questions. This appears to be an exception, however, and generally speaking, the incentives in local politics ensure that the council defers to the authority of the executive.

The Change-Continuity Paradox

This chapter suggests that the primary obstacle to police professionalization has been the lack of continuity in personnel and policies, itself a product of the politicization of policing. To be sure, some personnel and policy change is inevitable when there are divergent ideological beliefs and different spending priorities. The dramatic pendulum swings in Buenos Aires, for example, were a product of legitimate ideological differences. León Arslanián's approach was premised on the protection of human rights, and Carlos Ruckauf's on heavy-handed policing, or *mano dura* policies. One administration might believe in the limited-discretion approach, another in citizen-oriented professionaliza-tion, and a third in militarization. Regardless of whether the pendulum swings were justifiable or not, however, the analysis presented here reveals that exces-sive change has clearly served as an obstacle to police professionalization. The Buenos Aires police, like Mexico's municipal forces, were negatively affected by the dramatic changes. More important, however, much of the change ap-pears to have little to do with ideology and much more to do with distinguish-ing one administration from its predecessor. It is hard to argue that the many personnel changes with each passing administration are due to factors other than political loyalties and patronage.

One could also make the case that policy changes are justifiable because of resource limitations: new administrations are bound to have different spend-ing priorities. In many cases, however, the lack of policy continuity results in highly inefficient spending. Police stations are built and then abandoned. Equipment is purchased and then not used. Patrol cars and buildings are re-painted with new colors. One newspaper reporter estimated the cost of repaint-ing police vehicles in Hermosillo to be $400,000. Clearly, human, financial, and political capital are being wasted because of the lack of continuity.

Nonetheless, arguing for "continuity" in Mexican policing appears ill-advised given all the problems of corruption, ineffectiveness, and abuse laid out in Chapter 1. To the average citizen, it would seem that police commanders *should* be demoted, departments purged, and new policies developed and implemented. In fact, voters are likely to reward politicians who promise and deliver such change. This presents what might be considered the change-continuity paradox. Ward (2006) quotes one Brazilian police reformer as stat-ing, "The best way to not change anything is to change everything" (176). Ironi-cally, dramatic policy changes from one administration to the next have left intact the informal rules of patronage and tolerance of misconduct. Paradoxi-cally, what appears to be change only leads to the continuity of perverse incen-tives, and the lack of continuity in reform initiatives fails to produce meaning-ful institutional change.

Nonetheless, the goal should not be continuity for continuity's sake, a justification of the status quo, or an unnecessarily patient approach to reform. As mentioned above, maintaining leaders that achieved their positions through an unreliable promotion process is not necessarily desirable. Instead, Mexican policing requires a more evidenced-based approach to determining personnel and policies. Evaluations of personnel and policies would facilitate better decision making. Unfortunately, however, municipal governments find themselves trapped in a vicious cycle. As Geddes points out, public officials have little incentive to forgo the cost of patronage and invest in merit- based systems that will likely be abandoned by their successors.

Given that Chihuahua experienced greater reform continuity, it is useful to ask what is unique about Chihuahua? Does Chihuahua somehow differ from the other three research sites in terms of culture, politics, or economics? There are of course some differences, but none appear to satisfactorily explain Chihuahua's exceptionalism. It appears more likely that a confluence of positive factors, including substantial human agency, led to the greater continuity. In fact, when running for office in 2004, the PAN candidate Blanco Zaldivar was critical of the incumbent's efforts to seek CALEA recognition. He contended that the police department should be certified by its citizens—not by an external U.S.-based organization. Consistent with the informal rules of Mexican politics, Blanco Zaldivar actively argued against his predecessor's policies. Once in office, however, his pick to lead the department became convinced of the merits of CALEA accreditation and successfully argued for its continuity.

More important, Chihuahua's past continuity is no guarantee of future continuity. While Chihuahua's success attracted considerable attention during the mid-to-late 2000s (Mendoza and Salgado 2009; Sabet 2010), as of this writing Chihuahua's advances have been brought into question. Beginning in 2008, the state of Chihuahua became the center of a major conflict between the Sinaloa- and Juárez-based organized criminal groups. Although not as negatively impacted as Ciudad Juárez, Chihuahua City became victim to exceptionally high rights of organized crime-related violence. From 2008–10, there were an estimated 1,385 organized crime-related killings in the city, a tragically high number below only Tijuana, Ciudad Juárez, and Culiacán. Rising insecurity made it difficult to consider the city's police force as a success story. In 2009, the reformist police chief Lázaro Gáytan was pushed out for failing to deliver results and replaced by a retired military leader. Despite the fact that Chihuahua's police far surpassed other departments on a variety of indicators, Chihuahua's reforms neglected the robust accountability mechanisms (a topic that will be explored in Chapter 4) needed to protect it from organized crime infiltration. In addition, there is not a one-to-one correlation between police reform and crime reduction. While a more professional police force will be more effective at fighting crime in the long run, it remains dependent on the larger criminal justice system. Increasing crime and revelations of organized crime infiltration into the police placed police and political leaders under pressure to change course. As priorities shifted and as political leaders attempted to respond to a panicked electorate, several initiatives that played a role in the department's success were rolled back, including educational opportunities for officers, community policing activities, a CompStat-like program of accountability, and collaboration with a citizen public security committee that had channeled an enormous amount of human and financial resources to the department. Furthermore, with the change of administration in 2010, a new leadership team was brought in, and the incoming mayor expressed his support for the ostensibly more dramatic reform proposal of collapsing the municipal police into the state police.

A more thoughtful diagnosis would have found that the police department was infiltrated by organized crime because of the absence of more robust accountability mechanisms and was ineffective at reducing crime because of failed coordination with state and federal authorities. Rather than address these two obvious deficiencies, however, new leadership turned their attention elsewhere. As at the other research sites, the political and police leadership opted for a shake-up of policies rather than institutional change. The data presented here suggests that continuity was a key to Chihuahua's success; however, given the incentives in Mexican politics, there is no guarantee that there will be continuity in Chihuahua's future.

Conclusion

This chapter has shown that honest efforts at police reform confront a serious problem. Even provided good policy design and implementation, the success of reform policies will depend on the actions of future administrations. Unfortunately, however, the institutional incentives in Mexican politics—and particularly Mexican municipal politics—do not favor policy continuity. No-reelection, three-year administrations, a closed-party-list ballot of council candidates attached to the mayor's ticket, and almost-guaranteed supermajorities on the council combine with informal rules of clientelism and presidential-ism to create shortsighted policies, a lack of continuity, and little horizontal accountability.

Changing the paradoxical status quo of constant change appears unlikely in the short run. Removing the restrictions on reelection runs contrary to one of the great legacies of the Mexican Revolution. To this day, official documents are stamped with the message, "Effective Suffrage; No Re-Election" (*Sufragio Efectivo, No Reelección),* and public opinion polls consistently show opposition to such proposals.[14] As police leaders have traditionally preferred to limit the discretion of police officers who they do not trust, citizens prefer to limit the electoral periods of elected officials who they do not trust. Despite popular op-position, ending the no-reelection restriction for mayors (and legislators) was part of the Calderón administration's proposal for state reform and has at least garnered support among the political leadership.[15] Reforming the processes for electing council members and assigning seats to ensure greater horizontal ac-countability, however, has not been part of the reform agenda. On the contrary, the tendency has been to further centralize power in the executive in an effort to quickly address the many challenges facing municipalities. While central-ization of authority might facilitate policy design and implementation, it can be expected to further hinder institutionalization.

Although the evidence here illustrates the importance of the formal constitutional-choice rules, this chapter suggests that informal rules might have precedent over collective-choice and operation rules. This trend can clearly be seen in the failure to implement merit-based promotion criteria. Laws, reg-ulations, and formal rules have often been worked around when they are con-tradicted by the informal rules.

Where then can reform continuity come from? How can the vicious cycle be broken? First, despite the problems of a legal approach, building strong police institutions will require improved legislation. Even acknowledging the pri-macy of informal rules, there is no question that several of the problems con-fronting municipal police stem from inadequate legislation. Up until 2009, Hermosillo did not even have a specific set of regulations governing the police. Instead, operational rules were tacked on to the end of the city's municipal or-dinances (*bando de policía y gobierno*), and they contained blatant errors. To illustrate, prior to the 2009 reforms, the Hermosillo regulations constantly differentiated between transit and preventive police; however, in the section on sanctions for misconduct, the regulations only mentioned preventive police. It is also important to note that some formal policies have successfully constrained executive discretion. The divisions among A, B, and C agents in Mexicali did limit the discretion of incoming police leaders in naming their mid-level commanders. As such, it stands to reason that reformers should continue to improve and perfect existing legislation and regulations.

Second, an attitudinal shift is likely required that recognizes the need to build on previous efforts. Police interviewed were asked to identify past directors who had been important for the development of the police. Interviewees consistently and overwhelmingly gave such credit to the current administration. Given the dramatic increases in public security investments, this is perhaps not surprising; however, other evidence suggests that in an interview setting, study participants might have felt some obligation to show their support for the current administration. For example, one officer who felt that an earlier director had made important contributions hesitated before answering the question, and then asked nervously if his answers were confidential. He was not even criticizing the current administration; he was simply praising a past administration.

Although every annual report is full of the alleged successes of police reform, police leaders are surprisingly dismissive about their predecessors. In Tijuana, the chief commented, "The only thing of value that the past administration left was the people." He softened the statement somewhat in further comments, but then concluded, "there is nothing that can be salvaged from the previous administration." In the survey of eleven departments, two questions were included asking the department to summarize the advances of the previous administration and the current administration. While all eleven filled out the latter, only five of eleven departments answered the former, and all of these were of the same political party as their predecessor. Two wrote simply that they did even not know of the advances of the previous administration. It is hoped that empirical evidence about the deleterious effects of constant personnel and policy change will help foster needed attitudinal changes.

Third, actors external to municipal government can also influence the incentives that local officials confront. External actors can create negative incentives, as the following chapter will explore; however, they can also create positive incentives for reform continuity. As will be discussed in Chapter 6, citizens and civil society organizations can create pressure for greater reform continuity. In Baja California civic and business leaders, tired of constant changes in police leadership during previous administrations, pressured then-governor

Elorduy Walther (2001–07) to maintain the same attorney general for his entire six-year administration. Positive incentives for reform continuity can also come from the federal government. As will be discussed in Chapter 7, the creation of the Ley General del Sistema Nacional de Seguridad Pública (General Law of the National Public Security System) effectively altered the constitutional-choice architecture confronted by local authorities and required them to implement a series of reforms.

4 Organized Crime, the Police, and Accountability

2008, Year of (False) Hope[1]

Following a very violent 2007, there was optimism that 2008 would be different for Baja California. The front page of *Frontera* newspaper on January 1 ran an article entitled "2008, Year of Hope" (Ramírez 2008a). The city's new police chief was quoted as saying, "I believe that 2008, from my point of view, is going to be a historic year for Baja California and for Tijuana in particular" (Ramírez 2008b). There was no way of knowing at the time that it would be a historic year, but for the opposite reason: 2008 was the most violent year in the city's history. Perhaps this was foreshadowed by the positioning of the "2008, Year of Hope" headline below the lead article entitled "Police Kidnapped Because Corrupt." (Andrade 2008b). The year had begun with the New Year's Eve kidnapping and killing of one of Tijuana's delegation commanders, and the new chief had responded by acknowledging that it was likely because of involvement in organized crime. In answer to the question why reform efforts have not been more successful, perhaps the most obvious answer is the topic of this chapter: the threat posed by organized crime.

On April 22, 2008, General Sergio Aponte Polito, the ranking military officer in Baja California, took the unprecedented step of releasing to the public a letter directed to the attorney general of the state of Baja California detailing corruption allegations regarding all of the state's police forces (Aponte Polito 2008). The head of the state's anti-kidnapping unit along with two ministerial police and a Tijuana municipal police officer were accused of involvement in kidnappings. Municipal police from Rosarito were accused of participating in an attempt on their police chief's life. The letter alleged collusion between a binational car theft ring and the state's vehicle theft unit. Several cases were cited of police who had been caught red-handed in criminal acts but were set free by their colleagues. In Mexicali, the general described a group of officers who colluded with organized crime to safely land planes loaded with drugs for final transport across the border. The letter not only described the extent of corruption in the state's police forces, but it suggested that institutional channels to address such corruption were not functioning. The general stated clearly the question that many Baja California citizens had been asking for years: "How much deception does it take to know that those entrusted to enforce the laws are the very ones who weaken the law by their ties to organized crime?"

Nonetheless, the letter left many other questions unanswered. Some of the names listed in the letter could not be matched with actual police officers. Other charges were brought into doubt as those accused vehemently defended their reputations. Although many of the named officers were brought up on charges or fired, citizens were left with too little information and too many questions.[2] Aponte Polito himself was eventually removed from his post. These three outcomes (1) a perception of corruption, (2) a perception that anticorruption efforts are failing, and (3) uncertainty and a lack of information are central themes of this chapter, which illustrates how organized crime has undermined the professional development of the police.[3]

Insulating the police from infiltration requires counterbalancing the negative incentives provided by organized crime. Reformers must protect honest officers from organized-crime threats while raising the probability that collusion will be identified and punished. As discussed in Chapter 2, however, developing robust accountability mechanisms represents perhaps the most challenging aspect of police reform. In addition to the benign implementation challenges confronted by improving selection criteria, training, and equipment, and the collective action problems presented by reforming promotion criteria, developing accountability mechanisms also faces zero-sum opposition from those that benefit from corruption. Given these enormous implementation obstacles, the chapter explores three distinct hypothetical scenarios, whereby elected and appointed officials decide to (1) collude with organized crime, (2) confront organized crime, or (3) tolerate organized crime. Essentially, under the first scenario collusion comes from the top and can be expected to permeate the organization. Publicized reforms will be mere window dressing. Under the second scenario, officers are forced to weigh the incentives created by their police leaders against those offered by organized crime. Successful reform must create sufficient counterincentives to organized crime's threats and bribery. In the final scenario, while corruption is not encouraged from the top, there are few incentives to counterbalance the causes of corruption. This is perhaps the most common approach taken in Mexico today, which helps explain why several years into the Mexican government's war on organized crime, all the improvements to selection criteria, training, and equipment have failed to bring about honest, professional policing.

This chapter begins with a brief overview of organized crime in Mexico, the conflict as it affected the country from 2005–10, and criminal infiltration of the police. Following a theoretical and historical discussion of these three hypothetical cases, the chapter explores organized crime—police relations in Tijuana, where the police leadership during the Jorge Ramos administration (2007–10) engaged in a confrontational strategy with organized crime. After a brief discussion of organized crime–police relations at the other three sites, the chapter explores the weaknesses in accountability mechanisms in Mexico's municipalities and illustrates why many formal mechanisms have failed to produce accountability.

The Problem: Organized Crime, Violence, and Police Collusion

The current conflict among organized criminal groups has laid bare the ineffectiveness of the police and their frequent complicity in criminal activities. Organized crime-related violence is not a new phenomenon in Mexico. Cities such as Tijuana, Ciudad Juárez, and Culiacán have long been witness to violence and organized crime-related killings. In 1993 in Sinaloa, for example, there were reportedly 385 drug-related killings and over seventy kidnappings for ransom (Astorga 2005). Nonetheless, violence in Mexico has unquestionably reached unprecedented levels: the number of killings and kidnappings have far outpaced past incidence rates, the conflict has affected almost every state, and the brutality of the violence has shocked the conscience.

Organized crime has historically derived its economic resources from drug trafficking and, to a lesser extent, drug cultivation. Concern over drugs in Mexico can be traced back at least as far as a 1923 decree regulating opium, morphine, cocaine, and other drugs (Astorga 2005). During the WWII years, domestic opium production increased as global demand for the painkiller rose dramatically. While Astorga refutes the commonly held belief that the U.S. and Mexican governments actively promoted illegal drug production, he does note that much of the drug was destined for the United States, beginning a long history of northbound flows. Marijuana production and trafficking increased in the 1960s due to growing U.S. demand for the drug. It was not until the cocaine boom of the 1980s, however, that drugs afforded Mexican traffickers unprecedented windfall profits. Early on in the boom, Colombian organized crime trafficked cocaine by sea through the Caribbean. A U.S. law enforcement crackdown in Miami in the 1980s, however, made the expansive two thousand-mile U.S.-Mexico border a more desirable smuggling route (Fuss 1996). Colombian producers found a willing ally in Mexican drug traffickers such as Miguel Ángel Félix Gallardo, Ernesto Fonseca Carrillo, and Rafael Caro Quintero.

The history of organized crime in Mexico is full of divergent accounts that often disagree on the causes and nature of events. Nonetheless, it is commonly held that in the 1980s Sinaloan drug trafficker Miguel Ángel Félix Gallardo rose to become the "boss of bosses" among most Mexican drug traffickers. Following his arrest in 1989, it is believed that Félix Gallardo, with the help of allies still at large such as Juan José Esparragoza Moreno, called the major operators together (excluding the nascent Gulf organization) and divided Mexican territory and smuggling routes among them (Ravelo 2006; Blancornelas 2002).[4] By the late 1990s and early 2000s, experts typically divided organized crime in Mexico into four large criminal organizations: the Arellano Félix Organization based in Baja California, the Juárez organization based in Chihuahua, the Sinaloa organization based in Sinaloa, and the Gulf organization based in Tamaulipas (Bailey and Godson 2000). Of course, there were and continue to be numerous smaller operators that have at times cooperated with and at other times contested the authority of these larger organizations. In addition, the "cartels," as they were typically denominated, have always been subject to considerable *intra*-cartel conflict. For this reasons, the term *cartel*, which implies a high degree of cooperation, has always been, and is increasingly, something of a misnomer (Astorga and Shirk 2010). Finally, despite evidence of the 1989 pact, there has always existed considerable *inter*organizational conflict. Juan García Abrego, who operated in the northeast state of Tamaulipas until his 1996 arrest, is not believed to have been party to the 1989 pact, and the Gulf organization frequently fought criminal groups from Chihuahua and

Sinaloa for control of Nuevo Laredo. The Arellano Félix brothers, who assumed control of the Tijuana route, fought a long drawn-out battle with Joaquin Guzmán Loera and Ismael Zambada of the Sinaloa organization. At times, the interorganizational conflict has been over control of routes, but in other instances the conflicts have appeared more personal than business related.[5]

If diversity of interests and intra- and interorganizational conflict had always existed, by the mid-to-late 2000s it had become the predominant characteristic of organized crime in Mexico. Sinaloa-based Joaquín Guzmán Loera's strength had grown since his escape from a maximum security prison in 2001, and, in 2005, he led an ultimately unsuccessful bid to challenge the Gulf organization's control of Nuevo Laredo, which contributed to an estimated 228 drug violence-related deaths in the state that year (Merlos 2007).[6] The city gained international media attention when a new municipal police chief was killed less than twenty-four hours after taking office (Marshall 2005). In response to the violence, federal authorities assumed control of the city, and the municipal police, which was believed to be heavily infiltrated, was temporarily disbanded.

The violence was not limited to Nuevo Laredo, however. On the opposite end of the country, Guerrero also became a battleground between the Sinaloa organization and the Zetas, a paramilitary group founded as the enforcement arm of the Gulf organization.[7] The two groups also fought for control of the domestic drug market in metropolitan Monterrey, Nuevo León. In 2005, the head of Nuevo León's state investigations agency was killed after the arrest of Sinaloa operatives. In 2006 and 2007, there were 162 assassinations in the state, including a shocking number of thirty-nine police killings, which spread panic through the metropolitan area's various police forces (Campos Garza 2009).

By 2008, Guzmán Loera and his Sinaloa-based allies were engaged in an even more extreme conflict against the Juárez organization and its leader, Vicente Carrillo Fuentes, for control of Ciudad Juárez.[8] Despite the fact that these organizations were former allies, tied together in a group commonly referred to as the Federation, the conflict would grow to become the country's most violent, particularly after the defection of the Beltrán Leyva brothers from the Sinaloa group (Guerrero Gutiérrez 2009). The Beltrán Leyva brothers were considered to be part of the Sinaloa organization until the January 2008 arrest of Alfredo Beltrán Leyva. His brother Arturo blamed Guzmán for the arrest, violently split with the organization, and aligned his family with

Carrillo Fuentes. The ensuing conflict reached levels of violence that by comparison make the 2005 struggle in Nuevo Laredo appear to be a mild dispute. According to data released by the Calderón administration, in 2008 there were a stunning 2,118 organized crime-related killings in the state of Chihuahua, a number which grew to 3,345 in 2009, and reached 4,427 in 2010 (Presidencia 2011). Ciudad Juárez alone accounted for 2,738 of the 2010 killings (Presidencia).

Historically, the Sinaloa organization has also been involved in a third fight with the Tijuana-based Arellano Félix organization (AFO). While the two groups had established a tentative peace as of this writing in 2011, the Sinaloa group supported the defection of Teodoro García Simental from the AFO in 2008 and had been a partisan to the conflict affecting Tijuana. As of 2011, other conflicts continue to rage throughout the country, including violence between the Zetas and La Familia in the state of Michoacán, conflict between the Zetas and their former bosses in the Gulf organization in Tamaulipas and Nuevo León, and a fight for the control over what remains of the Beltrán Leyva organization in central Mexico. The conflict has been fueled by constantly shifting alliances among criminal groups in response to new threats. The maxim "my enemy's enemy is my friend" appears to explain the seemingly contradictory ability of criminal groups to make peace with old rivals so as to fight off immediate threats. Every major criminal group has made major changes in its alliances since just 2006, and, as a result, the violence has continually worsened. The Mexican government estimates that killings rose from 2,826 in 2006 to 6,837 in 2008, to 9,614 in 2009, and to 15,273 in 2010 (Presidencia 2011). Data is not available for 2005; however, *Reforma* newspaper's more conservative estimates place the number at 1,537.

Under President Felipe Calderón's leadership the federal government has responded to the violence by deploying over forty-five thousand military personnel, doubling the size of the federal police, and greatly intensifying counterdrug operations. Unfortunately, the deployments have not had the desired effect. Escalante's (2011) subnational comparison of organized crime killings and deployments finds that violence has consistently increased despite (or because of) Mexican military and police deployments. In Ciudad Juárez, Chihuahua, for example, a federal deployment, which at its peak in 2009 included an estimated 7,500 military officers and 2,300 federal police, was unable to stem the violence in the city. This was despite military reports contending that the first twenty-one months of the operation netted 2,150 arrests and the confiscation of 2,532 firearms. Military authorities claimed that forty-five of the arrestees had confessed to a total of seven hundred killings (Sánchez 2009).

As many observers have pointed out, the Mexican federal government's fight against organized crime has in the short and medium term probably exacerbated the conflict. Guerrero Gutiérrez (2009) argues that the arrests and extraditions of drug leaders have upset the balance of power between criminal groups, and decommissions of drugs have resulted in major financial losses during a period of growing costs. In the long term, however, the factors that have permitted the current violence are (1) the market forces that offer large rewards to those who can meet U.S. drug demand; and (2) a police, judicial, and political system that have allowed organized crime to grow in power and to operate with relative impunity. As evidenced in almost daily newspaper reports, police officers and employees of the justice system continue to undermine efforts to confront, arrest, and prosecute organized criminal leaders and operators. Ravelo (2006) concludes, "High level police, military, and government leaders have served as links in a long chain of protection created by powerful drug traffickers. This is why they can operate with impunity and their drug businesses—the cause of the whole country's violence—can flourish" (24). While law enforcement should be the solution to organized crime, it is instead part of the problem.

As discussed in the introductory chapter and the opening paragraphs of this chapter, there have been numerous cases of police involvement in organized crime. In the introduction, I mentioned the discovery of a "narconomina" or list of police on organized crime's payroll in Tabasco, Nuevo León, and Hidlago; a confrontation between municipal and federal police over the arrest of municipal officer involved with organized crime in Torreón, Coahuila; and revelations of infiltration by the Beltrán Leyva brothers into the highest levels of the federal attorney general's office. Examples abound, and the collusion at times borders on the absurd. The former head of Nuevo León's state police, Aldo Fasci Zuazua, offers his experience regarding the famous *narcomantas,* or banners directed at Mexican society, rival groups, and government officials:

> For several years we have seen that when there are executions there were
> no patrol cars present, so we initiated a review. We detected that yes, there
> were patrol cars [assigned], but that they had gone elsewhere. This obligated us
> to investigate what was happening with the police, how they had begun to

operate increasingly and shamelessly in favor of these groups [organized crime]. A concrete case; there is one that is a perfect example. In Nuevo León and another 16 states they simultaneously hung banners and nobody removed them. The municipal police did not remove the banners, and at that point you have to ask yourself, how is this possible? We called the dispatch, and we asked that they remove the banners, but they didn't do it. We even called the state police to remove them, and they were not only beaten, but the municipal police re-hung the banners. We had to send in the SWAT team and ask for the support of the Mexican military to remove them, it is absurd (Tapia 2009a).

Even though municipal police do not have technical jurisdiction over organized crime, they are essential to organized criminal operations. Fasci Zuazua explains the most common form of collusion:

To operate, organized crime requires information from police working on the street because they are the ones who know what is happening. It is a network of alert that they call "falcons," and they pass along information if the military is passing by or about police investigations, etc . . . and in this way organized crime protects itself (Tapia 2009a).

At slightly higher levels of involvement, police commanders will clear police out of an area where organized crime is operating, doctor police reports, and release or ensure the release of captured criminals. At the worst level, police will actually participate in organized criminal activities by providing security for drug shipments; kidnapping; carrying out homicides; and often using their uniforms, badges, and equipment to facilitate illegal activities. As such, honest police leaders not only have to confront organized crime, they have to confront their own police. Or, as Alberto Capella Ibarra, the former head of public security in Tijuana, said upon assuming his position, "We are from the beginning waging a war on two fronts" (Ramírez 2009). Given such infiltration, the following section seeks to understand why corruption is so pervasive by engaging in a theoretical and historical exploration of three hypothetical scenarios, including executive collusion with, confrontation with, and tolerance of organized crime.

Approaches to Understanding Collusion with Organized Crime

For the sake of parsimony, police and organized crime are often presented as unitary actors. It is common to hear residents quip that "*the police* are corrupt," a blanket statement that fails to recognize the diversity within the force. Citizens and commentators also tend to view organized crime as a large operation under the single direction of a powerful mafia boss. However, as evidenced by the discussion above, organized crime is better characterized by its divisions than by its organization. Such generalizations might offer useful explanations in certain situations; however, they risk glossing over important divisions within these groups.

At the local level, the key actors in state and municipal policing include (1) the executive, who is elected and appoints the police chief; (2) the police chief, who appoints his upper- and mid-level command staff; and (3) the operational commanders, who oversee policing operations by the final group: (4) the rank and file. Each of these actors, or groups of actors, has the option to tolerate, collude with, or confront organized crime (Bailey and Taylor 2009). As discussed above, there are varying degrees of collusion. The Knapp Commission (1972) investigating the New York City Police Department in the early 1970s famously made the distinction between grass-eaters, who passively accept bribe money when it is offered, and meat-eaters, who actively pursue corrupt exchanges. In a similar vein, actors pursuing a confrontation strategy can do so either aggressively or halfheartedly.

In theory, the executive, elected by his or her constituents, should represent the public, act in its interests, and refrain from pursuing a collusion strategy; however, a long tradition in political science has noted that it is far easier for a small group of individuals highly affected by public policy (in this case organized crime) to organize and affect the policy process than a large group of less intensely affected individuals (i.e., the general public) (Wilson 1980; Freeman 1965; Stigler 1971). Organized crime offers political leaders, police chiefs, and line-level officers both the carrot of bribe money and the stick of violence. As repeated in hundreds of journalistic accounts as well as academic writing, organized crime provides a choice between "*plata o plomo*," "the bribe or the bullet." The concept is summed up well by the former Tijuana chief of police Alfredo de la Torre, who on the day of his appointment and prior to his subsequent murder by organized crime in 2000, reportedly told a colleague, "First they send you a briefcase full of money. Then, if you reject it, they send you a briefcase with a gun" (Moore 2000). If the mayor decides to collude with organized crime, it is likely that he will appoint a police chief willing to do the same. The chief will in turn appoint operational commanders who will also collude or tolerate corruption.[9]

This produces one potential answer to the questions of why there is collusion between the police and organized crime and why the police have failed to professionalize: collusion between the police and organized crime is driven by corruption at the very top of the city and police hierarchy. Under such circumstances the unitary actor assumption appears reasonable: a corrupt mayor ensures a corrupt police force. Many commentators and members of civil society have tended to favor this explanation. It has certainly become the favored view to explain organized crime collusion during the PRI-dominated one-party system (Payan 2006a O'Neil 2009; Friedman 2010).

Luis Astorga's (2005) history of drug trafficking in Mexico from the early 1900s to the present reveals no shortage of examples of collusion between elected officials and organized crime. Health officials' reports written in the 1930s document the direct involvement of the governors of the Baja California territory in opium smuggling (Astorga 2000). In Chihuahua, Astorga cites a series of older articles from *El Universal* detailing the exploits of Enrique Fernández Puerta, known as the Al Capone of Juárez, who "came to control city hall and served as a stepping stone to enrich many individuals in public life, among them three governors" (Astorga 2005, 42). In Sinaloa, Astorga (2005) profiles the 1944 assassination of an anti-drug governor, Rodolfo T. Loaiza. The killer is caught, and although he later escapes, he fingers Loaiza's successor, General Pablo Macías Valenzuela, and other prominent politicians as the intellectual authors of the crime. In the following years, the media and popular opinion continued to accuse Macías of protecting the production and trafficking of marijuana and poppies. Perhaps due to the intervention of high-ranking generals on his behalf, as Astorga suggests, Macías was never charged for either the assassination or protecting drug cultivation. The story takes an ironic turn when the once-convicted killer of Loaiza ends up years later working as a bodyguard for another Sinaloa governor, Leopoldo Sánchez Celis, who governed from 1963 to 1968 and was also alleged to have ties to organized crime. One of Sánchez Celis's other bodyguards and personal friend was Miguel Ángel Félix Gallardo, who, as discussed above, would rise to become Mexico's boss of bosses by the time of his arrest in 1989.

Astorga argues that corrupt government officials were for many years able to dominate and control organized crime; however, he contends that the system of control began to fall apart in the 1980s as a product of two factors. First, the abusive and corrupt Federal Security Directorate (Dirección Federal de Seguridad—DFS) was disbanded in 1986 following revelations of its involvement in the killing of a journalist, and it was under pressure from the United States following the killing of DEA agent Enrique Camarena Salazar. According to Astorga, this powerful agency had both protected and subjugated organized crime; with its disbanding, the state lost its tool of control. Second, the dissolution of the DFS coincided temporally with opposition-party electoral victories at the state and local levels during the 1980s and 1990s, further limiting the ability of the centralized state to co-opt and control. One could add a third factor: the wealth and power of Mexican organized crime grew enormously as it became the preferred vehicle to traffic Colombian cocaine.

The shift in the state's power vis-à-vis organized crime and the increasing importance of governors and mayors has transformed the nature of collusion. Although the former governor of Quintana Roo, Mario Villanueva Madrid, is the only governor to have been successfully prosecuted for collusion with organized crime, Ricardo Ravelo (2006) details alleged links between state administrations and organized crime in Tamaulipas, Baja California, Chihuahua, Sinaloa, Sonora, Yucatán, Campeche, Jalisco, Michoacán, Morelos, and even Querétaro.

If the extent of past collusion is difficult to determine, it is even harder to know the extent of high-level corruption in contemporary Mexico. As in the past, there are few successful prosecutions, but there is no shortage of accusations. While never successfully prosecuted, critics have long held that the former mayor of Tijuana, Jorge Hank Rhon (2005–07), was involved with organized crime. Critics point to the involvement of his bodyguards in the killing of one of *Zeta* newspaper's cofounders and the 2011 discovery of numerous illegal arms on his property. In Michoacán, in May 2009, military and federal authorities arrested thirty-four public officials, including ten mayors accused of ties to La Familia. Federal judges would eventually absolve all but one of these (Avilés and Castillo 2010). During his 2009 campaign for mayor of the wealthy Monterrey suburb of San Pedro Garza García, a recording was released suggesting that Mauricio Fernández Garza had made a pact with the Beltrán Leyva brothers (Garza 2009). Fernández fought back against the charges and was elected; however, he has remained a lightning rod for controversy, first for attempting to create paramilitary groups, and then for his knowledge of an assassination prior to the body's discovery by the police. Despite the uncertainty about the degree of high-level collusion, I assume that there are mayors who collude with organized crime and that in these municipalities collusion and tolerance will extend throughout the police bureaucracy.

If, however, the executive sincerely wishes to *confront* organized crime (or support federal authorities in doing so), then a more complex relationship emerges, requiring a more thorough analysis of the specific incentives facing line-level officers. As discussed in Chapter 2, a police department is better viewed as a complex bureaucracy containing diverse interests and principal-agent problems than as a quasi-military organization where orders are given by the chief and then trickle down through the chain of command. A principal-agent approach notes that an agent, or subordinate, is supposed to act in the interest and under the command of the principal, in this case the police leader. Nonetheless, agents have their own interests. Because principals lack full information about the actions of their subordinates, agents can and often do exploit these "information asymmetries" to pursue personal interests contrary to those of the principal or the public (Klitgaard 1988). This principal-agent problem does not just exist between the mayor and the police chief, but down the entire hierarchy. The extent to which honest police leaders are able to minimizes principal-agent problems depends on the extent to which they can monitor police activities (reduce information asymmetries), create incentives for honest policing, enforce sanctions for dishonest policing, and inspire a culture of professionalism. While the unitary actor assumption seems reasonable under a corrupt mayor, an honest mayor scenario underscores the diversity of interests within the department.

To further explore these incentives, it is useful to think in terms of the equation offered in Figure 4.1 based on the (1) individual factors, (2) organizational factors, and (3) external factors discussed in Chapter 1. If organizational incentives raise the probability that officers colluding with organized crime will be caught and punished; if punishment means foregoing salary, benefits, and a pension; if officers have sufficient tools to protect themselves from organized crime threats; and if a sense of professionalism has embedded itself within police culture, then following a mayor's or police leader's confrontation strategy appears more likely.

Figure 4.1 also recognizes the importance of external incentives, including those created by organized crime. As discussed above, organized crime offers police the carrot of bribe money but also the very credible threat of reprisals. As such, the bullet or the bribe suggests an additional approach to understanding collusion: collusion between the police and organized crime is due to the ability of organized crime to monitor police, create incentives for corruption, and inspire a sense of fear. Consequently, as presented in Table 4.1,

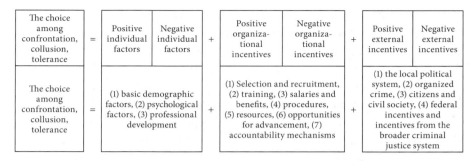

FIGURE 4.1. Choice among confrontation, collusion, and tolerance

TABLE 4.1. Hypothetical decisions of subordinates to collude, confront, or tolerate organized crime

	Provided corrupt leadership	*Provided confrontational leadership*	*Provided tolerant leadership*
Elected official	Collude	Confront	Tolerate
Police chief	Collude	Confront/Tolerate	Collude/Tolerate
Commanders	Collude/Tolerate	Conf./Collude/Tol.	Collude/Tolerate
Officers	Collude/Tolerate	Conf./Collude/Tol.	Collude/Tolerate

while a collusive mayor ensures a collusive police force, a confrontational mayor does not guarantee a confrontational police force. The strategies pursued by the chief, commanders, and line-level officers will depend on whether the monitoring, incentives, and professionalism fostered by the local government, citizens, and civil society are able to outweigh the monitoring, incentives, and fear offered by organized crime.

Thus far, I have considered an executive who *colludes* with and one who *confronts* organized crime. The third possible scenario entails a mayor who is *tolerant*. Tolerance provides no financial benefit to officials; however, it entails less risk, both from citizens and from organized crime. Absent a money trail, tolerance is harder for citizens to detect than collusion, and turning a blind eye to criminal groups also reduces the likelihood of becoming a target of such groups. Because drug trafficking, organized crime, and (until recently) drug sales are (were) all federal offenses, municipal leaders can easily justify a strategy of tolerance. Municipal leaders are able to rhetorically underscore their commitment to enforcing the law within their jurisdiction and defer all

responsibility for organized crime to higher levels of government. Such leaders can easily stress the "preventive" nature of preventive policing and leave
"reaction" to state and federal officials. In many ways, tolerance offers city
leaders the safest strategy: one that can be justified politically/legally and that
will not invite the ire of organized crime. It is for this reason that I suspect
that tolerance is the dominant strategy among municipal leaders.

A tolerance strategy does, however, leave police leaders, commanders, and
officers free to pursue collusive strategies (See Table 4.1). There are, unfortunately, numerous recent cases where police chiefs have been arrested for ties
to organized crime. In 2008 and 2009 examples include Saulo Reyes Gamboa,
former director of municipal police in Ciudad Juárez; Hugo Armando Resén-
diz Martínez, former assistant attorney general in Durango; Gerardo Garay
Cadena, former interim head of the Federal Preventive Police; Noé Ramírez
Mandujano, former acting director of the country's anti-drug agency (SIEDO);
Francisco Velasco Delgado, former head of the municipal police in Cancún;
Juan José Muñiz Salinas, former head of the municipal police in Reynosa;
former heads of the Morelos state police and the Cuernavaca municipal police, Luis Ángel Cabeza de Vaca Rodríguez and Francisco Sánchez González;
and José Fernando Sereno Victorio, former head of the Tapachula, Chiapas
municipal police, two weeks after the detention of his former superior, José
Manuel Cinta Solíswere. The former head of the Guadalajara police spoke
about this form of "tolerance" when he wrote, "And I see all around irrespon-
sible politicians who name and maintain police commanders that have stepped
on the other side [engaged in corruption] in full view of everyone, and they
hide it as long as they maintain order and don't cause problems with public
opinion" (Tamez Guajardo 2008).

The same logic can also be applied further down the chain of command. If
the elected official and the police chief both pursue tolerance strategies, then
this opens the door for mid-level commanders to opt for collusive strategies.
In addition, tolerant mid-level commanders make it easier for rank-and-file
officers to engage in collusion. Of course, while collusion affords protection
from one specific group, it makes officers vulnerable to attack from rival criminal organizations. Collusion is a safe strategy when one criminal organization
dominates a geographical area but risky when territory is contested. Given the
danger presented by organized crime, strategies of tolerance might be perceived as the safest choice for the vast majority of the police force. There is an
ugly but commonly cited expression, "*Si quieres llegar a policía viejo, hazte*

pendejo," which literally means "If you want to last to be an old police officer, pretend to be stupid."

In summary, this discussion has attempted to develop a theoretical framework in which to analyze differing police strategies toward the police and explain how organized crime has hindered police professionalization. While it is tempting to take the considerable evidence of police corruption and organized crime infiltration and assume political corruption across municipalities and across time, doing so fails to recognize the diversity of strategies employed across the country and the predominance of tolerant strategies. This chapter puts forward the following propositions:

- The amount of organized crime infiltration in the police will depend on the strategy adopted by the mayor and the police chief. Where the mayor has adopted a collusive or toleration strategy, infiltration is expected to be considerable.
- In administrations that adopt a confrontational strategy, the amount of organized crime infiltration in the police will depend on the ability of elected officials and police leaders to monitor, create positive incentives, sanction misconduct, and create a professional environment for their agents vis-à-vis the ability of organized crime to monitor, bribe, and threaten.

Methodological Concerns

Unfortunately, it is extremely difficult to determine the amount of organized crime infiltration, the strategy of mayors, and the responses of police to official and organized crime incentives. Interviews and surveys offer important but limited tools, and media reports rather than judicial proceedings, police investigations, or public commission investigations (e.g., the Knapp Commission) continue to be the main source of information available to academics and observers studying organized crime and the police.

The preceding examples of collusion relied heavily on derivations of the term *allegation*. It is important to recognize that no Mexican president and only one governor has been prosecuted for collusion with organized crime. In theory, the presumption of innocence should exonerate the above-mentioned public officials. It is important to note that organized crime has an incentive to spread misinformation. Allegations of corruption are a simple means to create doubt and undermine public trust in police leaders who threaten criminal interests. Ravelo (2006) quotes the noted organized crime prosecutor Santiago Vasconcelos, "This is the form in which the criminals operate: they seek to discredit and in so doing weaken the institutions." (73). More recently, organized criminal groups have increasingly sought to discredit public officials through *narcomensajes,* or narco-messages, hung in public places or left on the bodies of victims. For example, in Nuevo León in 2006, one such message left on a recently assassinated body read, "Attorney General: Don't act like an idiot, this is going to continue until you stop protecting the people of Héctor Huerta, El Chapo Guzmán and the [deleted word] 'La Barbi'" (Cedillo 2007).

Absent a judicial system capable of taking on such cases and credibly determining truth from political attack from organized crime machinations, such allegations come down to the word of a journalist, a rival politician, or even a convicted criminal against the word of a political or police leader. The fact that many citizens give more credibility to allegations by convicted criminals than political leaders is evidence of the lack of trust in both the political and judicial system. Absent greater trust in the state, many citizens are not inclined to afford such officials the presumption of innocence in the courts of public opinion. Astorga (2005) writes, "accusations, perhaps true or false, but rarely proved or disproved; cases that will almost never be investigated much less judged by the appropriate authorities, and others that will be simply forgotten or ignored—impose a need for distance, reserve, an attitude of methodic doubt, which the reader should adapt before entering into this history" (14). The statement is both a warning to the reader to be skeptical of allegations like the ones above and an admission of frustration over the many cases that are never resolved.

Failure to investigate and determine guilt also places in doubt the honesty of those men and women who have made great sacrifices to uphold the rule of law. It is hard to imagine putting one's life on the line, as many officers have done, for a public who has largely prejudged all police as corrupt. But citizens have become skeptical because several police "heroes" have turned out to be villains working on behalf of a rival cartel. The most famous of these examples is of course Mexico's former drug czar, General José de Jesús Gutiérrez Rebollo. Gutiérrez Rebollo had been praised as an accomplished leader in the fight against organized crime and drug trafficking; however, in 1997 he was arrested and found guilty of collaborating with the Juárez Cartel of Amado Carrillo Fuentes. He is not the only example. Guillermo González Calderóni, a commander in the now-extinct Federal Judicial Police, was credited with arresting the organized crime world's boss of bosses Miguel Angel Félix Gallardo in 1989 and cornering Chihuahua's powerful drug *cacique* Pablo Acosta in 1986. Nonetheless, Calderóni was accused of corruption and was forced to flee the country in the early 1990s when he was discovered to have an unexplainable amount of wealth (Astorga 2005). Although Arturo Durazo Moreno was credited with several important drug arrests as head of the Mexico City police during the late 1970s and early 1980s, he is perhaps Mexico's most legendary corrupt cop (González G. 1983). With these cases at the forefront of the public's mind, successful police are as suspect as ineffective officers. Felipe Calderón's top police official Genaro García Luna has repeatedly faced accusations of corruption and ties to organized crime (Hernández 2008). The problem of misinformation causes damage in both ways: honest police can be perceived as corrupt, and corrupt police can be perceived as honest.

On the one hand, this chapter hopes to help fill part of this gap in our knowledge of organized crime—police relations. On the other hand, this research suffers from the same methodological challenges. This chapter focuses on organized crime–police relations in Tijuana, which has been the center of operations for the Arellano Félix organization (AFO) since the early 1990s. In addition to basing the analysis on an important case, there is also a methodological advantage to focusing on Tijuana. Newspapers in the other three research sites have self-censored themselves in the face of threats from organized crime. Only in Tijuana does the weekly paper *Zeta* continue to conduct investigative journalism into organized crime and police corruption issues. As such, the following analysis of Tijuana is based on a review of articles from *Zeta* and *Frontera* newspapers in addition to interviews with police, police leaders, journalists, and members of civil society. Following the analysis, the chapter will explore the other three cases and discuss similarities and differences.

Police-Organized Crime Relations in Tijuana

There has been a long history of police and government collusion with organized crime in Tijuana.[10] As late as the 1980s, Blancornelas (2002) suggests that the federal attorney in Baja California (delegate of the Procuraduría General de la República), José Luis Larrazolo Rubio, largely controlled drug trafficking in the state. Blancornelas writes of Larrazolo's tenure in Baja California, "Like all the feds of his time period, he loved to torture low level criminals, open routes for drug traffickers, and charge high rates for his services. While he was in Tijuana, the mafia flourished, abuses spread, and injustice erased the law" (37). However, consistent with the conclusions of Astorga's national-level analysis discussed above, organized crime's strength vis-à-vis government actors in Baja California changed in the 1980s and 1990s as the power of government actors waned and organized crime's grew. This change was visible in Baja California with the rise of the Arellano Félix organization in the late 1980s and the 1990s. (See Table 4.2 for a time line of select events in Tijuana.)

In the above-mentioned pact organized by Miguel Ángel Félix Gallardo, the Tijuana *plaza* was given to Jesús Labra, who in turn appeared to turn over operations to his nephews in the Arellano Félix family.[11] Benjamín Arellano Félix became the head of the organization, and his brother Ramón developed a reputation as the family's ruthless enforcer. Blancornelas (2002) concludes that collusion between the authorities and the Arellano Félix operation was evident early on. He relates how *Zeta* first reported on the Arellano Félix family in 1985. Much to his dismay, he observed state police deployed throughout the city buying up all the copies of the edition to keep it from the public. Blancornelas offers additional evidence, such as a 1994 incident whereby corrupt state officials escorting the youngest brother Francisco Javier and another AFO leader, Ismael Higuera Guerrero, found themselves in a confrontation with corrupt federal officials escorting Héctor Palma of the Sinaloa organization. The two AFO members were arrested at the time; however, both were let go despite photos of the arrest.

In addition to detailing collusive links, Blancornelas (2002) also profiles the threats meted out by the AFO. A common strategy was to appear in the middle of the night and shoot up a house or business to send a warning. *Zeta's* own offices were the target of such an attack, as was a home where the wife of a governor was staying, the homes of police officers, and the residences of the brother of a former state attorney general (Blancornelas). Such threats were not hollow, however. María Idalia Gómez and Darío Fritz (2005) profile the efforts of Dr. Ernesto Ibarra Santés, a federal official in Baja California, to bring down the organization in the mid-1990s. A massive and carefully planned operation based on months of secretive investigation was foiled at the last minute, and Ibarra Santés returned to Mexico City defeated. Waiting for him at the airport, however, were AFO assassins, and Ibarra Santés was killed (Gómez and Fritz).[12]

Blancornelas (2002) concludes that neither federal, nor state, nor municipal authorities were willing or able to confront the AFO. He writes,

TABLE 4.2. Timeline of select events in Tijuana's recent history

1985	• *Zeta* newspaper first reports on the Arellano Félix family.
1988	• *Zeta* co-founder Héctor Félix Miranda is killed.
1993	• Francisco Arellano Félix, the oldest of seven brothers, is arrested by Mexican federal authorities in Tijuana.
1994	• Five elite federal antidrug police are killed; their deaths are blamed on the AFO and corrupt state police. • PRI presidential candidate Luis Donaldo Colosio is shot and killed in Tijuana. • Reformist Tijuana police chief accredited with cleaning up the police force Federico Benítez López is killed.
1996	• Federal prosecutor Ernesto Ibarra Santés is killed after a failed attempt to arrest AFO operatives.
1997	• Eighty-seven federal police operating in Baja California are replaced by military personnel. • Celebrated state investigator Odín Gutiérrez Rico is killed, allegedly by the AFO. • Blancornelas is shot four times in an assassination attempt. He survives and is provided with army protection.
2000	• Tijuana police chief Alfredo de la Torre is killed • AFO leader Ismael Higuera Guerrero is apprehended.
2002	• Ramón Arellano Félix is killed in Mazatlán, Sinaloa • Benjamín Arellano Félix is apprehended by the military in Puebla. • Federal authorities apprehend forty-one state and municipal law enforcement personnel in a surprise operation. All but nine are eventually released.
2004	• *Zeta* associate Francisco Ortiz Franco is killed by former bodyguards of newly elected mayor Jorge Hank Rhon.
2005	• Murder of fifteen-year-old Sara Benazir Chagoya Ruíz mobilizes civil society.
2006	• Kidnappings of Asian businessmen George Koi Choy and Yong Hang King threatens the city's maquiladora industry. • The Citizen Public Security Council and its president, Jesús Alberto Capella Ibarra, lead a fifteen-day march through the state protesting insecurity. • Francisco Javier Arellano Félix is captured by the U.S. Coast Guard in international waters while fishing off the Baja California coast.
2007	• Jorge Ramos is elected municipal president and appoints civil society activist Alberto Capella Ibarra to lead the Secretariat of Public Security.
2008	• Eduardo Arellano Félix is arrested by Mexican federal authorities in Tijuana. • A violent rift emerges in the AFO between Luis Fernando Sánchez Arellano and Teodoro García Simental. • Capella Ibarra steps down and is replaced by Lieutenant Colonel Julián Leyzaola Pérez.
2009	• The military captures Santiago Meza López, *el pozolero*, responsible for dissolving hundreds of victims' bodies in acid. • Garcia Simental is captured following arrests earlier in the year of lieutenants Ángel Jácome Gamboa and José Filiberto Parra. • Leyzaola and General Alfonso Duarte are recognized by *Zeta* as People of the Year and win public praise from U.S. officials and the business community.
2010	• García Simental's brother José Manuel and principal lieutenant Raydel López are arrested. • Captain Gustavo Huerta succeeds Leyzaola as Secretary of Public Security.

Frequently reading or hearing of or about Arellano Félix has become familiar in our country, even common, as if one was to speak about a musical group or some football team with a recap of their recent season. But in reality they had more power and intelligence than three federal governments combined, more than 10 attorney generals, hundreds of federal commanders, thousands of Mexican police, and many U.S. officials. Their recipe: bribery. Something like water for chocolate . . . corruption (33).

A 2002 *New York Times* article puts it even more bluntly, "It has been said, not entirely in jest, that of every 10 police officers in Tijuana, 11 were on the cartel's payroll in the 1990's" (Weiner 2002). Through the use of both carrots and sticks, the Arellano Félix family maintained solid control of the Tijuana *plaza* and successfully fended off attempts by the Sinaloa and Juárez organizations to enter the Tijuana market.

By the mid-to-late 2000s, the game had changed for the criminal family. In the 2000s the AFO would become a primary target of U.S. and Mexican authorities. Most significantly, Ismael Higuera Guerrero was arrested in 2000 and Benjamín Arellano Félix in 2002. While not a product of federal efforts, the organization's main enforcer Ramón Arellano Félix was killed in 2002. By 2005, the Fox administration bragged that it had detained (although not necessarily successfully prosecuted) two of the organization's leaders, five of its financiers, eleven cell leaders or lieutenants, forty-eight of the AFO's killers or *sicarios*, and thirty-three government officials accused of colluding with the AFO (Fox 2005). Most of these government officials were police officers arrested in 2002. Federal authorities called many of Baja California's police leaders to the state police academy for what was promoted as a training and evaluation. After checking weapons at the entrance, federal authorities arrested over forty police and flew them to Mexico City for questioning (Fox). While many, including the director of the Tijuana municipal police Carlos Otal, were never brought up on charges, it was hoped that the dramatic arrests represented a newfound commitment to addressing corruption. In August 2006, the subsequent leader of the organization, Francisco Javier Arellano Félix, was arrested, and in October 2008 the last of the brothers Eduardo Arellano Félix was captured by federal police. Although the mantle of leadership formally passed to a nephew, Luis Fernando Sánchez Arellano, challenges began to surface from within the organization.

Traditionally, the AFO had been made up of a number of cells loyal to the Arellano Félix family but with a degree of operational independence; the

United Nations Office on Drugs and Crime (UNODC 2002) labeled the AFO's structure a "clustered hierarchy." With the decline of the Arellano Félix brothers, one of the organization's cell leaders, Teodoro García Simental, challenged Sánchez Arellano's leadership, producing a major rupture in the organization. Concurrently, the Sinaloa organization, which had always been the AFO's chief rival, sought to strengthen its presence in Baja California by cultivating ties to the García Simental camp (Camarena 2008). Clearly the conditions of the game had changed for the Arellano Félix family leadership, which had to fight off federal and U.S. pressure, an insurgency within its ranks, and the entrance of an external organization.

The internal division turned violent by the spring of 2008, when a sustained shoot-out between the two rival groups resulted in sixteen deaths and many more injuries. Following a lull in violence over the summer, the killings escalated dramatically in the fall. By the end of the year there had been 882 homicides, of which an estimated 614 were organized crime-related, up from 310 homicides, of which 176 were estimated to be organized crime-related in 2007 (*Zeta* 2009a; Presidencia 2011). After months of fighting, which had left both camps drained of human and financial resources, in December 2008 it is believed that the two groups called a truce and agreed to respect one another's territory. The truce was an uneasy one, and conflict largely continued at lower levels until the capture of García Simental and his principal lieutenants at the end of 2009 and early 2010.

Police–Organized Crime Relations During 2008 and 2009

Under increasing pressure from civil society, the federal government, and the military, there was cautious optimism that the incoming administration of Jorge Ramos (December 2007–November 2010) would be more serious about tackling police corruption and developing a professional police department than his predecessor. Despite the dramatic federal arrests of local police in 2002, cartel infiltration only seemed to increase under the 2004–07 municipal administration of Jorge Hank Rhon. As mentioned above, Hank Rhon had consistently been under suspicion of ties to organized crime, and subsequent evidence does suggest that criminal cells successfully took advantage of Hank Rhon's poorly implemented enlargement of the police force to enroll their members in the police. In response to a wave of violence in early 2007, the Calderón administration deployed 3,300 federal police and military personnel to Tijuana. While such measures were taken throughout the country, in Tijuana

the military took the extra step of confiscating the guns of all of Tijuana's officers, leaving the police force without weapons for close to a month (McKinley
2007). Although the official statistics do not bear out the assertion, popular
perception holds that crime decreased during this time period.

Upon arrival in office, the Ramos administration responded to the crisis in
the police force by appointing as his Secretary of Public Security Jesús Alberto
Capella Ibarra, a civil society activist who had headed the state's citizen public
security council. Capella Ibarra was so outspoken that upon his selection as
secretary, gunmen shot up his house in an attempt to scare or assassinate the
civic leader-turned-police chief. The attack failed when Capella Ibarra used the
automatic assault rifle left by his bodyguards to fend off the assailants, propel-
ling the young lawyer to stardom status in the national and international
media. For the position of police director and operational commander, the administration appointed a lieutenant colonel from the military, Julián Leyzaola
Pérez. The colonel sought to bring military-style discipline to the force and
took an active role in day-to-day operations, participating in police actions and
meeting daily with all district commanders. The two appointments from more
trusted backgrounds were meant to reassure Tijuana's citizens.

In early January 2008, weeks into the new administration, members of an
AFO cell attempted to rob an armored car along one of Tijuana's principle
transit routes (Ovalle 2008a). Under the direct leadership of Leyzaola, a police
pursuit was initiated, the transit route was shut down, and the robbers were
forced to flee without their cargo. The operation detailed in the following
day's newspaper was surprising to members of Tijuana's society for two reasons. First, the municipal police had successfully prevented a major criminal
act, and second, the director of the police had personally joined and then led
the operation. The incident suggested that the new leadership would not select
the traditional options of tolerance and collusion, but would instead confront
organized crime.

Had the story ended there, it might have been on balance a very positive
outcome. Instead, messages were broadcast over the police radio threatening
that anyone who participated in the operation would be killed. Only a few
hours later, the commanders ordered by Leyzaola to close off the transit route
were assassinated. In attempting to carry out one of the killings, organized
crime triggermen opened fire on the wrong house, killing a woman who lived
there and wounding her husband and child. The gunman recognized the error and turned their weapons on the correct house, killing police commander

Margarito Saldaña along with his wife and twelve-year-old daughter (Salinas and Ovalle 2008; Ovalle and Villegas 2008). The killing of an apparently honest officer (as evidenced by Saldaña's humble home and limited financial resources) seemed to break from a history of targeting double-crossing police but sparing families.

This cycle of crime, police response, and reprisal would repeat itself several times in the following months. Organized crime was used to impunity and had no intention of giving an inch, even for rather small offenses. When a twenty-year-old youth who claimed to have "connections" was detained in early April 2008 for driving a car without license plates, a municipal officer accompanied by another individual arrived at the district police station where the youth was being held and attempted to negotiate his release. To the commanding officer's credit, the two men were arrested and transported to the central police station. Minutes later an armed group of an estimated ten men opened fire on the district station, and three days later a group attempted to assassinate the police commander at his home (Andrade 2008).

History would repeat itself again in March. Throughout early 2008, organized criminal cells had been using tow trucks to drag away ATMs. The acts were brazen and symptomatic of the degree of impunity with which organized crime felt it could operate in Tijuana.[13] Believing they were responding to a grocery store robbery, an elite police unit arrived at 4 AM to find a tow truck guarded by armed men pulling away an ATM. A firefight, ensued and two of the criminals were detained and arrested despite threats that there would be retribution. The next day, the mid-level officer in charge of the operation was assassinated immediately outside the police station on his way home from work (Cordero 2008). Of the four remaining officers who participated in the arrests, three resigned in fear and one was transferred to another area.

Despite these reprisals, throughout 2008 and 2009 Leyzaola continued to pursue a confrontation strategy, facilitated by improved cooperation among municipal, state, federal, and military authorities. Constitutional changes in 2008 allowed municipalities to play a more active role in addressing local drug sales and consumption, and Leyzaola specifically targeted the AFO's local drug business. *Zeta* (2009f) reports that when the AFO threatened commanders to make them stay away from a drug-selling stronghold, Leyzaola sent the police into the zone en masse. Facing a continued threat to their operations, a somewhat-united AFO opted for an intimidation strategy. Following a tactic that had proved successful in removing Ciudad Juárez's police chief in 2008, the AFO threatened to randomly kill innocent police until Leyzaola resigned. Seven officers were killed in April 2009 in what were believed to be coordinated attacks between the Sánchez and García factions, and another three officers were randomly shot in July (*Zeta* 2009f; 2009g). Leyzaola, however, refused to step down.

Having failed to intimidate the secretary, García Simental's faction developed plans to assassinate him. As a military officer, however, Leyzaola lived on the military base, which afforded a degree of protection not available to many civilian police chiefs. Intelligence reports leaked to the media suggest that there was a plan to use a car bomb to attack the secretariat's vulnerable installations, which was reportedly foiled when the secretary moved operations to a more secure location. In November 2009 a more elaborate plan was uncovered by military and police personnel involving dozens of organized crime *sicarios* who had been tracking Leyzaola's movements. They planned an attack on his vehicle in which they would be dressed as military personnel and use high-powered .50 caliber rifles (*Zeta* 2009i).

Based on the above evidence, it appears that the Ramos administration and, more importantly, the police chief Leyzaola adopted a confrontation strategy. There is always the possibility that Leyzaola was targeting one group while favoring another; however, most members of civil society interviewed felt that he was engaged in a genuine confrontation strategy. It was even reported that Leyzaola's corrupted assistant director told his criminal handlers that the chief could not be corrupted. In Finnegan's (2010) account, Leyzaola related that a military colleague came to him as an emissary of a criminal group looking to make a deal. Leyzaola claimed that he held a gun to the emissary's head, personally escorted him on a flight to Mexico City, and had him arrested. Nonetheless, even as Leyzaola pursued a confrontation strategy, many of the men and women under his command face conflicting incentives. Evidence of collusive corruption between the police and organized crime continued to come to light. It is worth reiterating and mentioning a few of the events of 2008.

- General Sergio Aponte Polito took the unprecedented step in April 2008 of sending an extensive letter to the press detailing allegations of corruption against individual police officers and police leaders throughout the state.
- In June 2008, three police officers were detained along with fifty-five others in a police raid of what would become known as the

"narcobautizo," a baptism for the child of a member of the AFO (Andrade 2008c).

- In July 2008, Mexicali police detained a band of kidnappers, two of whom were Tijuana municipal police (Murillo 2008).

- In November 2008, the federal attorney general's office announced the arrest of nineteen municipal police. All nineteen were commanding officers, including one of the force's assistant directors.

- In December 2008, an officer working for a kidnapping gang with ties to García Simental used his authority to pull over a vehicle and abduct the driver (*Zeta* 2009c).

While there is evidence of collusion and outright criminality by the above-mentioned officers, a far more common strategy among line-level police officers appears to have been tolerance. As mentioned above, it is easy for officers to use their lack of jurisdiction as justification for turning a blind eye to organized criminal activity and avoiding dangerous confrontation. *Zeta* describes an event from August 2008 illustrative of the fear felt by municipal officers. At the time, Leyzaola personally led over a hundred municipal patrol cars in pursuit of an armed criminal convoy. According to *Zeta,* it was supposedly announced over the police radio that the group included García Simental. The patrol cars began to slow down and some pretended to get lost, until:

> All of a sudden, all the patrol cars had fallen back and the federal group that was supposed to have cut off passage at a specific street in the neighborhood never arrived. The convoy escaped. The official version was that the armored plating on the secretary's truck prevented it from catching up. The non-official version was that he was left with three men against three cars with criminals and opted to retreat (*Zeta* 2009h).

Tolerance also appears to be a safer strategy than collusion. As previously alluded to, when officers accept a bribe, they might escape the bullet from one organized criminal group, but they become a target for an opposing group. When the rift emerged in the AFO in 2008, corrupt officers found themselves on either side of that division and hence a legitimate target of the rival gang. In April 2008, a major shoot-out took place between the two rival groups. Sixteen people were killed in the incident, including a municipal police officer (*Zeta* 2008). *Zeta* alleged that ten other municipal police participated on both sides of the fighting. It is believed that of the thirty municipal police killed in 2008, the majority were partisans in a war between the two factions.

As such, just within the Tijuana municipal police department one can observe confrontation, tolerance, and collusion with two different criminal factions. The key to explaining these contradictory strategies is to understand the differences in the incentives faced by Leyzaola and those faced by his subordinates. As a political appointee, Leyzaola is more sensitive to mayoral and civil society pressure, and, as a military officer, he is subject to military pressure from the commanding military general in Baja California. The failure to produce results can be cause for removal. While Jesus Alberto Capella Ibarra, the civil society advocate appointed secretary of public security, was originally a popular choice, his lack of police experience quickly became a liability. After one year of poor results he was pushed out and replaced by Leyzaola. In addition, while the former military officer no doubt faces considerable risk by pursuing a confrontation strategy, he does have bodyguards and is able to live on the army base for added protection.

The incentives confronted by Leyzaola's subordinates, however, are entirely different. They face only limited pressure from civil society, as citizens have limited information and few tools with which to hold rank-and-file police accountable. On the other hand, as the above assassinations indicate, police officers are highly subject to the bribes and threats of organized criminal operations. In early 2009, two mid-level officers confessed to being paid between $500 and $700 a month to facilitate criminal operations. The arrested officers contended that they did not collude by choice, but that they would be killed if they did not cooperate (*Zeta* 2009e). In May 2009, another mid-level officer, Abel Santos Salazar, was killed on his way to work; reports by *Zeta* (2009g) suggest that he was assassinated for refusing to work with organized crime. It should be mentioned that most police in Mexico are not allowed to carry a weapon while off duty, making them particularly vulnerable to attack. Several assassinated officers, including the mid-level commander who prevented the above-mentioned ATM robbery, were killed immediately before or after their shift.

As a different type of "principal" in a principal-agent relationship, organized crime has also proven adept at overcoming information asymmetries. In theory, if a police operation is carried out by masked police officers, the criminals should not know exactly who carried out the operation and be unable to issue reprisals. As one officer interviewed explained, however, "the problem is the other police officers," who report information back to the cartels.[14] Although, Tijuana has been converting to a more secure communications system, organized crime has been able to monitor and communicate with the police by listening to police radios with a police scanner that can be easily purchased. In all of the above-mentioned cases, organized criminal elements announced threats over police radio.

The Tijuana case illustrates the dilemma for a mayor or police chief who has selected a confrontation strategy. A successful strategy requires a holistic approach to police reform.

- To overcome information asymmetries and identify infiltrated officers, police chiefs require a trustworthy mid-level command structure (i.e., a merit-based system of promotions) with reliable evaluation methods. To prevent future infiltration, police chiefs require strict selection criteria and mechanisms for incoming cadets.

- To counter the desirability of bribes, both carrots and sticks are required. Bribe money would be worth less if salaries and benefits were improved. Equally if not more important, however, are accountability mechanisms that will increase the probability that misconduct will result in a loss of salaries, benefits, and pension, and even possible jail time.

- To counter the threat of organized crime is perhaps the most challenging. Doing so requires removing infiltrated officers from the force, securing radio communications, protecting officers while they are on duty by giving them adequate equipment (e.g., bulletproof vests, assault rifles), revising operational procedures, and protecting officers who have been threatened (by permitting them to carry their weapons off duty, providing bodyguards, or even relocating them). While outside the jurisdiction of local police chiefs, countering the threat of reprisals also requires aggressive prosecutions of police killings.

Absent these enormous policy changes, tolerance and collusion will continue to remain the dominant strategy for line-level officers, despite the presence of a confrontational police chief. Arguably, Leyzaola pursued all of these strategies; however, Tijuana lacked an effective and reliable means to identify and sanction police misconduct. The previous chapters have discussed the challenges of improving selection criteria, raising salaries and police benefits, and creating a merit-based promotion system. Absent from this analysis thus far, however, has been a discussion of accountability mechanisms. Following a brief discussion of organized crime–police relations in the other three research sites, this chapter explores the challenges of creating effective accountability mechanisms to detect, sanction, and prevent misconduct. As such tools are lacking in Tijuana, it appears that Leyzaola, in coordination with military and federal authorities, resorted to harsh interrogation techniques and human rights abuses. While numerous corrupt police were identified and sanctioned, it appears that innocent officers were falsely charged, and organized crime infiltration undoubtedly continues.

Tijuana as Compared with Chihuahua, Mexicali, and Hermosillo

Tijuana is without question an extreme case, not representative of the situation in the country as a whole, but nonetheless comparable to other hot spots like Ciudad Juárez and Culiacán, which are also operational centers for large criminal organizations. Tijuana does, however, offer a unique and interesting case study because of the confrontation approach pursued by Leyzaola in coordination with military and federal officials. Baja California was one of the first to experiment with a flexible unified police command, whereby Leyzaola worked closely with and in subordination to the military commander for Baja California, General Alfonso Duarte. In the other research sites, the local police forces played a far less proactive role in the Mexican state's conflict with organized crime and largely limited their activities to enforcing municipal regulations. While legally justifiable, such a limited interpretation of their responsibilities toward providing public security set the stage for a tolerant strategy toward organized crime.

Mexicali and Hermosillo

In theory, organized crime-related violence should be worse in Mexicali than it has been. Given its location along the border, Mexicali cannot escape its fate as a transit point for drugs headed to the U.S. market. In September and October 2008, two human and drug smuggling tunnels were discovered by state and municipal authorities. Had they been completed, they would have connected houses in Mexicali with houses in the U.S. city of Calexico. In early October of that year, Mexican federal authorities arrested five presumed drug traffickers in Mexicali; this was in coordination with the U.S. Operation Money Train, which resulted in thirty-five total arrests of operatives tied to the Sinaloa cartel. In December, responding to anonymous tips, the military decommissioned 5.6 tons of marijuana being warehoused in Mexicali. U.S. Customs and Border Protection also reported a number of major drug seizures at the Calexico point of entry in 2009, including a three-ton shipment in November of that year (Morosi 2009, CBP 2009).

At the time of the division of Mexican territory among drug traffickers in 1989, scholars differ on whether Mexicali was given to Joaquín Guzmán Loera or Rafael Chao López. As the Arellano Félix organization grew in power in the 1990s, however, their influence also grew in Mexicali. As their power waned in the 2000s, traffickers affiliated with the Sinaloa organization came to reassert control of the *plaza*. The Sinaloa cartel's Vicente Zambada Niebla was believed to be responsible for operations in Mexicali in the late 2000s; however, the violent rift between the Beltrán Leyva brothers and the Sinaloa cartel on the national level was reproduced on a smaller scale in this border city. Arturo Salazar, a nephew of the Beltrán Leyva brothers, is believed to have sided with his relatives, while Víctor Serrano Galván aligned himself with Zambada Niebla. Written in early 2009, a *Zeta* report (2009d) speculated that Zambada controlled 60 percent of the flow of drugs, Beltrán Leyva 30 percent, and the AFO 10 percent.

The city has not escaped this organized crime presence unharmed. There is abundant evidence of illegal activities, an official per capita crime rate that is actually worse than Tijuana's, and increased gang conflicts. When kidnappings soared in Tijuana, there was a spillover effect in Mexicali. Although all three were rescued, two Mexicali businessmen were kidnapped in April 2008 and a third was taken in July. Despite its location along the border, however, Mexicali has avoided the worst of the violence that has plagued nearby Tijuana. There were only an estimated 129 organized crime-related killings in Mexicali between the years of 2007 and 2010, as compared with 1,667 in Tijuana and 1,415 in Chihuahua City (Presidencia 2011).

Respondents interviewed offer different explanations for the relative safety of the city. The most common explanation is that Mexicali has never been the center of operations for the violent Arellano Félix organization. While the city has known periods of violence when the Sinaloa cartel and the AFO vied for its control, it is believed that the AFO became too weak to effectively contest the *plaza*. Other observers joke that the city's harsh desert climate is simply too extreme for drug traffickers. Pointing to the large drug shipments mentioned above, however, many fear that authorities have quietly colluded with or tolerated organized crime to protect the sanctity of the state capital (Marosi 2009). Historically there is evidence to suggest that this is the case; in 2004 a former police chief during the 1990s, Antonio Hermenegildo Carmona Añorve, was sentenced to thirty-six years in prison for collaboration with an AFO cell. More recently, allegations by General Aponte Polito suggest that during the Samuel Ramos administration (2005–07), high-ranking police commanders facilitated drug shipments through the municipality.

The presence of organized crime with relatively low levels of violence presents a situation similar to that of Hermosillo. Hermosillo has a reputation as a safe community, relatively free from the threats of organized crime. This perception is reflected in a newspaper article from mid-2008 noting a convoy of thirty federal police vehicles passing through Hermosillo. The twist of the article was that the police were not in Hermosillo as part of an operation against drug traffickers; rather, they were just stopping to pick up some of Sonora's famous steak before continuing on to the more dangerous Baja California (Ponce 2008). It is true that in relative terms, Hermosillo has experienced less violence than the other research sites. Similar to Mexicali there were a relatively low 112 organized crime-related assassinations between 2007 and 2010 (Presidencia 2011). The city has also experienced less derivative violence; from 1995-2007, there were only thirteen reported kidnappings in Hermosillo. Finally, a systematic review of *El Imparcial* articles in 2008 produced no public revelations of police connections to the major organized criminal groups and only two allegations of corrupt ties to local drug dealers.[15]

Despite the relative calm in Hermosillo, many interviewees were less optimistic about the city's ability to avoid violence and the negative impact of organized crime. In fact, the optimistic tone of the aforementioned newspaper article was undermined by the discovery of a dead body in Hermosillo along with two others in Nogales, Sonora, just four days later. In early 2007, the capital city suffered a series of attacks on its police officers. In March, municipal officer Hero Arturo Gálvez Acosta was killed; he was reported to have been found with a message pinned to his body by a knife in his chest that read, "Look [expletive], the problem is not with the government, it is with Arturo Beltrán and the 'Barbie;' all the judicial and municipal police that are with him are going to die" (Diario del Desierto 2007). Unlike Tijuana, such messages had been a rarity in Hermosillo. At that time, Arturo Beltrán Leyva was one of the primaries in the Sinaloa organization and, according to Ricardo Ravelo (2006), dominated drug trafficking in the Sonora area. The intellectual author of the assassination was attributed to Francisco Hernandez Garcia, who had once been an associate of the Sinaloa cartel but was believed to have broken with the organization and aligned himself with the Gulf and Zetas. Several police took the threat seriously, including thirty-eight who left the force that same March (Imparcial 2008c). A total of thirty police were killed from throughout the state in 2007, including six from Hermosillo, of which at least three deaths were attributable to organized crime (Imparcial 2008a).

Rumors and allegations of organized crime infiltration go all the way up to the city mayor. While the rumors are impossible to verify, it is alleged that criminal organizations made large contributions to the mayor's election campaign in exchange for the appointment of a compromised officer as operational commander of the preventive police during the 2006–09 administration. The same rumors suggest that the police force was so much in the pocket of criminal groups that much of the force received a Christmas bonus from organized crime. While perhaps just conspiracy theory, the allegations offer observers a compelling explanation as to why Hermosillo was not harder hit by the violence. Other interviewees provided alternative explanations. Some pointed to Hermosillo's distance from the border. Others argued that Sonora has always been somewhat free territory shared by different criminal organizations. Still others contended that organized crime has no incentive to upset the political and economic elites in the state capital.

Chihuahua

Of the three research sites, Chihuahua's experience has come closest to Tijuana's. While nearby Ciudad Juárez had always been plagued by organized crime violence, the Chihuahuan capital had been a safe city with a low crime rate. In 2008, however, the violent conflict involving the Juárez organization, the Beltrán Leyva brothers, and the Zetas against the Sinaloa organization brought unprecedented violence to Chihuahua City. Early in 2008, several state investigative police officers were assassinated in the capital, and in March of that year, the city was witness to its first major confrontation between federal authorities and an organized criminal group holed up in a safe house. Authorities began to note the presence of criminal gangs, such as the Sinaloa-affiliated Mexicles and the Juárez aligned Aztecas, who had previously limited their operations to Ciudad Juárez. From 2007 to 2010 there were 1,415 organized crime-related killings in the city, which on a per capita basis yields a higher rate than Tijuana. The municipal police have not escaped the effects of the conflict. Four municipal police officers were killed in the first month of 2009, including one of the city's four regional commanders. Unable to stem the rising insecurity in the city, Lazaro Gaytán was forced to step down as director after five years in the post to be replaced by a retired military officer. The killings would continue, however. By the end of summer 2010, the department reported that sixteen more officers had been killed, including several high-level commanders.

The violence plaguing Chihuahua has raised doubts about the professionalism of the Chihuahua municipal police department. If in fact the department was one of the best police forces in the country, as its city and police leaders claimed, why was it not more effective at preventing such devastating violence? Moreover, why did this professional department include officers with links to organized crime? The infiltration of organized crime in Chihuahua's police force in many ways reveals the unfortunate flaw in Chihuahua's professionalization efforts and the efforts currently underway across the country. While Chihuahua had made unprecedented strides in terms of training, investment, education, citizen participation, operational procedures, use of technology, etc., it had made only minimal advances in developing accountability mechanisms and addressing corruption. The following section explores why existing accountability mechanisms across the research sites have failed to address problems of corruption and organized crime infiltration.

Accountability Mechanisms

Preventing collusion with organized crime depends on the ability of elected officials and police leaders to (1) create positive incentives, (2) monitor and hold police accountable, and (3) create a professional environment for their agents vis-à-vis the ability of organized crime to (a) bribe, (b) threaten, and (c) monitor those same agents. As part of this equation, effective accountability mechanisms are necessary to identify and punish corrupt officers and increase the likelihood that those engaging in future corruption will be caught and punished. Mechanisms to ensure accountability can take a number of different forms. As Robert Varenik (2005) points out, such mechanisms can be organized under distinct auspices; focus on either individual cases or systemic problems; and employ reactive, proactive, or preventive measures.

The U.S. literature on police accountability mechanisms has tended to focus on whether such mechanisms fall inside or outside of the police department (Walker 2000; Kutnjak Ivković 2005). Advocates of external oversight argue that an internal agency has no real motivation to uncover police misconduct whose revelation would serve as a black eye to the police and police leaders. Of course, police leaders with a long-term perspective might recognize that it would be far more advantageous to suffer a bad reputation in the short term to achieve a good reputation in the future, but, as the preceding discussions have illustrated, the short term is far more salient given the three-year time horizon of administrations and the urgency of the current security crisis. Not surprisingly, there are no shortages of examples of ineffective internal mechanisms (Sherman 1974; Walker; Kutnjak Ivković; Arias and Zúñiga 2008).

While external agencies can be expected to have greater independence, they suffer from a different set of limitations (Bayley 1990). Walker (2000) points out that the creation of a fully independent Office of Municipal Investigations founded in 1981 in New Orleans failed to prevent the New Orleans Police Department from developing a national reputation as one of the most corrupt police forces in the United States. In addition, many police in favor of internal accountability mechanisms contend that external agencies will be biased against the police. They might, for example, rule that an officer used excessive force without understanding the danger in confronting potentially violent individuals. In the extreme, detractors of external oversight argue that police will not respond to calls for assistance or put themselves at risk if they feel that they do not have the full support of the department and the law. In Colombia, the leadership of the Colombian National Police resisted and undermined one such external citizen-led oversight commission (Varenik 2005).

In addition to the oversight mechanism's location, a second key point of variation is whether the agency focuses on "rotten apples" or the "rotten barrel." Historically, police chiefs have favored individual-level explanations for police corruption. A focus on individuals suggests that incidences of misconduct are isolated, deviant behavior, and the product of a few rotten apples. Such an approach is extremely problematic, however, if the institutional incentives within the department encourage misconduct, in other words, if the barrel is rotten (Sherman 1974). If systematic incentives for misconduct exist, removing corrupt officers and replacing them with ostensibly more honest recruits will fail to bring about an honest police force. In New York in the 1960s, investigations into corruption in the city's narcotics division led to a gradual transfer of almost the entire staff of the division. Three years later a study found continued corruption, and personnel were again replaced. Despite these personnel changes, corruption continued (Sherman). Similar problems have plagued purges in Mexican police forces (Uildriks 2010). According to the analogy, placing a perfectly good apple inside a rotten barrel will lead to the rotting of the apple.

In recognition of both the dangers presented by rotten apples and a rotten barrel, a robust disciplinary regime requires a focus on both. As Martínez, Bellalta, and Montt (2008) point out, such an approach was adopted in Hong Kong by the now-famous Independent Commission Against Corruption (ICAC). While not focused exclusively on police, the ICAC has been hailed as a successful model for oversight. It not only investigates corrupt activity, but also conducts preventive audits to identify ways to reduce corruption, and even conducts outreach and educational activities to change attitudes about corruption (Lai 2000).

Even among those agencies that only investigate individual officers, there are still variations in strategies, divided by Varenik (2005) and others into reactive, proactive, and preventive strategies. Reactive investigations occur as a result of a complaint against an officer, and might only examine the specific alleged act of misconduct. Complaint-based systems are the most common, but they are problematic for a number of reasons. Complaints frequently come from criminal suspects rather than impartial witnesses and are notoriously difficult to substantiate after the fact (Kutnjak Ivković 2005). The success of complaint mechanisms often depends on the willingness of police to report fellow officers (Varenik 2005); however, police culture and a code of silence typically discourage officers from doing so (Sherman 1974; Drummond 1976; Azaola Garrido and Ruíz Torres 2009, Suárez de Garay 2009). Finally, incidences of corruption and organized crime infiltration are unlikely, or at least far less likely than other forms of misconduct, to be reported. Analyzing data from the International Crime Victim Survey, Kutnjak Ivković finds that of the respondents who reported that they had been asked to pay a bribe across the globe, only 5 percent stated that they had reported the incident. To offer another example, at the time of high levels of corruption in the New York City Police Department in the 1970s, corruption allegations made up only 5.7 percent of complaints (Kutnjak Ivković).

Proactive investigations require no such complaint, can be initiated at any time, and offer investigators greater leverage and flexibility. Rather than try to investigate an act that has already occurred, proactive investigations and sting operations allow investigators the opportunity to observe misconduct first-hand and build stronger cases against corrupt officers. Preventive measures use supervisor evaluations, citizen complaints, psychological evaluations, and other information to identify "early warning signs" that an officer might be at risk of abusing authority. Rather than take punitive action, early warning signs allow a department to reassign officers, refer them to additional training, or send them to psychological treatment to prevent misconduct from occurring. In summary, accountability mechanisms can vary in their auspices, their objective, and their approach.

All four cities have incorporated their accountability agencies into the municipal government rather than inside the police force or outside of the government. It should be mentioned, however, that there are also state-level human rights commissions, which, while focused on human rights abuses rather than corruption per se, have greater autonomy from the government and function more like an external accountability mechanism. In theory, location outside the police force should give agencies some autonomy in carrying out their investigations. While there is some variation across the research sites, accountability mechanisms in all four sites have tended to favor investigating individual officers (i.e., rotten apples) rather than systematic factors that encourage misconduct (i.e., the rotten barrel). In addition, all four sites have tended to implore reactive, complaint-based approaches over proactive and preventive measures. This began to change somewhat in 2008 and 2009 with federally promoted reforms centered on confidence control tests, a topic that will be discussed in Chapter 7.

In Mexicali, investigations are done by the statutory auditor, or *sindicatura;* in Tijuana they are performed by an internal affairs unit within the *sindicatura;* in Hermosillo the internal affairs unit is located within the city's comptroller's officer, or *contraloría;* and in Chihuahua they are performed by an office in the secretariat of the city government. At all four sites, the agency is responsible for receiving and investigating citizen complaints against the police or any other public servant. The investigations typically consist of a statement from the complainant, a response from the accused officer, statements from any witnesses, and any investigative activities undertaken within the time and personnel constraints of the agency. If there is sufficient evidence to validate the complaint, a hearing will be held where the charges and evidence will be presented. The officer will have a chance to defend him- or herself with the presence of an attorney, and the agency will make a decision regarding culpability.

In Tijuana and Mexicali, the agency has the power to determine if actions substantiated by the investigation warrant removal from the force. In Chihuahua and Hermosillo, the agency lacks this authority and instead makes recommendations to a commission organized *within* the police department, called the Honor and Justice Commission. It is this commission, presided over by the police chief, which has the final say on culpability and subsequent punishment. There are slight differences in the composition of the Honor and Justice Commission in Chihuahua and Hermosillo. In Chihuahua, the commission is made up of two appointees of the municipal president, the police chief, a city council member, and a member of the governmental public security commission. In Hermosillo, the commission includes the chief of police, a senior officer in the force, a city council member, and a member of the Citizen Public Security Committee.

Despite serious design limitations, these agencies offer some degree of accountability and provide citizens with a place to voice complaints. In Chihuahua, for example, the department received 557 complaints in 2007, which represented six complaints for every ten officers; 55.6 percent of which led to an investigation.[16] It should be mentioned that these numbers are not comparable across cities; a high number of complaints could be the result of a strong outreach campaign to encourage criticism and citizen input, and a low number could be a product of an unpublicized investigative agency. Also the total number of complaints does not distinguish between substantiated and unsubstantiated grievances or between serious and nonserious allegations.

The agencies can point to certain success stories. In Mexicali, investigators at the *sindicatura* used a cell phone video of police beating a detainee to remove officers from the force. The officers had their faces hidden; however, the video allowed investigators to identify a janitor who could be seen on camera witnessing the event. The janitor helped identify the agents and they were found guilty and fired.

While these agencies represent a step toward accountability, they have not been an effective tool in addressing day-to-day corruption or organized crime infiltration—the largest issue undermining the credibility of the police and preventing its professionalization. Day-to-day corruption and bribe taking exists at each of the research sites (although to different degrees), yet because of the reactive, complaint-based process, interview respondents in these agencies report that corruption investigations make up only a small percentage of their work. Officials point out that citizens who participate in corruption are as culpable as the officer and unlikely to file a complaint. As a consequence of design, corruption ends up being a low priority. Proactive investigations are in some cases legally possible, but they appear to be few and far between. Furthermore, none of the agencies had the legal authority to conduct sting operations, use wiretaps, or subpoena witnesses.

In addition, because the agencies focus on rotten apples rather than the rotten barrel, numerous red flags might be repeatedly dismissed despite collective evidence of a very real problem. Baja California's human rights commission reported coming up against this problem in Tijuana. In 2007, they received a number of complaints from detainees contending that the police had planted knives or weapons on them and that they had been falsely charged. From the department's perspective, an individual detainee carrying a weapon obviously has an incentive to lie, claim that the weapon was planted, and try to avoid charges. The cases boiled down to the word of the officer against the word of the detainee. The commission staff, however, wondered how there could be such a jump in complaints without there being some truth to the allegations. While disciplinary action could not be taken against individual officers absent proof of misconduct, efforts could have been made to prevent such actions in the future. The commission had advocated for a police policy forbidding officers from carrying unofficial weapons to be followed by random spot checks of police cruisers; however, the recommendation was ignored.

Most important for the focus of this chapter, in practice oversight agencies do not investigate allegations of ties between the police and organized crime, without a doubt the priority concern for cleaning up the police. Agency officials argue that they are responsible for "administrative faults," and, as involvement in organized crime is a federal criminal offense, it is the providence of the federal attorney general's office. The federal government, for its part, reports that it lacks the manpower, capacity, geographical reach, and local knowledge to be the primary tool to combat local organized crime infiltration. Despite their enormous importance, investigations of police-organized crime collusion have almost completely fallen through the cracks. In other words, the current status quo is not only for municipal police to reject responsibility for assisting in the fight against organized crime but to reject responsibility for addressing organized crime infiltration into their own departments! Local assertions of a lack of jurisdiction are somewhat disingenuous. For example, the Tijuana agency's legal mandate tasks it to investigate and resolve the situation if "a member or element does not comply or violate one of the requisites to remain in the police" (Ayuntamiento de Tijuana 2004). Criminal activities clearly violate these requirements. A more productive and legally viable route, employed by only a few departments in Mexico, is to conduct a parallel investigation.

In addition, all of the agencies suffer from insufficient human resources. Only Monterrey and Guadalajara have developed large oversight agencies, while the other cities have agencies staffed with only a handful of people. Chihuahua, despite all of its advances in other areas, has one of the smallest internal affairs agencies with only five employees, less than one employee for every two hundred officers. Given the perceived pervasiveness of police misconduct, these numbers are insufficient for internal affairs to take on a more proactive and preventive role. In 2009, Tijuana's internal affairs department had only slightly more than one employee for every two hundred officers. Partially as a result of understaffing, several high-profile cases referred to the internal affairs agency failed to result in the dismissal of known corrupt officers from the force. For example, four removal proceedings before the city's statutory auditor failed to remove Luis Hernández Jaime from the force until he was finally arrested by federal officials for the assassination of fellow officers on behalf of García Simentel's group (*Zeta* 2009b).

Labor protections for government employees that are not *de confianza,* or trust employees, are rigid, and police departments must clearly prove that an officer engaged in misconduct. Fired employees are able to appeal their firings before an administrative court, and in several cases the Tijuana police department was required to reinstall fired officers and even pay back wages. Part of the problem is an effective internal affairs agency without sufficient resources and meaningful investigative powers capable of developing cases that can stand up in administrative courts.[17] The other part of the problem is that the bar for firing officers appears to be too high. In response to this problem, the Calderón administration pushed through a constitutional amendment carving out an exception for police firings. Currently, former officers can still win severance packages for unjustified firings; however, departments no longer have to reinstall officers. While the constitutional changes offered a quick fix, the real problem is that internal affairs departments lack the ability to gather evidence that can hold up to legal challenges.

Several interview respondents also contend that oversight agencies lack sufficient autonomy or incentive to bring police misconduct to light. In two of the cities, Hermosillo and Chihuahua, while the investigation occurs outside of the police department, the decision to fire or sanction an officer falls to the department itself, more specifically the Honor and Justice Commission, which is headed by the police chief. Agency personnel in Chihuahua expressed concern that they did not have final say over whether an officer should be removed from the force or sanctioned. In addition, organizing the oversight agency outside of the police force does not guarantee its objectivity. As one journalist in Hermosillo explained, "The thing is that public security, the comptroller, internal affairs, at the end of the day are all part of the municipality. So, if the comptroller and internal affairs were to beat up on public security, they would be beating up on their own municipality—on their own administration. This is why they don't find errors, failures, and problems, because they are the same." Although it is tempting to dismiss such an argument as overstated, it resonates with the findings presented in Chapter 3 that Mexico's municipalities are governed by a strong municipal president without checks and balances. As a result, it is the municipal president rather than the police chief who is at the end of the day responsible for improving public security. A scandal that reflects poorly on the police chief also reflects poorly on the mayor, creating incentives to keep dirty laundry from being aired by either the municipal government or the police department. A similar concern was expressed in Mexicali, where, during the 2007–10 administration, the head of the statutory auditor was a political insider in the PAN party. The agency head's brother was the state Secretary of Public Security, and his other brother was the head of the PAN in Baja California. Such a political appointee, it was argued, could not have the incentive to be too effective in his oversight.

A city council member in Hermosillo alleges a similar problem in that city. Mentioned earlier was the role of a citizen and a city council member on Hermosillo's Honor and Justice Commission. As these two members make up half of the commission, it would seem that they would guarantee a certain degree of objectivity. In addition, under the Gándara Camou administration (2007–09), the city council member sitting on the commission was actually from the opposition party, providing an additional incentive to address police misconduct. He argued, however, that in order to prevent him from obtaining the case file, polemic cases did not make it from the municipal comptroller to the commission. To support his argument, he cited a complaint of sexual harassment made by four female police against a supervisor that was covered in the news but never came before the commission (Contreras 2008). Not wanting to give the political opposition such ammunition, the council member alleged that the case was held up by the administration-controlled comptroller. The council member further argued that while he did have a vote on the commission, he frequently was on the losing end of a 3-to-1 vote, where the senior officer and the representative from the Citizen Public Security Committee (appointed by the mayor) both voted with the director of the police. While it is difficult to evaluate the veracity of these charges, similar expressions of a lack of confidence in the oversight agencies were common among interview respondents both inside and outside of the police.

The inability to address salient corruption concerns suggests the presence of an informal rule tolerant of corruption. As has been illustrated in other arenas, even smart policy design does not ensure effective implementation. In this case, organization outside the force does not ensure autonomy, and incorporation of citizens does not ensure objectivity. There are other examples of such avoidances. Mexicali and Hermosillo require their officers to file annual asset declarations. This could in theory be an important tool to raise red flags if officers are living far beyond their means; however, interview respondents contend that rules are avoided by placing assets in the name of spouses and family members. Absent sufficient manpower to perform audits and verify if asset declarations match living styles, the asset declarations do not have their intended effect.

In Mexicali, police are required by law to report other officers if they are seen engaging in illegal activity such as bribe taking. Failure to do so is, legally speaking, cause for removal from the force, and yet the *sindicatura* reported not receiving a single complaint from officers about corruption. The current system has also failed to instill in superior officers a sense of responsibility for the actions of the men and women under their command. When asked what he was doing to address corruption among his subordinates, a zone commander in Hermosillo replied flatly, "I do not have the legal faculties to investigate corruption. That is the responsibility of the comptroller." In another interview with a shift commander, the officer responded to a question asking if he had ever reported a subordinate for misconduct:

Have you ever reported an officer?
"Yes, if they commit infractions, I'll punish them.
For what types of things?

Things like not reporting pulling over a vehicle, not paying attention, failing to show respect.

What about for bribes?

I've never confronted it . . . The thing with bribes is that there are two participants—the person who gives and the person who receives, but that is the job of the comptroller [to investigate].

The responses (which not only justify bribery) suggest an abrogation of responsibility and at best a misinterpretation of the law. Ensuring the honesty and trustworthiness should *first* be the responsibility of supervising officers and then the responsibility of the investigating agency. In practice, this order of responsibility has been reversed, and, unless the investigating agency can prove misconduct, which it rarely can, these supervisors, operating under informal rules tolerant of corruption, have stated that they not going to address the problem.

This failure further highlights the problem discussed in the previous chapter of not having an effective merit-based promotion procedure to determine rank within the agency. If an inadequate mechanism is in place to ensure that officers of proven probity are the ones being promoted, then the command hierarchy cannot be expected to offer an effective tool against corruption. From this vantage point, it is possible to offer a complete answer to the two realities of Mexican police reform presented in the introduction. Yes, enormous strides have been made in improving selection criteria, education levels, training, equipment, salaries and benefits, and even procedures, but without (1) a merit-based process to ensure an effective command structure, and absent (2) an oversight agency that reduces the incentives for misconduct and raises the probability that misconduct will be identified and punished, the outcome of the equation presented in Figure 4.1 remains collusion or tolerance with organized crime and police misconduct more generally. Add to this equation a failure to protect officers from organized crime reprisals and the outcome is almost overdetermined.

Tijuana's Alternative Approach

Given the failure of past administrations to clean up their departments, an incoming mayor and police chief like Ramos and Leyzaola confront the same institutionalization problem discussed in Chapter 3. In theory, they could invest in creating a robust internal affairs department, but doing so would take time to produce results and be dependent on the following administration. Confronting a security crisis in the short term, and faced with a three year administration, they adopted a different approach. Leyzaola all but ignored the city's internal affairs department and created his own internal vetting unit. As a result of internal departmental efforts, the administration reported in July 2009 that it had purged 430 officers, or almost 18 percent of the force. While impressive, the number is not entirely accurate: a plurality (205) was made up of officers who voluntarily resigned. The administration contended that these officers were involved with organized crime and resigned because they saw the writing on the wall. This is surely the case in some instances; however, other resignations were the product of fear or simply normal attrition. In addition, 105 of the total announced officers were suspended and in the process of removal, but had not actually been removed. Only sixty-four of this total had been formally fired, and twenty of these were not fired by the police force until after they were arrested by federal authorities.[18]

Of greater concern were the methods employed to detect misconduct. Absent a reliable investigations agency, Leyzaola and the military were accused of using torture, forced confessions, and unreliable witnesses to build cases against suspected officers. Twenty-five municipal police officers arrested in early 2008 took their case to Mexico's human rights commissions and the Inter-American Commission for Human Rights, alleging that they were tortured with beatings and electric shocks applied to their genitals and forced to sign statements that they could not read (Díaz 2009; Finnegan 2010). Of another group of sixty-two officers from around the state arrested in July 2009, roughly forty had been released by the courts by early 2011 (Dibble 2011). Torture and extralegal actions only represent the opposite extreme of looking the other way to corruption, the approach employed at the other three research sites. Both abuse and negligence are derived from the absence of institutional mechanisms capable of identifying and investigating officers involved in illicit activities.

It is difficult to evaluate Leyzaola's administration of Tijuana's police force. By the end of his term in 2010, he was viewed as both a hero and a villain (Finnegan 2010; Alvarado 2010). His advocates note that he was one of a handful of municipal police chiefs who had joined the fight against organized crime, and his coordination with the military in particular, but also with state authorities appeared to offer one of the few cases of successful interagency cooperation in all of Mexico. In 2009 and 2010, authorities from all three levels of government effectively dismantled the García Simental organization, arresting him and two principal lieutenants in 2009 and his brother and another remaining lieutenant in 2010. By the end of 2010, authorities led by the military could claim that they had decommissioned 270 tons of marijuana passing through Baja California in that year alone (Ramírez 2010). There is a widespread belief that the security situation improved dramatically despite continued high levels of organized crime-related killings, and Leyzaola won effusive praise from the *Zeta* newspaper, several U.S. officials, and the Tijuana business community.

On the other hand, critics who placed high value on the protection of individual rights and police officers who appear to have been unjustly accused of collusion could only view the improved perception of security as bittersweet. Because of constitutional changes made by the Calderón administration, absolved officers had no way to regain their jobs after having been fired from the force. Others contended that the security improvements were overstated. While organized crime-related killings in the city dropped from a high of 614 in 2008 to 399 to 2009, they rose again to 472 in 2010 (Presidencia 2011). Tijuana was still clearly an important drug trafficking *plaza*, and there was evidence of Sinaloa and La Familia operations in the city. Still others speculated that Leyzaola was not has honest as he appeared, alleging that he had chosen sides in the organized crime conflict and favored the AFO over García Simental. Under pressure from both sides, the incoming administration of Carlos Bustamante Anchondo chose not to rename Leyzaola but nonetheless promoted his deputy Gustavo Huerta Martínez to continue Leyzaola's efforts. Leyzaola himself would briefly serve as head of the state police before being named to lead Ciudad Juárez's police force in 2011.

Regardless of whether one views Leyzaola as a hero or villain, it is clear that institutional means are needed to reliably identify and sanction corrupt officers. Recognizing the problem of organized crime infiltration and the failure of local authorities to clean up their police forces, in 2008 the federal government began to promote a nationwide vetting program referred to as trust control, or *control de confianza*. In order to receive a large federal subsidy, municipalities must send their officers in groups of one hundred to take medical, toxicological, psychological, and lie detector tests and submit asset declarations. The use of the lie detector at the municipal level represented a new step in Mexican policing that was previously utilized by only a very few agencies. These efforts will be reviewed in greater detail in Chapter 7; however, the underlying conclusion is that there is no test that can accurately and reliably distinguish corrupt officers from honest officers. Trust control tests are an important tool, but they can only work effectively if combined with robust internal affairs units that use the tests as part of an "early warning system" that raises red flags for investigation. Absent sincere efforts to develop such investigative capacity, it appears likely that the two realities of Mexican policing will continue well into the foreseeable future.

Conclusion

Recognizing that organized crime represents a fundamental challenge to police professionalization, this chapter explored organized crime–police relations in greater detail and asked why insulating the police from infiltration and developing robust accountability mechanisms has proven to be so difficult. I argue that provided a strong organized crime presence, the degree of organized crime infiltration of the police will depend upon:

- The decision of the mayor and police chief to confront, collude, or tolerate organized crime
- Efforts by the city leadership and the police chief to monitor, create positive incentives, sanction misconduct, and protect officers
- Efforts by the organized crime to bribe, threaten, and monitor police.

While historically most municipal administrations and police chiefs in Tijuana have selected tolerance or collusion strategies, it appears that during the Ramos administration, the police opted for a confrontation strategy. However, the administration had a difficult time protecting officers from organized crime reprisals. As evidenced by the events reported in this chapter, organized crime's willingness to employ violence ruthlessly offered it a powerful trump card capable of overriding efforts at professionalization. Furthermore, the city's internal affairs agency abrogated its responsibility to address organized crime infiltration, and instead of investigating misconduct, the police leadership relied on harsh interrogation techniques and forced confessions.

The importance of accountability mechanisms, or rather the problem of not having such mechanisms, is also highlighted by the Chihuahuan case. Chihuahua's CALEA certification, merit-based promotion, salary increases, investment in equipment, and investment in education and officer training did not protect the agency from organized crime infiltration or allow it to effectively confront criminal groups.

Addressing corruption within the police force is without a doubt the most difficult of the police reforms needed in Mexico. Unfortunately, for every successful example like Hong Kong's ICAC, there are dozens of failed accountability mechanisms (Macaulay 2002; Meagher 2004; PDDH 2007; Arias and Zúñiga 2008). It is far easier to develop training programs and improve selection criteria then to reverse a long history of extortion and bribery. Improving training, salaries, equipment, promotion criteria, operational procedures, selection criteria, etc., while not entirely without opponents, are essentially win-win reforms in that both the police leadership and rank and file benefit. Tackling corruption, however, requires confronting the many officers who use their badge to extort money from citizens and criminals, and the powerful organized crime syndicates that need corrupt officers to operate. As such, reformers face a major dilemma of police reform. Addressing corruption prior to addressing the comparatively easier reforms is perhaps unlikely to succeed in the face of rank-and-file and organized crime opposition.[19] Nonetheless, these easier reforms will be insufficient to achieve an honest, professional force capable of confronting organized crime.

5 Citizens and Their Police: Vicious Cycles

Citizens: Part of the Problem and Part of the Solution

This chapter considers the role of citizens in perpetuating the problems of corruption and ineffectiveness in the police. This is a somewhat controversial hypothesis to consider, as citizens are often victims of police corruption and ineffectiveness rather than perpetuators and enablers of these problems. In many cases, citizens are, in fact, clearly extorted by police, and there is a real danger of "blaming the victim." Nonetheless, this chapter provides evidence that police and the citizens they serve are locked in a vicious cycle fueled by day-to-day bribery and corruption. At the end of the day, a focus on citizens' role in perpetuating corruption and ineffectiveness is not entirely negative, as it suggests that there is also a positive role that citizens can play in institutional change.

Citizens are potentially able to impact the effectiveness of the police and police reform efforts through four categories of action or inaction: (1) compliance with the law, (2) coproduction of public security, (3) support for the police politically and financially, and (4) oversight of the police to ensure its accountability. Through these actions, citizens can help build a better police force. By contrast, it is difficult to imagine an effective, professional police force emerging in a society where compliance is low, where citizens do not report crimes or provide the police with information, where there is resistance to paying taxes and ensuring the police have sufficient resources, and where there is inadequate citizen oversight or the opportunity for oversight.

This chapter first establishes the importance of these categories of citizen action and documents major deficiencies in each area. Recognition that citizens are part of the problem suggests the presence of several vicious cycles reinforcing a status quo of police ineffectiveness, abuse, and corruption, on the one hand, and citizen noncompliance, failure of coproduction, and low support on the other. I argue here that this vicious cycle is primarily perpetuated by day-to-day corruption and bribery for citizens to avoid traffic tickets and other legal violations. This is supported by evidence that experiences with bribery impact attitudes of corruption tolerance, which fuels further corruption, and additional evidence that experiences with bribery lower citizens' evaluations of the police, which reduces the probability that citizens will cooperate with and support the police.

The research benefits from qualitative evidence collected by the author at the four research sites, but it also takes advantage of public opinion polling conducted by the Latin American Public Opinion Project's (LAPOP) AmericasBarometer and by the Instituto Ciudadano de Estudios sobre la Inseguridad (ICESI). The LAPOP study is a national sample that allows for comparisons with similar surveys in the rest of the Americas and includes some attitudinal measures that are not part of the ICESI survey. The ICESI study is a victimization survey conducted nationwide with representative samples for fourteen cities throughout Mexico, including three of the research sites: Tijuana, Mexicali, and Chihuahua.

Compliance, Coproduction, and Support

Ordinary citizens impact policing and public security first and foremost through legal compliance. Obviously criminals have little interest in following the law; however, compliance is also a concern among those citizens who generally consider themselves to be law-abiding. These individuals may wish to avoid or evade a wide array of laws, ordinances, and regulations requiring registering vehicles, complying with traffic laws, paying taxes, obtaining proper licenses, complying with alcohol sales legislation, properly disposing of waste, and refraining from buying stolen and pirated goods, to name a few. The more law-abiding society is, the more the police can focus their attention on serious crime. Furthermore, while isolated violations of a given law might have little public impact, widespread violations combine to create severe public security concerns, and they might even produce an environment that fosters more serious crime. Most important for the topic of police reform, a highly compliant society will be less tolerant of police corruption and ineffectiveness, whereas a less-compliant society can be expected to exploit the lack of police professionalism to allow citizens to avoid law enforcement and bribe police officers when necessary.

Second, numerous public goods cannot be purely "produced" by a public agency and "consumed" by clients; rather, it is desirable, and at times necessary, for citizens to play a role in the production process, or for the good to be "co-produced" (Davis and Ostrom 1991). There are several ways in which citizens can contribute to the public good of security, including reporting crime, providing information to the police, serving as witnesses, and taking preventive measures. Despite the common perception that most crimes are solved by CSI-style sleuthing television detectives, in fact, research clearly shows that the vast majority of cases are resolved because the victim, witnesses, or accomplices come forward with information (Chaiken, Greenwood, and Petersilia 1977; Cosgrove and Wycoff 1997, Bieck and Oettmeier 1998). In other words, the police cannot be effective without the actions of citizens.

Third, citizens can provide the police with needed political and economic capital by supporting tax increases and/or directing more resources toward the police department. Virtually all the aspects of reform discussed in this book, including improving selection criteria and cadet training; taking officers off the street for in-service training; improving equipment, salaries, and benefits; developing robust accountability mechanisms; and even creating merit-based promotion procedures require political capital and economic resources. As discussed in Chapter 3, municipalities rely on the federal government for the majority of their revenues despite their legal faculties to raise a greater percentage of their income from property taxes, fines, and fees.

Fourth, citizens also have an important role to play in overseeing the police. Numerous authors have found that citizen oversight and participation is essential for efforts to combat corruption (Carothers 1999; Johnston 2005; Peruzzotti and Smulovitz 2006). Citizens can use both elections and more direct means to create incentives for professional policing. These include submitting complaints to oversight agencies, contacting representatives, attending public meetings, reducing information asymmetries through watchdog activities, and participating in formal oversight mechanisms. These four groupings of actions by citizens are summed up in Table 5.1.

TABLE 5.1. Citizens' actions to promote police effectiveness and facilitate reform

	Citizens' actions
Compliance	• Respect the law regardless of enforcement and encourage others to do the same
Co-production	• Report crime, provide information, serve as witnesses, take preventive measures
Support	• Support tax increases for the police
Oversight	• Vote, file complaints regarding corruption and abuse, participate in public meetings, contact representatives.

Deficiencies

Unfortunately, there are clear deficiencies in all four of these areas. While citizens' behavior is perhaps rational given the incentives they face, the evidence here suggests that the actions and inactions of ordinary citizens have inadvertently helped fuel Mexico's current insecurity and contributed to the lack of police professionalization. To begin, compliance with a wide variety of laws appears to be relatively low. Proper registration of vehicles is an interesting case in point particularly affecting the four research sites. The North American Free Trade Agreement (NAFTA) allowed for continued protection of Mexico's auto industry through quotas and tariffs on used car imports until 2025. In recent years, Mexico has experimented with allowing older cars into the country and reducing import tariffs; however, it remains difficult to legally import used vehicles (Chu and Delgado 2009). Although the restrictions are good for Mexico's domestic auto industry (an important part of the Mexican economy), they are bad for Mexican consumers, many of whom would prefer to purchase cheaper used vehicles from their northern neighbor. This has created a large black market for used cars that are not properly imported or registered in Mexico (Chu and Delgado).[1] In an additional twist, politically protected consumer groups have formed throughout Northern Mexico and created their own parallel licensing systems. Political authorities have been ambivalent about enforcing a law that hurts organized constituents' pocketbooks, and even when they do, corrupt officers are happy to take bribes to look the other way. Despite the seemingly innocuous nature of the violation, noncompliance actually produces a major security challenge as it also facilitates the sale of stolen cars and makes it harder to track vehicles, including those driven by members of organized criminal groups. Furthermore, the practice presents a security risk to officers as it deprives the police of reliable information during traffic stops.

Another illustrative example can be found in the informal economy. Rather than buy a variety of goods ranging from used car parts to electronics in the formal economy, many citizens prefer to buy these parts in informal markets for considerably less. Because the establishments are not under regulation, the origin of their goods cannot always be determined, and extremely low prices are at times indicative of stolen merchandise. In this case, the lack of compliance creates a large market for stolen goods, incentives for theft, and even a means for organized crime to launder money (Naylor 2004). Pirated goods produce similar challenges. A study of 933 survey respondents in four urban areas in Mexico (Mexico City, Monterrey, Guadalajara, and Tijuana) found that 76 percent of respondents had bought pirated goods (25 percent of whom did so always or almost always) even though 82 percent recognized that buying pirated goods "fosters criminality" (ACCM 2009). In fact, Gómez (2009) profiles the predominant role of the organized crime group La Familia in the state of Michoacan's pirated goods business.

Coproduction also appears to be deficient. Through its victimization survey of over forty-five thousand individuals, ICESI (2010) estimates that only 22 percent of crimes in 2008 were reported to authorities, and they find similar percentages for 2004 and 2007, 23 percent and 21 percent respectively.[2] By contrast, similar surveys in Chile find that 42 percent of crimes are reported (Dammert 2005). This is not to say that the police are not receiving calls for services; on the contrary, police press releases regularly complain that residents abuse and improperly use emergency call numbers (equivalent to 911 in the United States). For example, Chihuahua reported that in 2009, 60 percent of calls to its call center were not police emergencies (Ayuntamiento de Chihuahua 2010). A study from February 2010 found that of 55,873 calls in that month, 31,803 (or 56 percent) were "false," including 6,390 calls attributed to kids making a practical joke; in 7,232 cases police responded but were unable to find a problem at the reported location; and 12,325 calls were made by people seeking general information (Ayuntamiento de Chihuahua). As such, surveys of police also reveal a recognized need for greater citizen participation to effectively combat insecurity (Nájera Ruíz 2006; Moloeznik, Shirk, and Suárez de Garay 2009; Moloeznik, Shirk, and Suárez de Garay 2011).

As discussed in Chapter 3, there is also a lack of local financial support for the police, and the majority of municipal resources come from federal transfers. Prior to the federal public security subsidy for Mexico's municipalities, known as SUBSEMUN, police departments lacked resources to purchase basic equipment. As one member of civil society complained, "People pay thousands of dollars of property taxes in the U.S., but in Mexico the rates are very low and many people don't pay. It's a problem of co-responsibility. Those that complain about the property taxes are the ones that are targets of kidnapping and are demanding that the government solve the problem."

Finally, as evidenced by the corruption, abuse, and ineffectiveness of the police, citizens have clearly been unable to effectively hold the police accountable. Citizens are not attending public meetings in large numbers, they submit relatively few complaints of corruption to internal affairs agencies (despite large numbers of complaints of abuse), there is a dearth of citizen watchdog efforts, and transparency laws have not been fully taken advantage of. Of course, as will be discussed in the following chapter, the ability for citizens to hold the police accountable is largely determined by the political opportunities available to them; nonetheless, it appears likely that citizens have undervalued their potential role in overseeing the police more directly.

Vicious Cycles

Recognition that citizens are often times not compliant with the law, not co-producing public security, not supporting the police, and not holding the police accountable begs the question: why? Answering this question is essential to understand how citizens and reformers can alter the status quo. I argue here that the primary determinant of these shortcomings is day-to-day corruption and bribe payment. In light of Mexico's security crisis, the attention of most scholars and policy makers has understandably focused on organized crime–police collusion. While the deleterious effects of organized crime discussed in the previous chapter are considerable, day-to-day corruption and bribery might pose an even greater challenge to institutional change. I argue here that citizens who experience corruption firsthand are more likely to think that corruption is inevitable, thus undermining norms of compliance. Moreover, they are less likely to trust the police, reducing coproduction and support for the police. In other words, day-to-day corruption perpetuates the vicious cycle governing the relationship between citizens and their police.

Evidence of Corruption

There is plenty of evidence of day-to-day bribe solicitation and payment in Mexico. First, Transparencia Mexicana (TM 2011) has conducted a series of studies documenting the quantity and amount of bribe payments in Mexico. According to their 2010 report, surveyed individuals who tried to avoid a traffic ticket (of a total sample of 15,326 households) reported paying a bribe 68.0% of the time, an increase over four previous iterations of the study dating back to 2001. Second, in a comparative study, the LAPOP AmericasBarometer asks respondents throughout Latin America if they have had a bribe solicited by a police officer in the last year. The survey asks about bribe solicitation rather than bribe payment as a means to avoid response bias from study participants who might be hesitant to admit to paying or offering a bribe. Of the data presented in Figure 5.1 for fourteen major Latin American nations, solicitation is highest in Mexico, where 18.5 percent of respondents reported a bribe solicitation in the last year. The average across the fourteen countries was 8.8 percent, and Chile saw the lowest rate of bribe solicitation at only 1.7 percent.

Data from ICESI offers a view of corruption that distinguishes among police departments and among major metropolitan areas. The survey asks

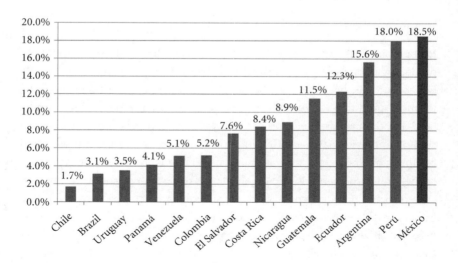

FIGURE 5.1. Mexican bribe solicitation in comparative perspective

NOTE: There is some concern with the data from Peru, which has a high percentage of missing values. The population of respondents who have had a bribe solicited might be higher in Peru. Sample sizes are typically around 1,500 respondents per country.

SOURCE: AmericasBarometer 2008; Latin American Public Opinion Project.

respondents in fourteen municipalities if they are aware of a given police force. If they respond yes, they are asked a short battery of questions about the agency, including if someone from that department has solicited a bribe from them. Methodologically this is a correct approach, as respondents cannot opine about a department that they do not know of; however, it does limit comparability as some cities (e.g., Mexico DF) have considerable missing data, while other cities have very little (e.g., Tijuana). The question also does not specify when the solicitation would have occurred, which likely introduces some error.

Although data is not available for Hermosillo, ICESI's survey reveals that 21.5 percent of respondents in Tijuana (25.2 percent excluding respondents unfamiliar with the police) report having paid a bribe to the preventive police, 14.5 percent (23.5 percent) in Mexicali, and 2.8 percent (4.2 percent) in Chihuahua (See Table 5.2). The lower percentage of bribes in Chihuahua is, on the one hand, consistent with a more professional police force, but, on the other hand, the dramatic difference is likely driven principally by the division of labor between preventive and transit policing in Chihuahua and Baja California. In Chihuahua, the municipal preventive police are not legally empowered to enforce traffic violations, a responsibility reserved for the state traffic police. And, in fact, 25 percent of Chihuahuan respondents reported having had a bribe solicited from the state traffic police. In fact, across the cities, respondents were far more likely to have had a bribe solicited from transit police, with percentages ranging between 18 percent and 33 percent, or between 24.7 percent and 41.2 percent excluding respondents unfamiliar with the transit police. In contrast to Chihuahua, traffic violations are a responsibility of Baja California's municipal police. In both Tijuana and Mexicali, there are units within the local police specifically responsible for traffic violations; however, the rest of the force is also permitted to enforce traffic violations. As a result, municipal police in Mexicali and Tijuana have more opportunities for corruption than those of Chihuahua. Regardless of opportunity, the high levels of reported solicitations are cause for concern.

Why Are There Such High Levels of Bribe Solicitation?

Conventional wisdom places the blame for police corruption squarely on the shoulders of the police. There are of course many cases where citizens are the *victim* of corruption (Anteo 2007). They might, for example, be extorted by the police despite having violated no law. Alternatively, police might inflate the consequences of a small violation to pressure citizens into paying a bribe. However, there are also many cases where citizens who have in fact violated

TABLE 5.2. Bribe solicitations

	Bribe solicitations from preventive police			
	Bribe solicited	No bribe solicited	Do not know of or missing	Total
México D.F.	8.6%	51.9%	39.5%	100.0%
	169	1020	776	1965
Urban Mexico State	7.9%	44.2%	47.9%	100.0%
	148	828	896	1872
Guadalajara	7.2%	63.0%	29.8%	100.0%
	131	1140	538	1809
Monterrey	6.0%	54.0%	40.0%	100.0%
	108	972	721	1801
Chihuahua	2.8%	64.9%	32.3%	100.0%
	48	1101	548	1697
Acapulco	14.6%	58.2%	27.2%	100.0%
	238	950	444	1632
Toluca	10.3%	54.6%	35.1%	100.0%
	166	881	566	1613
Cd. Juárez	11.9%	62.1%	26.0%	100.0%
	187	977	408	1572
Tijuana	21.5%	63.7%	14.8%	100.0%
	369	1093	254	1716
Culiacán	6.5%	67.0%	26.5%	100.0%
	111	1153	456	1720
Cuernavaca	7.7%	52.9%	39.4%	100.0%
	134	916	681	1731
Oaxaca	5.1%	56.6%	38.3%	100.0%
	96	1076	728	1900
Cancún	9.8%	51.4%	38.8%	100.0%
	149	782	589	1520
Mexicali	14.5%	47.2%	38.3%	100.0%
	256	832	675	1763

NOTE: The survey first asks respondents if they are aware of the "local preventive police" and then if they have had a bribe solicited from them. If individuals unaware of a specific police department are excluded, the valid percentages of those having paid a bribe increase.

SOURCE: Data from ICESI-ENSI6 Urbana

the law unilaterally *offer* bribes to the police to avoid sanctions. Police interviewed, government officials, and members of civil society all agreed that because bribe payments are so common, it is usually not necessary for police to actually solicit a bribe. Instead, they typically wait for citizens to offer. As the following quotes from a diverse set of actors suggests, citizens are victims, but they are often also willing participants in corruption:

- There is one that receives but there is also one that gives. There are five million government officials in this country and one hundred million outside of the government. Did such a small percentage really corrupt the whole country? To dance the tango you need two; for corruption you need two. (Police administrator)
- Nobody has asked me for a bribe. Perhaps they want to, but they wait for you to offer. So who is to blame? Society is losing its values. The narcos are not here by coincidence, they were allowed in. (Newspaper editor)
- We say that a society has the crime that it deserves, well it also has the police that it deserves. (University professor)
- The society needs it [bribery]. We need it. You are never going to change things training the police because it's a social problem . . . . The law moves with money. This is how we are. (Journalist)
- We can't get rid of it. The citizen is not afraid [to offer a bribe]. It is he that offers the bribe first. (Police officer)
- Citizens are involved in the corruption but nobody says that society is failing like they say that the police is failing. (Police administrator)

In surveys, the police place far greater blame on citizens for widespread corruption when responding to the question, "Who do you think fosters corruption more, citizens or the police?" While a plurality (49 percent) of Ciudad Juárez's police said both, 42 percent placed the blame on citizens compared with only 6 percent who blamed the police (Moloeznik, Shirk, and Suárez de Garay 2011). Metropolitan Guadalajara's police responded similarly: 44.3 percent said both, 50.7 percent blamed the citizens, and only 5.0 percent blamed the police (Moloeznik, Shirk, and Suárez de Garay 2009). This alternative perspective is perhaps surprising in the face of conventional wisdom of police culpability.

The blame game is not terribly productive, however, as it obscures the self-perpetuating cycle of corruption. In theory, officers and citizens who engage in corruption should face consequences. There is, perhaps not surprisingly, considerable evidence to support the importance of enforcement. Research in "deterrence" has found that variation in the likelihood and cost of punishment impacts both crime (Becker 1968) and corruption (Olken 2005). In a status quo where the probability that police or citizens will be punished for corruption is extremely low, corruption is a rational strategy: police augment their income and citizens avoid higher penalties and save time.

Nonetheless, a purely enforcement-based explanation to legal compliance is unsatisfactory, as it leaves much of the variance in lawful and unlawful action unexplained. As Tyler (1990) writes, "Citizens have been found to obey the law when the probability of punishment for noncompliance is almost nil and to break laws in cases involving substantial risks" (22). In surveys, Mexican survey respondents often blame the culture for the high levels of corruption (Bailey and Paras 2006). In fact, some evidence points to the importance of cultural acceptance of illegal behavior in a poor enforcement environment. In an innovative natural experiment in a nonenforcement environment—diplomatic immunity for parking tickets in New York City—Fisman and Miguel (2007) find that there is enormous cultural variation in legal compliance. Germany, for example, had one legal violation per diplomat per year while Kuwait had 249.4. Although the authors find that culture matters far less once an enforcement regime was enacted in New York City, in the specific case of bribery, "enforcement" is particularly challenging as it requires a mechanism to police both citizens and the law enforcement officials themselves.

Given the limitations of both a purely enforcement or purely cultural approach to compliance, some scholars have looked to more nuanced models that embrace the vicious cycle that appears to exist between poor enforcement and cultural attitudes. Tom Tyler (1990) argues that norms of legal compliance depend on the legitimacy of the police and the law. He writes, "In each case citizens who accept the legitimacy of the legal system and its officials are expected to comply with their dictates even when the dictates conflict with their self-interest" (26). A series of interesting studies in the United States has provided evidence for the link between legitimacy and legal compliance. In his 1990 study in Chicago, Tyler finds a statistically significant relationship between a battery of questions measuring legitimacy and an additional battery measuring obligation to follow the law. Sunshine and Tyler (2003) replicated the study in New York and found similar results. Other studies have identified an empirical link between respectful treatment by police officers and compliance with the law (Mastrokski, Snipes, and Supina 1996). McCluskey

(2003) finds that controlling for other factors, citizens who receive respectful treatment from authorities are more than twice as likely to comply with police commands. As such, a distrusted and illegitimate police force (in addition to being ineffective in its own right) might prevent the internalization of norms of compliance in the broader citizenry. Given these findings, one could only imagine the impact police accepting bribes would have on norms of compliance generally and attitudes toward corruption specifically.

A collective-action approach also helps elucidate the mutually reinforcing relationship between culture and enforcement. Citizens who refuse to pay bribes must suffer the costs of not paying a bribe (e.g., higher fine, time lost) but they will not gain the benefits of a more professional police force if everyone else still plays by the old rules of the game. The same logic applies for police officers.

This link between cultural attitudes and enforcement is visible through an analysis of the AmericasBarometer survey data, which ask respondents if they agree with the statement, "As things are right now, it is sometimes justifiable to pay a bribe." A sizable minority of Mexican survey respondents, 27.2 percent agreed with the statement, demonstrating a degree of tolerance toward bribery or at least its inevitability. In comparative perspective, Mexican respondents are on par with their peers in Argentina (28.6 percent) and Nicaragua (28.2 percent), and above the fourteen country Latin American average of 17.7 percent. Interestingly, those who reported that they have had a bribe solicited from them in the last year were more likely to express tolerance or acceptance of corruption. Of those who had a bribe solicited from them, 43.1 percent reported that they felt paying a bribe was justifiable, compared with only 23.7 percent of people who have *not* had a bribe solicited from them. This suggests that corruption prevalence might foster corruption tolerance, which makes future corruption more likely.

This relationship holds up in a logit regression controlling for several additional factors, including a number of demographic factors such as education, income, sex, age, gender, region of the country, and size of locality. In addition, I control for tolerance of patronage and support for violating the law to improve security, as tolerance of corruption is also expected to correlate with other attitudes prioritizing outcomes over the rules. Sampson and Bartusch (1998) argue that residents living in areas of "concentrated disadvantage" or high crime/low income/low opportunity areas exhibit "legal cynicism," or a lack of faith in the law. As a proxy for "concentrated disadvantage," the regression controls for respondents who report that drugs are sold in their neighborhood.

Given that drug dealing is perceived to occur with the knowledge and complicity of the police, residents of such neighborhoods are presented with further evidence of the pervasiveness of corruption. Those with a stronger moral compass are expected to reject corruption, and consequently, as a very imperfect proxy, religiosity is included in the analysis. A breakdown of all the variables is provided in Appendix B.

Bribe solicitation is one of the few variables that consistently has a statistically significant relationship with corruption tolerance, regardless of how the model is specified. The model presented in Table 5.3 predicts that if other factors are held at their means, those who have not had a bribe solicited from them have only a 24.35 percent chance of agreeing that bribes are sometimes justifiable, whereas those who have had a bribe solicited have a 40.67 percent chance of agreeing, a difference of 16.32 percent.[3]

TABLE 5.3. Logit regression on corruption tolerance

	Coefficient	Std. Error	Odds ratio	Estimated probability change
Bribe solicited (0,1)	.756***	.166	2.130	**.1632**
Confidence in justice system (cont)	−.050	.045	.992	−.0175
Break law for security (0,1)	.074	.147	1.077	.0147
Tolerance of patronage (0,1)	.434***	.113	1.544	.1911
Drugs in the neighborhood (0,1)	−.419**	.173	.658	−.0874
Education (1–5)	−.032	.067	.968	−.0128
Gender (0,1)	−.045	.140	.956	−.0092
Income (1–11)	−.020	.034	.980	−.0159
Religious (1–5)	.115*	.054	1.122	−.0021
Age (1–5)	−.127**	.060	.881	−.0765
Size of community (1–5)	.019	.053	1.019	.0112
Northern states (0,1)	.434*	.210	1.544	.0895
Southern states (0,1)	.261	.220	1.298	.0530
Central states (0,1)	.419**	.206	1.521	.0796
Constant	−.915	.662	.400	
n	1,190			
Nagerkerke R^2	.086			

NOTE: See Appendix B for an explanation of variable *operationalization*. The odds ratio can be interpreted as a respondent who has had a bribe solicited has 2.130 greater odds of feeling corruption is justifiable than someone who has not had a bribe solicited. Probability changes are based on differences in the probability of tolerance between those who have had a bribe solicited and those who have not. Predicted probabilities are based on a one standard deviation difference from the mean for those variables that have more than two values. * p<.05; ** p<.01; ***p<.001

SOURCE: Data from the AmericasBarometer by the Latin American Public Opinion Project (LAPOP), www.LapopSurveys.org.

Income, education level, gender, confidence in institutions, size of the city, and willingness to bend the law to improve security are not found to have an independent relationship with bribery tolerance. In many ways the null findings for income and education are very encouraging, as they suggest that corruption is not more accepted among low income or low education segments of the population. There is evidence, however, that living in a community with drug dealing increases tolerance of corruption. Younger respondents are also more likely to feel that bribery is justifiable, which presents a concern for long-term attitudinal change. There is a 7.65 percent probability difference in agreement between those in the 45–65 age range and those in the 18–24 category. Respondents in central western states offer the lowest level of acceptance, and northern and central (e.g., Mexico City) residents are significantly more likely to tolerate bribe payments.

While there is a tendency for citizens to blame the police for corruption and for the police to blame citizens, this analysis suggests that many citizens are in fact tolerant of corruption and that experiences with corruption helps foster this attitude: bribery leads to tolerance, and tolerance leads to more bribery. In other words, bribery is best viewed as a self-perpetuating cycle.

Corruption's Additional Impact

In addition to affecting corruption tolerance, experiences with corruption also have a dramatic impact on confidence in and satisfaction with the police, perpetuating a second vicious cycle. Police need citizens to be effective; however, citizens are unlikely to report crime, come forward with information, or serve as witnesses if they distrust the police or view them as incapable (del Valle Martínez 2004). When the above-cited ICESI victimization survey asked why crimes were not reported, 39 percent of respondents felt that it would be a waste of time, 16 percent did not trust the authorities, and 10 percent saw the process as too bureaucratic (ICESI 2010). As one interviewee from civil society stated, "We don't report crime, because we do not trust the authorities. The Mexican people have become a distrusting people . . . As a result, we turn lax, and become complicit." The consequence is noted by Ruíz Harrell (2007), who writes "without the trust of the population whom they are told to serve, police and public ministers are condemned to ineffectiveness" (143).

Recognizing a degree of attitudinal acceptance of corruption, interviewed officials and even many members of civil society felt that citizens were willing to tolerate a degree of corruption if it meant that their cities would be safer. Some commentators have even gone so far as to suggest that the Mexico should return to "pacting" with organized crime, or grant impunity in exchange for assurances of peace. A preference for results over process is encapsulated in the infamous Brazilian expression "rouba mas faz," commonly translated as "he steals but he gets things done." Manzetti and Wilson, for example, ask why many citizens in Latin American countries continue to support corrupt governments. They contend that when there is a historical legacy of clientelism, citizens will tolerate corruption in exchange for tangible benefits (Manzetti and Wilson 2009). In fact, an older academic literature, sometimes referred to as *functionalist,* viewed corruption as a necessary evil for successful governance and economic development (Huntington 1968; Leff 1964).

While there is evidence that policing outcomes do in fact impact citizens' satisfaction with their police (Reisig and Parks 2002), a large literature in U.S. policing studies has found that citizens also tend to evaluate the police based on "procedural justice" (Tyler 1990). In other words, citizens are as concerned with the fairness of the justice system as with outcomes. For example, research in the United States has found that citizens evaluate officers who wrote them a speeding ticket well if they were treated with dignity and respect (Correia, Reisig, and Lovrich 1996). And, of course, the biggest obstacle to procedural justice in Mexico is corruption. Silva Forné's (2009) research illustrates how bribe solicitation negatively affected respondents' satisfaction with the local police in the city of Nezahualcoyotl, State of Mexico. These findings apply to government legitimacy more generally. Morris (1991) finds a relationship between perception of corruption and low trust in government, and Seligson's (2002) research uncovers a similar relationship in other Latin American countries.

Using the ICESI survey results, it is possible to measure the impact of corruption experiences on satisfaction toward the police. Figure 5.2 presents the bivariate relationship between having a bribe solicited and dissatisfaction with the police across the fourteen surveyed cities. As can be seen in the figure, there is a substantial difference in the evaluation of the police between those who have been a victim of corruption and those who have not. Across the research sites, 69.1 percent of those who have not had a bribe solicited from them are unsatisfied with the police compared with 90.8 percent of those who have had a bribe solicited, a difference of 21.7 percent. This gap varies from a low of 11.5 percent in Chihuahua (where there are fewer reported incidences of bribery) to a high of 33 percent in Mexicali.

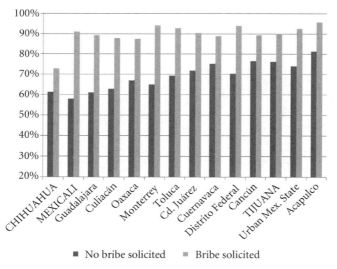

FIGURE 5.2. Percent dissatisfied with the local police
SOURCE: ICESI-ENSI6 Urbana

Of course, these observed differences do not take into account other factors, including evaluations related to policing outcomes. I include four measures of insecurity in the analysis. It seems logical that victims of crime might not evaluate the police well (Dean 1980); but a non-victim might have little confidence in the police merely because of a *perception* of insecurity. It is also common to distinguish between egocentric evaluations, based on one's perception of how one is personally affected by violence, and sociotropic evaluations, based on one's perception of how the community as a whole is affected by violence.[4] Finally, there is a temporal dimension to evaluating the police. Respondents might evaluate the police well despite insecurity if they perceive things to be improving. As a result, this analysis distinguishes among four aspects of insecurity: was the respondent a victim of crime (objective – egocentric)? Was his/her life affected by crime in the last year (perceptive – egocentric)? Does he or she regard the city as safe or as insecure (perceptive – sociotropic)? And is crime worsening or improving (perceptive – temporal)?

Table 5.4 presents the results from the pooled logistic regression analysis of data from all fourteen cities, controlling for the four insecurity measures, confidence in institutions, support for federal anti-crime strategy as a proxy for public security ideology, media consumption, education, income, gender, and age.[5] The

TABLE 5.4. Pooled model of respondents' satisfaction with the police using logistic regression

	Estimate	Std. Error	Odds ratio	Estimated probability change
Bribe solicited (0,1)	1.306***	0.084	3.693	0.179
Sociotropic perception (0,1)	0.472***	0.05	1.603	0.09
Egocentric perception (0,1,2)	0.271***	0.031	1.312	0.095
Victim (0,1)	0.085	0.047	1.089	0.015
Crime worsening (0,1,2)	0.157***	0.037	1.17	0.06
Media consumer (0,1,2)	0.097*	0.047	1.102	0.033
Support policy (0,1)	−0.476***	0.079	0.621	0.077
Confidence in institutions (cont)	−0.908***	0.033	0.403	0.36
Education (1,2,3)	0.112***	0.032	1.119	0.041
Income (1–5)	0.037	0.028	1.038	0.026
Female (0,1)	−0.088*	0.043	0.915	0.016
Age (1–5)	−0.063***	0.018	0.939	0.045
Constant	1.339***	0.202		
	0.203			
Nagerkerke R^2n	13,422			

NOTE: See Appendix C for an explanation of the variable *operationalization*. The odds ratio can be interpreted as a respondent who has had a bribe solicited has 3.693 greater odds of being unsatisfied with the police than someone who has not had a bribe solicited. Probability changes are based on differences in the probability of dissatisfaction between those who have had a bribe solicited and those who have not. Only confidence in institutions is an interval level variable, and, in this case, change is the difference between probabilities at approximately one standard deviation on either side of the mean. * $p < .05$; ** $p < .01$; ***$p < .001$
SOURCE: Data from ICESI-ENSI6 Urbana.

results suggest that bribe solicitation is the second-most-important individual factor affecting respondents' evaluation of the police (after confidence in other institutions of government). Holding all other variables at their mean, a respondent who has had a bribe solicited from him or her is estimated to have a 90.9 percent chance of being unsatisfied with the police versus a 73 percent chance for someone who has not had a bribe solicited, a difference of 17.9 percent. Sociotropic and egocentric perceptions of crime do have an estimated impact on satisfaction with the police; however, this is far less so than experiences with corruption. Temporal evaluations have a slight estimated impact, and, perhaps surprisingly, actual crime victimization has no estimated independent impact.[6]

While not the focus of this chapter, the other variables also produce interesting findings (and non-findings). As expected, those with greater confidence in other institutions of government and the criminal justice system are consistently more likely to evaluate the police positively. Those supportive of the federal government's campaign against organized crime were also more likely to evaluate the police well. While the variable testing media exposure does not distinguish among the types of news sources, I find that the variable has no relationship with police satisfaction. Although certainly not definitive, this finding is inconsistent with the common perception in police departments that the media is to blame for the police's poor image. Those with more education are slightly more likely to be dissatisfied with the police, as are younger respondents.[7]

The findings here run contrary to conventional wisdom positing that citizens will tolerate corruption if it produces results, and suggests that experiences with bribery have a detrimental and substantial impact on citizens' views of the police. The finding has important policy implications. As discussed above, the police cannot be effective without citizen compliance, co-production, and support. If the police are distrusted and viewed poorly, then citizens will be less likely to report crimes, come forward with information, and support the police politically and financially. Building trust, however, has proven to be difficult for political and police leaders. Many have sought to do so by increasing police presence and taking a tough approach to crime, in other words by focusing on the outcomes of policing. However, many citizens might realize that such measures will not be effective if the police force is corrupt. Day-to-day bribe solicitations and payments, while perhaps less harmful than collusion with organized crime in the short term, offer citizens direct evidence that the police are willing to place money over the law, and it is only a short logical leap to conclude that money can also ensure impunity for criminals.

Conclusion

Discussions of improving law enforcement and professionalizing the police too often occur in a vacuum isolated from the citizenry; however, this analysis has shown that citizens are part of the current problem and will have to be part of the future solution. Police leaders will have a hard time tackling corruption if they do not recognize that citizens—including high-powered economic and political elites—are accustomed to bribing their way out of legal compliance. Police leaders will also find it difficult to improve police effectiveness without a citizenry that works with the police and provides it with the information and resources necessary to prevent and solve crimes.

Recognition that many citizens are not complying with the law and not working with and supporting the police creates a serious dilemma for advancing police professionalization. Much of this study, the literature, and popular perception have placed the blame for this problem on the police. However, how can the police be expected do their job if even those citizens who consider themselves to be law-abiding are regularly violating the law, if ordinary citizens are the very ones offering bribes, if information is not forthcoming, and if resources are scarce? One could oscillate back and forth between these two points of blame without recognizing that there is clearly a vicious cycle complicated by a collective-action problem at work. Corruption and ineffectiveness drive distrust, which inhibits citizens from coming forward with information about criminal activities, and encourages citizens to offer bribes when they themselves are caught violating the law. The consequence is continued ineffectiveness and greater corruption—reinitiating the cycle. The question should, therefore, not be one of where to place the blame, but rather how to stop these vicious cycles and even reverse them. This analysis finds that addressing day-to-day corruption is the best place to start.

Tackling day-to-day corruption is no easy task given that citizens are accustomed to paying bribes and police are accustomed to the supplemental income. While police reform advances have been made in selection criteria, cadet and in-service training, and police equipment, the preceding chapters have clearly shown that both the promotional process and police oversight have been the two neglected areas of meaningful reform. Not coincidentally, these are the two areas that need to be strengthened to address day-to-day bribe payment. How can this status quo be altered? One potential approach is through the fourth arena of public participation: direct accountability to citizens.

6 Civil Society and the Police: Stopping the Vicious Cycle

The Potential of Civil Society

The previous chapter identified a vicious cycle whereby police corruption and (to a lesser extent) ineffectiveness fuel citizen dissatisfaction, which drives noncompliance, lack of coproduction, and insufficient support for the police. Ironically these shortcomings further incentivize corruption and ineffectiveness. The presence of a vicious cycle means that change has to come from both citizens and the police. In the search for ways to turn back the cycle and even convert it into a virtuous one, this chapter asks if organized civil society can encourage compliance, coproduction, and support. There is no agreement on a definition of the term *civil society*;[1] however, I use the term here to distinguish organized, citizen-led efforts to impact public security from the day-to-day behavior of ordinary citizens discussed in the previous chapter.

I also explore in this chapter the fourth potential role of civil society: holding the police and city and police leaders accountable. Over two decades of democratic local elections suggest that the vote by itself has been an insufficient tool to incentivize the reforms necessary to combat corruption, ineffectiveness, and abuse: a conclusion that appears to hold true for much of Latin America (Ungar 2011). This chapter asks if there are more direct mechanisms for citizens and civil society to hold the police accountable. Through a focus on formally established citizen public security committees, which have emerged as the primary mechanism for citizen participation in the policy arena, I explore the efforts and activities of civil society in each of the four research sites. I argue that the vicious cycle can be (and in some cases has been) reversed if civil society promotes compliance, coproduction, and support in exchange for the political opportunity to monitor, evaluate, and hold public officials accountable. Unfortunately, however, I find that this compromise pact has rarely survived because (1) political leaders would prefer the benefits of compliance, coproduction, and support without strings attached, and (2) slowly evolving cooperation through repeated interactions between civil society and governing authorities is interrupted by the change of administration.

From Vicious to Virtuous Cycles

Political and police leaders have reluctantly come to the inevitable conclusion that they need community compliance, coproduction, and support to be effective. However, because of citizen distrust, governments have had a hard time promoting these positive behaviors. If citizens perceive that the police and governing authorities do not respect the law, then it will be difficult for those same authorities to encourage legal compliance. Unlike government officials, however, civil society leaders have the moral authority to promote compliance and combat legal cynicism. There have been several interesting civil society efforts to boost support for the law in Mexico. The relatively new term "a culture of lawfulness" (*cultura de la legalidad*) can now be found in speeches, educational curriculum, newspapers, and public discourse. A sizeable network of government and civil society groups has developed educational initiatives to promote such a culture in schools, police, media, civil society, and the business community.[2] The Mexico City-based México Unido Contra la Delincuencia (Mexico United Against Crime—MUCD) leads workshops with business groups, sponsors an annual poster competition, and has collaborated with educational and police institutions in promoting a culture of lawfulness. In conflictive Ciudad Juárez, the civil society group Plan Estratégico de Juárez (Strategic Plan of Juárez) has asked residents to sign a pact committing themselves to respecting the law. Furthermore, the group has developed a campaign to discourage the driving of illegally imported and unlicensed cars, a major concern discussed in the previous chapter.

Civil society organizations can also serve as a conduit for more effective coproduction. Recognizing the need for greater citizen involvement in public security, several administrations have attempted to organize neighborhood groups to such an end. Unfortunately however, many residents are suspicious of government outreach efforts; Mexico has a long history of governmental abuse of such organizations for clientelistic and partisan purposes (Padilla Delgado 2000; Cornelius, Craig, and Fox 1994). Even when clientelism does not predominate, residents complain that organizing efforts are empty attempts to create an appearance of governmental concern for security in the neighborhood. One official responsible for organizing community groups reflected this concern, stating "We go to the community and the people there say, 'You don't do anything. All you do is come in and organize us.'" By contrast, civil society efforts to foster coproduction are less likely to be subject to the perception of partisan manipulation and clientelistic intentions. In fact, groups like Mexico United Against Crime have run numerous campaigns offering support to victims of crime and urging them to report crime.

Finally, organized civil society can be a source of financial and political support. International and national philanthropic foundations offer an underutilized source of funding for innovative reform efforts. In the United States, several foundations helped fund the famous Knapp Commission in New York City, the Laura Spelman Rockefeller Memorial Fund subsidized the development of uniform crime reports, and the Ford Foundation helped establish the Police Foundation (Fogelson 1977). In Brazil, de Mesquita Neto (2006) profiles the Instituto São Paulo Contra a Violência (São Paulo Institute Against Violence), which runs a crime stoppers call center, supports community policing efforts, facilitated the development of geo-referenced crime maps, and participated in the founding of a national network of human rights observatories (de Mesquita Neto 2006). Also in Brazil, Ward (2006) discusses how the Federal University of Minas Gerais, the Fundação João Pinheiro, and the Minas Gerais military police collaborated to raise police education standards.

In the arena of political support, civil society organizations can help offset the primary obstacle to police professionalism discussed in Chapter 3: the lack of reform continuity. Civil society's commitment to certain projects offers a way to ensure that future administrations face pressure to continue successful initiatives. In Chapter 3, I discussed the importance of continuity in dramatically reducing violence in Bogotá, Colombia during the administrations of Antanas Mockus and Enrique Peñalosa in the 1990s and 2000s. After Mockus's second term, Luis Eduardo Garzón was elected mayor. Of a different political persuasion, Garzón showed only limited interest in the public security agenda of his predecessors. However, Mockus and Penalosa's initiatives had fomented active public participation in the policy arena, and their Unified System of Violence and Criminal Information offered an engaged citizenry reliable information about crime trends. When crime began to rise, citizen and civil society pressure forced Garzón to reverse course and continue the policies of his predecessors (Moncada 2009). In the Mexican context, research by the author in other policy arenas reveals numerous examples where civil society organizations helped ensure program continuity across administrations (Sabet 2008). While not always recognized, clearly there is a role for civil society in promoting compliance, coproduction, and support. Perhaps more important, however, there is also a role for civil society in promoting accountability.

From Sleeping Giant to Watchdog

The public has been referred to by Douglas Arnold (1992) and others as a sleeping giant that when awakened and angered can dramatically redirect the ship of state. In the U.S. experience, public anger and civil society activism were and continue to be key ingredients to police reform (Sherman 1978). Fogelson (1977) contends that, beginning at the close of the nineteenth century, civil society led the first wave of reform in U.S. policing. Warren Sloat (2002) describes in rich detail the role of the Reverend Charles Parkhurst and the Society for the Prevention of Crime in promoting police reform during this early time period. The Society hired detectives to investigate vice and police corruption and promoted grassroots community groups organized into a City Vigilance League. Parkhurst and the Society's efforts were the driving force behind the state senate's Lexow Commission investigations into police and political corruption, which issued three thousand subpoenas, heard almost seven hundred witnesses, and produced ten thousand pages of testimony, bringing to light in stunning detail the excesses and abuses of the city's police force (Fogelson). As Parkhurst said at the time, "It's the duty of the policeman to watch the people, and it's the duty of the people to watch the policeman" (Sloat, 64). Similar civil society activism such as the Citizens' Municipal Association of Philadelphia, the Baltimore Reform League, the Chicago Civic Federation, and the Los Angeles Committee of Safety sought to promote change in other U.S. cities.

The Lexow Commission was only one in a long history of many special investigative commissions that would expose police misconduct and foster reform, including the famous 1972 Knapp Commission in New York City and the 1991 Christopher Commission, established in the aftermath of the Los

Angeles police beating of Rodney King (Kutnjak Ivkovic. 2005). In some cities, citizens and civil society have successfully pushed for the creation of permanent citizen oversight agencies. Samuel Walker (2000) profiles several successes, including the San Jose Independent Auditor, the Special Counsel to the Los Angeles County Sheriff's Department, the Minneapolis Citizen Review Authority, the San Francisco Police Commission and Office of Citizen Complaints, and the Oregon Police Internal Investigations Auditing Committee. There is a risk of overstating the effectiveness of citizen oversight. Fogelson (1977) contends that civil society in the early twentieth century only produced temporary change, and Walker profiles the many challenges that citizen oversight mechanisms have confronted. Nonetheless, citizen and civil society pressure were and continue to be a major catalyst for reform in the United States.

Although civil society actors in Mexico and Latin America have had less luck holding their governing officials accountable, there is evidence of the sleeping giant impacting Mexican public security policy. In 1984, public disgust at a scandal involving the Federal Security Directorate (DFS) in the killing of journalist Manuel Buendía was a factor in the dissolution of the agency (Cisneros 2008).[3] In 1989, anger over the assassination of lawyer and human rights activist Norma Corona led to the creation of the National Human Rights Commission and legal reforms in the state of Sinaloa (Cisneros 2008). The more recent June 2008 kidnapping and killing of the fourteen-year-old son of wealthy businessman Alejandro Martí (with the involvement of federal police officers) seemed to represent a similar breaking point. As civil society organizations planned a major nationwide protest against insecurity, in August 2008, federal, state, and municipal governments, along with members of civil society and representatives of the news media, signed a National Agreement for Security, Justice, and Lawfulness, which committed the government to a number of needed reforms with time lines for implementation. A year-and-a-half later, public anger in Ciudad Juárez over the early 2010 killing of fifteen residents—mostly minors—at a party celebrating a high school sports victory (exacerbated by erroneous statements from the Calderón administration suggesting that the youths were involved in organized crime) galvanized civil society and sent state and federal authorities scrambling for new solutions. After several days of meetings between the Juárez public and Calderón and his cabinet, governing authorities announced the beginning of the *Todos Somos Juárez* (We Are All Juárez) program, a federal, state, and municipal government commitment to address both the security and social concerns of the city (Silva 2010).

These examples suggest that when the sleeping giant is awakened, Mexican society is able to demand accountability from its governing officials; however, it is less clear if the public is able to ensure the effective day-to-day implementation of new reform initiatives.[4] Outside of these dramatic events, there is a sense among many Mexicans that they have little impact on their own government. When Mexican survey respondents were asked whether they agreed with the statement that governing officials care what people like them think, the median survey respondent tended to disagree.[5]

Following the extensive literature on social movements, I posit that local civil society's impact will depend on opportunities from above and pressure from below (Tilly 1978). As to opportunities from above, this research asks if there is a political opportunity for citizens to affect public security problems. Even a well-organized and capable civil society might not be able to hold police accountable if there is insufficient political opportunity. Consistent with the theoretical approach adopted throughout this book, political opportunity is expected to manifest itself in two ways: through the formal and informal rules. The formal rules entail laws and regulations governing citizen public security councils in each of the four cities. The 1995 law establishing the National Public Security System included a section on promoting public participation in the public security policy arena and recommended establishment of a committee for citizen consultation and participation (Diario Oficial 2005). The form, structure, and impacts of the subsequent committees have varied; however, most large municipalities and all four of the research sites have created some form of formalized citizen committee.

The informal rules are evident through the actions taken by individual mayors or police chiefs to facilitate or hinder civil society efforts. As discussed above, there are several good reasons political and police leaders might embrace civil society. Committees and participating civil society organizations could help by educating about the law, discouraging illegal activities, and promoting law-abiding behavior. They could facilitate coproduction efforts and promote neighborhood watch organizations, after-school youth programs, drug rehabilitation groups, and prevention efforts. They could support tax increases for the police or mobilize resources from voluntary philanthropic institutions, the business community, and civil society. However, facilitating a civil society role in these areas is not necessarily the same as providing civil society and the public with the information and tools to effectively monitor, evaluate, and oversee police and government actors. Herein lays the tension in the relationship between public officials and members of civil society. Public officials and police leaders stand to benefit from public participation that facilitates compliance, coproduction, and support; however, they might stand to lose by allowing citizens a mechanism to hold them accountable. As Ramos García (2006, 189) concludes in his study of civil society impact on public security, "social participation has been temporary and conditioned by the political priorities of the government in office."

Of course, formal and informal political opportunity represents only part of the equation; human agency and civil society mobilization is still required to exploit such openings (Tilly 1978). While Mexican civil society had grown in size and strength in recent decades (Castro Salinas 2001), its development has been stunted by a history of co-option and clientelism (Verduzco 2003; Sabet 2008). As a result, the country's nonprofit sector has lagged behind the rest of Latin America (Verduzco, List, and Salamon 1999), and its philanthropic community has been particularly weak (CEMEFI 1996). A still-nascent civil society might not know how to effectively exploit and/or expand existing political opportunities.

Analysis: Civil Society in the Four Research Sites

This analysis examines citizen municipal public security committees in each of the four cities and the state-level public security citizen council in Baja California.[6] When placed in comparative context, the formal rules governing the committees did not provide them with strong legal authority. They were neither investigative commissions, like the famous New York City Knapp Commission, which was given prosecutorial powers and the ability to subpoena witnesses to testify under oath, nor were they citizen review boards, like San Francisco's Office of Citizen Complaints, an independent body with the legal authority to investigate police misconduct. Moreover, as evidenced in Table 6.1, there was variation in the formal rules across the four cities. Baja California, Mexicali, and Tijuana's committees' governing regulations were relatively strong compared to Hermosillo and Chihuahua's, and they provided the committees with over twenty-five different attributes, including the authority to comment on policies, access information, propose policies, encourage participation, report irregularities, and evaluate and oversee public security policy

TABLE 6.1. Formal rules governing the citizen public security committees in the four research sites as of 2009

	Mexicali	Tijuana	Hermosillo	Chihuahua
Name	Comité Ciudadano de Seguridad Pública	Comité Ciudadano de Seguridad Pública	Consejo Consultivo Ciudadano de Seguridad Pública	Comité Ciudadano de Seguridad Pública Municipal
Legal status	Governed by municipal regulations	Governed by municipal regulations	No municipal regulations.	Governed by municipal regulations
Authority	Moderate • Comment on policies • *Evaluate the police and programs* • Propose policies • Review monthly reports • Report irregularities • Promote professionalization • Encourage citizen participation	Moderate • Comment on policies • *Evaluate the police and programs* • Propose policies • Review monthly reports • Report irregularities • Promote professionalization • Encourage citizen participation • *Conduct studies on public security*	Mixed • Comment on policies • Make recommendations • Report irregularities • Recommend police for recognition • Support the police • Conduct educational campaigns • *Member of the Honor and Justice Board*	Weak • Propose and comment on plans • Analyze programs and conduct follow-up • Present recommendations
Participants	6 nonpartisan citizens and 5 government officials	28 nonpartisan citizens and 11 government officials	No procedure. Selected by the mayor.	Divided into 7 subcommittees, each contains a citizen president and official secretary plus additional citizens
Terms	Three-year post with one reelection. Overlaps administration by one year.	Three-year post with one reelection. Overlaps administration by one year.	Not defined	Not defined
Meetings	Once a month	Once a month	Once a month	Once a quarter
Year created	1999	1999	2007	2004
Financing	Mix of public and private	Mix of public and private	None	None
Additional committees	DARE Board Business Alliance Board	None	None	None

and programs. The three committees had been in existence since 1999; they had access to public and private resources, and the terms of the commissioners overlapped incoming administrations by one year to ensure continuity. Despite their name, all five committees also included governmental participation, which had its advantages as it gave the citizen commissioners access to their public officials.

Hermosillo's committee had only been in existence since 2007, and it did not have its own founding legislation or internal regulations.[7] Instead, the committee's legal basis was derived from an ambiguous state law. The committee had many of the same responsibilities as the Tijuana and Mexicali committees; however, descriptions of its functions omitted language suggestive of oversight authority, such as "evaluate the police and its programs." Commissioners were appointed by the mayor, and their terms coincided with the administration. Despite these limitations, the committee president was given one of four seats on the Honor and Justice Board, which hears all cases of police misconduct, a significant formal authority not present in the other three cities. On paper, Chihuahua's committee was the weakest of the four. Its functions were limited, commissioners' terms were undefined, and the committee, founded in 2004, was only required to meet once a quarter.

The formal rules governing the committees are still only part of the political opportunity structure. Interviews with members of the committees, police administrators, and members of civil society in the four research sites reveal that informal political opportunity varied considerably across the sites and across different administrations within the same site. In the state of Baja California, the political opening was significant under the Eugenio Elorduy Walther administration (2001–07), but small under the José Guadalupe Osuna Millán administration (2007–13). In Tijuana there was some opportunity under the Jorge Hank Rhon administration (2004–07), but almost no opportunity under the Jorge Ramos administration (2007–10). In Mexicali, the business and academic community experienced a greater window under the Samuel Ramos Flores administration (2005–07) than the Rodolfo Valdéz Gutiérrez administration (2007–10); however, the Valdéz Gutiérrez administration was more open to local neighborhood organizing efforts. In Hermosillo, the informal opening was relatively small under both the Ernesto Gándara Camou (2006–09) and Javier Gándara Magaña (2009–12) administrations. In Chihuahua, the opening was considerable under the Juan Blanco Zaldívar (2004–07) and Carlos Borruel Baquera (2007–10) administrations, but declined with the arrival of a new police chief. As will be demonstrated below, variation in informal support in cities where the strength of civil society and the formal rules are relatively unchanged allows for a clear illustration of the importance of informal mayoral support.

The strength of civil society is the last variable in this three-part equation, but unfortunately, it is a subjective and difficult concept to measure. Absent a strong history of nonprofit and philanthropic organizations, Mexican civil society is dominated by business chambers, professional associations, and academic institutions, which all four of the sites have in fairly equal numbers. An indicator based on counting the number of organizations operating in the arena of public security in Chihuahua in 2004 would have erroneously concluded that Chihuahua's civil society was very weak. Nonetheless, when the citizen committee was formed, many organized groups were drawn into the public security policy arena by the political opportunity. As a result, in 2007, the committee claimed that it had attracted the participation of around fifty organizations. In fact, of the four cities, only Tijuana could claim a long history of organizations concerned specifically with public security issues, such as the Centro Binacional de Derechos Humanos (Binational Human Rights Center). Absent a more nuanced measurement, interviews and media reports suggest that civil society capacity does not vary dramatically across the research sites. The following sections explore how the formal rules, informal discretion of political leaders, and civil society interact to encourage or discourage coproduction, support, and accountability.[8]

Encouraging Coproduction
There is evidence that civil society organizations and citizen participation committees in three of the four cities play an important role in promoting coproduction among the wider population. Recognizing both the need to help communities organize and the inability of government to serve as a credible organizer, Mexicali's Citizen Public Security Committee (Comité Ciudadano de Seguridad Pública) found a compelling way to overcome the distrust problem. Using the neighborhood watch model developed in the United States, Mexicali's committee replaced the government in promoting neighborhood organization. These local groups were asked to identify crime concerns, call the police to report crime, and participate in prevention efforts. If a problem arose with the police, the citizen committee was able to serve as a more autonomous interlocutor between citizens and police authorities. For example,

the committee had two lawyers on staff to attend to citizens' concerns. As one of the committee organizers reported, if the neighborhood watch group calls the police and the police never arrive, the lawyers are able to review the dispatchers' records and determine why. In addition, because the program is operated independently of (although in cooperation with) the local police, it is not entirely dependent on a given administration. As a result, when the PRI government of Samuel Ramos took over from a PAN administration in 2005 and sought to organize its own neighborhood organizations as part of a new program called Citizen Alliance (Alianza Ciudadana), the citizen committee's neighborhood watch groups continued to function.

As a result of this independence, Mexicali's experience contrasts with that of the local council in Tijuana. There, the Hank Rhon administration also recognized the credibility problem and enlisted the help of Tijuana's Citizen Public Security Committee in organizing neighborhood groups. Unfortunately, however, the following administration of Jorge Ramos (2007–10) was not interested in the groups organized by his predecessor. Absent autonomy from the municipal government, committee members reported that the three-year organizing effort was essentially dropped. Beyond the citizen committees, civil society organizations and the business community have also tried to encourage coproduction. Traditionally, business leaders in Mexico's northern cities have been hesitant to recognize the gravity of the security problem for fear of discouraging tourism and business investment. However, as the situation worsened in the mid-2000s, the perception of insecurity could no long be minimized, and the business community overcame its ambivalence to play a more active role in recognizing and addressing security concerns. In Tijuana, for example, the Chamber of Commerce (Cámara de Comercio CANACO) initiated a program called "*Ponle dedo al ratero*," which it roughly translates as "target the criminal." Through the program, CANACO works with the police to publish and disseminate something akin to a most-wanted list of burglars involved in commercial robberies. Many Tijuana business groups have also played an active role in Alianza Civil (Civil Alliance), a coalition of fifty-five organizations active in public security issues and crime prevention.

In Chihuahua, the committee's subcommittee on community policing promoted the installation of surveillance cameras linked to the police department. In addition, a subcommittee focused on family issues worked with victims of domestic violence to help respond to and prevent future victimization.

Providing Support

Perhaps the most interesting civil society initiatives entail actions to support the police financially and politically. In Mexicali, a supportive role began with the DARE program, a youth educational program designed to help kids resist drugs, gangs, and violence. Mexicali was one of the first Mexican municipalities to adopt the DARE program in 1998, and the department would eventually become the national training center for preparing Mexican DARE police officers. The DARE model requires that interested police departments establish a citizen board to oversee the program. Board members are asked to provide work, wisdom, and/or wealth. As such, Mexicali board members, through their own contributions and fund-raising, have paid for student books, bonuses for DARE officers, computers, and DARE patrol cars. The board meets every two months, oversees the finances and program implementation, and leads fund-raising efforts in the community. DARE's citizen board was used as a model for Mexicali's Business Alliance (Alianza Empresarial), which was created in 2005. The Alliance is a group of leaders in the business community that raises money for the police. In addition to overseeing an annual police raffle, they have donated bulletproof vests and police vehicles, built a gymnasium for the police, and facilitated housing loans for officers.

Perhaps the most impressive example of civil society support for the police can be found in Chihuahua. Upon its creation in 2004, the Chihuahuan committee was divided into seven subcommittees, with membership determined to best mobilize community resources in support of the police. For example, a subcommittee on certification, made up of businesspeople and university faculty familiar with ISO-9001 certification processes, worked closely with the department's newly created Center for Quality to help ensure that the department effectively negotiated the certification process for ISO-9001 and CALEA. In a similar vein, the subcommittee on dignifying the police included members of the restaurant business association and housing development association. The restaurants organized to provide discounts to police and their families, and the developers worked with the department to provide home loans to officers. The subcommittee also oversees a police- and firefighter-of-the-month award. Education leaders invited to participate on the professionalization subcommittee have provided the police access to the city's educational resources. This relationship has facilitated courses on computing, administration, and high school equivalency, and led to the development of technical, college, and master's degree programs for police.

Even in Hermosillo, the weakest of the five committees, business leaders participating on the committee were able to obtain discounted and donated paint for a large scale anti-graffiti campaign. Clearly, the citizen committees and complementary groups like those found in Mexicali offer important means to mobilize and channel societal support for the police. While these groups' contribution to the police is significant, they perhaps serve an even more important function: changing the relationship between police and citizens and potentially interrupting the vicious cycle. When asked why he works with the police despite their negative public image, a citizen committee member in Chihuahua responded that he is, "working to change that attitude—to work with the police and help them become better." Or as one interview respondent in Mexicali eloquently put it, he works to ensure "that society sees the police officer as someone that takes care of me rather than someone that screws me."

Accountability

Despite these examples of civil society efforts to promote coproduction and support, I find less political opportunity for real oversight and accountability. The most promising experiment in citizen oversight occurred in the state of Baja California during the administration of Eugenio Elorduy Walther (2001–07). Baja California's state council was established in 1999, and it is made up of citizens drawn from the leadership of the municipal committees (along with government officials). The state council's formal governing regulations gave it responsibility for evaluating police performance, but more important, Elorduy took citizen evaluation seriously. He ensured that the state's attorney general and secretariat of public security attended every meeting, gave the council access to these agencies to conduct multiple public evaluations, allowed committee members a central place in policy discussions, and provided them with a significant operational budget (complemented by other sources).[9]

Governing authorities have always made some statistical indicators available to the public, but officials have determined what indicators to present and how to present them. For example, in its annual report, a given administration might indicate a drop in assaults and ignore an increase in car theft. During the Elorduy administration, however, the council was afforded access to the government's raw data, and council members were allowed to present the information as they saw fit. The result was a series of studies that brought to light many of the deficiencies of the criminal justice system in the state.[10] In interviews, members of the council agreed that the evaluations, which were published and disseminated, produced significant impacts on policy and funding. They also allowed civil society to better target its demands on public officials. For example, according to one councilmember, data revealing that only a small percentage of federal detainees were ever brought before a judge allowed the council to pressure federal authorities for more successful prosecutions following a subsequent federal operation.

The success of Baja's council was also due in part to a strong, committed civil society that was able to take advantage of the political opportunity provided by the Elorduy administration. As discussed in Chapter 4, following a deterioration in the security situation in 2006, members of the council became alarmed that the government was not proactive enough in its response to the rising violence. As a result, the council organized a fifteen-day March for the Victims of Insecurity through the most populous areas of Baja California. In many ways the council became the voice of the public in issues of security in the state, and the state's news media regularly covered the actions of the council.

In summary, Baja California's council was successful because (1) the formal rules gave it the authority to conduct evaluations, (2) the Elorduy administration was supportive of citizen evaluation and oversight, and (3) Baja California's civil society was willing and able to take advantage of this political opportunity. While the formal rules and civil society strength have remained relatively constant, the informal political opportunity changed with the departure of Elorduy and the initiation of the Osuna Millán administration in 2007. Since the Osuna Millán administration took over, no such citizen evaluation has been conducted. While the citizen council continues to operate, its power has declined in the absence of a greater informal political opportunity.

There are unfortunately, few other examples of effective citizen oversight. The Chihuahua committee's efforts to support the police did open certain windows for accountability; for example, a subcommittee led by members of the academic community oversaw an internal survey of the police department and a complementary survey in the community. While the results were not made public or widely disseminated, evident frustration among officers regarding promotion requirements allowed the committee to push for a more merit-based process in which they were given an oversight role. In Mexicali, committee members contended that they are able to hold government officials to account, but they did so outside of the public purview and in the context of committee meetings. Committee members in all four of the research sites argued that they must walk a fine line. Given their dependence on informal support from the executive, actions that upset an administration might cause informal political opportunities to contract. One committee president summed up this inherent tension: "The positions that we take at times are not very agreeable to the authorities, but it is one of our responsibilities."

Hermosillo's experience illustrates the barriers to greater civil society oversight. Concerned that short-lived municipal administrations had little incentive to undertake long-term planning and investment, a citizen group called Hermosillo 2025 proposed empowering the citizen committee with a degree of control over the procurement process and responsibility for approving equipment purchases. Upon further analysis, however, they concluded that the committee was not up for the task, referring to it derisively as the "complacency committee" instead of the "citizen committee." Instead, they pushed for the creation of a stronger and more independent citizen board. Promoters argued that a citizen procurement board would not only prevent corruption and ensure efficient use of funds but provide a long-term vision to investment in public security. Unfortunately, they pitched the proposal to four administrations but failed to see it adopted. One member of the group was forced to conclude in an interview, "Society doesn't have any weight. The authorities are not accustomed to listening to civil society. They see us as a threat—that they are going to lose their authority."

Despite the weakness of the committee in Hermosillo, de jure it has an important power not present in the other cities: a member of the citizen council holds one of four seats on the Honor and Justice Board that hears all disciplinary cases. Unfortunately, however, this important formal power has not led to citizen accountability. Under the Gándara Camou administration (2007–10), the citizen member was appointed by the mayor, and interviewees alleged that the representative always voted with the police chief. Under the subsequent administration, the representative from the citizen council was actually a government official! Because the citizen councils include government participation, the Gándara Magaña administration contended that it was perfectly in accordance with the law for the representative to be one of the governmental members of the committee. As a result, the legal advisor to the city became the committee's representative.

In summary, despite the political opportunity to foster coproduction and to provide support, there is less of an opportunity for meaningful oversight. Dependence on the discretion of the mayor or police chief has prevented the committees from effectively holding government officials accountable. While it might be hoped that an active civil society could check the power of the executive, civil society is also subject to executive authority.

Citizen Observatories

The relatively new phenomenon of citizen observatories represents another potential avenue for increased accountability. The 2008 National Agreement for Security, Justice, and Lawfulness included a commitment to create citizen observatories to oversee the agreement and the progress in addressing public security problems. Unlike the citizen public security councils, whose mission is broad and somewhat ambiguous, the observatories' goal is (at least in theory) more focused: to identify, develop, and track reliable indicators of police and criminal justice system performance. While new to Mexico, observatories emerged in Colombia in the 1990s and have since expanded throughout much of Latin America with financial support from foundations, development aid organizations, and development banks (CISALVA 2008). They have emerged as a popular tool precisely because of the lack of reliable indicators on which to evaluate the success or failure of public security agencies and policies.

The need for better statistics has particular resonance in Mexico, where crime statistics are collected by a variety of different agencies, each of which holds only a piece of the crime puzzle. For example, municipal and state police departments have one set of crime statistics based on the number of calls for emergency assistance and the number of arrests. State and federal attorney general offices, however, provide different numbers for the same crimes based on the number of people that have formally filed a report, or *denunica*. A victim of crime might call the police and submit a *denuncia* to the attorney general's office, only submit a *denuncia* and not call the police, or do both. As a result, to obtain correct indicators, the police and the attorney general's office have to sit down together and merge their data. Interviews suggest that in many places, this does not happen. Even if the agencies do share their information, citizens might not see the final product. The problem of reliable indicators even impacts homicide statistics. Although homicides are the easiest indicator to track, the statistical agency INEGI and the National Public Security System provide different numbers (Escalante Gonzalbo 2009). Furthermore, and particularly at the local level, data is not made available in a consistent and reliable way across administrations that would allow for effective citizen evaluation.[11]

The objective of the observatory, therefore, is to bring government officials from the different agencies responsible for gathering information together with technical experts in civil society and develop common methodologies for tracking and disseminating information. The observatories offer considerable promise; with valid, reliable information, citizens would have an important tool to hold their elected and public officials accountable. However, the observatories confront the same basic problem as the committees: despite formal access to information laws, they still depend on the discretionary cooperation of governing officials. Immediately following the 2008 agreement, critics worried that the observatories would amount to one more government attempt to co-opt civil society and divert public anger (Gandaria 2008). The federal Secretariat of Public Security asserted itself as the agency responsible for organizing the observatories, causing interviewed members of civil society to express concern that the head of public security sought to control the process. As one member of civil society stated, "They were supposed to promote the observatories, not control them."

At the federal level, the national observatory was established involving many of the country's best universities and several civil society organizations, including groups like Mexico United Against Crime. Initial efforts to monitor the implementation of the National Agreement for Security, Justice, and Lawfulness produced useful public information; however, the more ambitious objective of setting up a true observatory to track indicators on crime and to evaluate police and criminal justice performance has been elusive. While the Observatorio Nacional Ciudadano de la Seguridad, la Justicia y la Legalidad (Security, Justice, and Legality National Citizen Observatory) formally existed and had attracted the participation of many key actors, more than three years after its creation the observatory had yet to settle on indicators and make available its results.

At the time of this writing, there was also no local observatory in Sonora, and only limited advances had been made in Baja California and Chihuahua. Interestingly, the Chihuahua's observatory is promoted by the same actors that were central to the municipal public security committee. Despite the legal obligation to share crime statistics, the observatory's promoters struggled for over a year to get the necessary data from both the municipal police and the attorney general's office. While they were somewhat successful, they had still not been able to obtain a combined database made up of information from both the city and the attorney general's office. An interviewed member of the observatory reported that the data has not been released because the city alleges that it cannot release state data, and the state alleges it cannot release city data.

Consequently, while the observatories do have considerable potential, they have yet to emerge as an important tool for citizen oversight and accountability. It seems likely that with time they will become more effective, but they might not overcome the fundamental opposition from authorities—what one observer called the "opacity consensus."

Discussion: Formal Rules, Informal Discretion, and Civil Society Strength

This analysis confirms the importance of the formal rules, informal discretion of political leaders, and civil society strength. All three of these factors were present in relatively successful committee experiences in Baja California, Mexicali, and Chihuahua. Nonetheless, the research suggests the primacy of the informal discretion of political leaders. Despite formal rules to the contrary, an active civil society in Baja California was dependent on the support of Governor Elorduy, and its effectiveness declined with the arrival of Osuna Millán. The same phenomenon occurred in Chihuahua and to a lesser extent in Tijuana and Mexicali. At the time this research began, Chihuahua's committee was the strongest and most active of the four research sites. In some ways, this was surprising because the formal rules governing the Chihuahua committee were actually weaker than those of the other committees. The difference appeared to be the product of a strong civil society and a supportive administration. The idea for the committee actually came from civil society; Chihuahua's local chapter of the business owner's association COPARMEX pushed the idea with the incoming Blanco administration in 2004. Blanco liked the idea and created the committee. When the administration changed in 2007, the counselors successfully lobbied Blanco's successor Borruel (from the same political party) for the committee's continuation. However, in 2009, Borruel left the presidency in a bid for the state governorship around the same time that the police department's reformist civilian police chief was replaced by a retired military officer. Despite the fact that Chihuahua's committee had provided the police with an impressive amount of in-kind services and support over the course of two administrations, the new police chief began to speak of the problem of too many isolated initiatives and the need to consolidate and focus community efforts. The committee saw its window begin to close.

Herein lays the unfortunate irony of civil society-led accountability. In theory, civil society oversight should allow for a more meaningful evaluation of administration policies in addition to pressure for continuity of effective programs and personnel, the principal governance challenge identified in Chapter 3. In practice, however, citizen committees are also subject to the mayoral tendency to reinvent public programs every three years.[12] Civil society might not only fail to ensure the continuity of programs, but its own opportunity for voice, participation, and oversight might close shut with the change of administration or leadership.

Consider the above-mentioned effort in Tijuana to organize neighborhood associations that was subsequently halted by the Ramos administration. Instead of building on previous efforts, the administration announced a new outreach program to the city's high-crime communities called Comunidad Segura (Secure Community). Not only was the committee, whose membership overlapped into the new administration, unable to sell the incoming political leadership on the importance of continuing its work, but the committee found itself isolated. It was not invited to participate in Secure Community, and more important, the city stopped paying rent, telephone, and electricity for the council's offices. The ironic twist to this reduction in political opportunity was that the former president of the committee, Jorge Capella Ibarra, was the city's new police chief. A formal rule of overlapping administrations, a supposed ally in the chief-of-police post, and a strong civil society failed to ensure continuity.[13]

Hermosillo's experience also suggests the primacy of informal discretion. While the formal rules grant a member of the citizen committee a place on the Honor and Justice Board, the Gándara Magaña administration circumvented the spirit of the rules and imposed a government official on the position. In short, rather than executive accountability to the civil society, civil society remains dependent on the executive.

How can this civil society–continuity dilemma be solved? Experiences in Mexicali suggest that citizens might be able to obtain a larger political opportunity if they can reverse the nature of dependency. In particular, when governing authorities *depend* on civil society for resources, citizen councils might be able to leverage this dependency to create opportunities for oversight. In Mexicali, because the DARE citizen board provided the police with substantial resources, it was able to influence government decision making in a way that other civil society initiatives were unable to do. Like many policies, most community outreach programs typically only last the three years of a given administration; however, the DARE program in Mexicali has outlasted five. Given the operational pressures on the police, there are strong incentives to exploit all available officers and slowly chip away at a program like DARE by reassigning personnel to operational duties. Despite these incentives, the DARE board successfully ensured that DARE officers were assigned to the program full time. Moreover, the board successfully advocated for the creation of a DARE commander at the equivalent rank of captain, meaning that he or she could not be outranked by other operational commanders. It would be hard to imagine local authorities fulfilling these commitments if they did not depend on the board financially. Although the outcome was different in Chihuahua, the Mexicali experience suggests that greater citizen financial support for the police might offer the best way to reverse dependency on executive discretion.

What About the Role of the Media?

If one of the obstacles to effectively monitoring police and public officials is the lack of reliable information, then it is impossible to ignore the essential role of the media. Unfortunately, however, there is no shortage of evidence that the media has largely failed to fulfill this role. The most salient explanation is a well-justified fear of organized crime. Joel Simon, the executive director of the Committee to Protect Journalists, adapts the familiar *"plata o plomo"* expression to the case of journalists. "It's a well-worn phrase in Mexico, one that's all too familiar to the country's journalists. It means, simply, we own you. Take our plata (slang for money) and publish what we tell you. Or we kill you" (Lauría et al. 2010, 1). The quotation not only suggests that journalists have failed to provide citizens with reliable news, but that they have been corrupted into providing misinformation.

There is disagreement on the number of journalists who have been killed or disappeared as a result of their profession. Writing in September 2010, the Committee to Protect Journalists estimates that "More than 30 journalists and media workers have been murdered or have vanished since December 2006 [when Calderón took office]" (Lauría et al. 2010, 5); however, other sources place the number much higher. The national newspaper *El Universal* counted twelve journalists killed in 2009 alone (El Universal 2009), and Reporters Without Borders (2010) counted eleven in the first nine months of 2010. Regardless of the actual number, it is clear that the profession has been severely threatened by organized crime.

In addition, state and federal authorities have largely failed to protect threatened journalists and investigate their deaths. Lauría et al. (2010), for example, profile the April 2010 abduction, torture, and killing of José Bladimir Antuna García, a crime reporter for *El Tiempo de Durango*. Prior to his death, Antuna García had received numerous threats, a colleague of his had been killed, and he had been fired on by an unknown assailant. Despite this clear danger, Antuna García's report to the police was ignored, and he was never provided protection. While an official investigation was opened into his assassination, the study finds that virtually no detective work was ever carried out. Antuna García's former boss was quoted as saying, "They know perfectly well who killed him. They don't need an investigation. They are either afraid of who did it or they are in business with them" (Lauría et al., 11). Unfortunately, very few of the journalist killings have led to arrests and prosecutions, and even those few have raised suspicions of scapegoating. In 2006, following a spate of journalist killings, the Fox administration established a special prosecutor's office for crimes against journalists; however, in four years it had yet to produce a single successful prosecution.

Operating in an environment where organized crime offers a credible threat and the authorities no protection, journalists and media outlets argue that they have no choice but to self-censor. In some extreme cases, such as Reynosa (also profiled in the Committee to Protect Journalist report), local media did not even report on a spate of major public shootouts between the Gulf organization and the Zetas in February 2010. In Ciudad Juárez, the main paper *El Diario* provoked a national debate by publishing an editorial conceding to the power of organized crime. The editorial read:

> Leaders of the different organizations that are fighting for control of Ciudad Juárez: The loss of two reporters from this publishing house in less than two years represents an irreparable sorrow for all of us who work here, and, in particular, for their families . . . We want you to explain to us what you want from us. What are we supposed to publish or not publish, so we know what to abide by. You are at this time the *de facto* authorities in this city because the legal authorities have not been able to stop our colleagues from falling.[14]

But the problem facing the local media goes well beyond organized crime threats. Although there is evidence of civic journalism in Mexico, Sallie

Hughes (2006) also finds what she refers to as authoritarian and market-based journalism. There is a long tradition of "authoritarian journalism," whereby the media acts as the voice of the government; however, this does not necessarily imply overt state coercion. Writing about the media in 1997, Raymundo Riva Palacio describes the perverse incentives in the industry at the time. First, with relatively small circulations, the media depended heavily on government advertising. The threat of advertising withdrawals implied bankruptcy for many outlets. As president José López Portillo famously said in 1982, "I don't pay for you to hurt me." Second, newspapers and reporters frequently charged government agencies for positive stories as a means to increase newspaper revenues and top off reporters salaries. Riva Palacio notes that such practices were not generally viewed as unethical.

On the other hand, many observers note a dramatic change in Mexican journalism and place the press at the forefront of the country's democratic transition (Hughes 2006; Lawson 2002). Independent, investigative journalism from the country's major national newspapers, magazines, and television stations provide Mexico's citizens with reliable and informative news coverage. And yet, it is not clear that civic journalism is the dominant trend at the local level, where the practice of paying for positive press coverage continues. Particularly in the arena of public security, market incentives have led to the rise of the *nota roja,* or the red press. A play on words derived from yellow journalism, red journalism is characterized by bloody images of assassinations complemented with little more than the basic facts. Sold at about a third of the cost of regular newspapers, the red press far outsells its traditional counterpart.

To explore the local media in the four research sites, this research project systematically examined public security news coverage by at least one primary newspaper in each of the four cities: *La Frontera* and *Zeta* in Tijuana, *La Crónica* in Mexicali, *El Imparcial* in Hermosillo, and a mix of *El Diario* and *El Heraldo* in Chihuahua.[15] Interviews were also conducted with editorial staff and journalists from these and other papers.

In many ways, the newspapers and their reporters do an excellent job with limited resources in a dangerous work environment. Dedicated crime reporters are often the first to the scene of the crime, and one or two journalists submit several stories each day. Interviewed journalists state that they typically work ten hours a day, are always on call, do not spend time with their families, are treated poorly by the police, and receive only a small salary for their efforts. Despite these challenges, some journalists have emerged as successes. In 2009, Mexicali reporter Juan Galván won a Mexico Journalism Award from the Federation of Mexican Journalist Associations for his dangerous work covering a police operation to free kidnap victims. Juan Galván not only writes for Mexicali's *La Voz de la Frontera* newspaper, but he runs a radio program and website/blog on security issues (La Voz de la Frontera 2009). In fact, one can cite several examples where newspapers broke very valuable news stories. For example, *La Frontera* (Tijuana) broke a story on corruption in the repair and maintenance of police vehicles, *La* Crónica (Mexicali) was the first to publish General Aponte Polito's letter condemning corruption in the state's police forces, and *El Heraldo* (Chihuahua) has published numerous articles revealing flaws in the state's new criminal justice system.

Of all of the newspapers, Tijuana's *Zeta* clearly stands apart. While criticized by officials as muckraking journalism, *Zeta* is perhaps the only paper in the country that continues to investigate and analyze local organized crime problems. It has paid a high price for doing so. One of its founding editors, Héctor Félix Miranda, was killed in 1988; another editor, Francisco J. Ortiz Franco, was killed in 2004; and its other founding director, Jesús Blancornelas, barely survived an attack in 1997 and spent the rest of his life under constant protection. Nonetheless, *Zeta* has survived and thrived since its founding in 1980, and Blancornelas received two national journalism awards and the UNESCO World Press Freedom Prize (Granados Chapa 2010).

Other news outlets have been unwilling to sustain similar risks. Hermosillo's *El Imparcial* was one of the first newspapers to publically announce that it would no longer cover organized crime following the disappearance of its photographer Alfredo Jiménez Mota in 2005. The paper argued that a life is worth more than a newspaper story, and furthermore, the paper's leadership hoped that such a public announcement would create sufficient alarm and pressure to resolve the case. Nonetheless, at the time of writing, Jiménez's disappearance still remains unsolved. Chihuahua's news media has also been targeted by violence. In August 2006, Enrique Perea Quintanilla, a reporter for Chihuahua City's *El Heraldo* and El *Diario* newspapers, who had also started his own publication, *Dos Caras,* was found tortured and killed. Furthermore, all of the journalists interviewed for this research stated that they or their colleagues had been threatened by organized crime and/or government officials. As one reporter in Tijuana stated, "We can't report everything that we know. I would have suffered five assassination attempts if I had published everything." Another in Chihuahua offered, "If the police cannot even protect themselves, how am I going to protect myself?" A third in Hermosillo, noting the impunity given crimes against journalists, stated, "If I disappear, it's no big deal. It's just one more reporter—nothing else. You have to take care of yourself because no one is going to take care of you." In short, organized crime and corruption clearly pose a threat to the news business.

As a result, self-censorship has occurred through a variety of means. Several of the papers have a policy where they do not use anonymous sources and only publish material that can be attributable. On the one hand, this does avoid the problem of publishing false information based on unreliable sources. On the other hand, however, it ensures that sensitive material will never be published. Instead, the papers' primary sources of information come from official statements by the police department and municipal leadership. Articles are extremely short, typically two to four brief paragraphs, and are normally limited to just *what* happened rather than *why* something happened.

However, as suggested above, organized crime is only part of the problem. Journalists interviewed freely recognize that they rarely conduct medium or long-term investigative journalism. All the journalists interviewed (again with the exception of *Zeta* reporters) focus their attention almost entirely on covering the day's crimes for the next day's news. To illustrate this problem, an editor of one of the newspapers admitted that they rarely take advantage of new local transparency legislation because transparency requests might take two weeks—far beyond their immediate deadlines.

In addition, the practice of paying for positive press coverage is still common. These articles do not appear as paid advertisements and are indistinguishable from other articles. This practice continues to help top off reporter's salaries, which, perhaps surprisingly, are considerably lower than police salaries. This "pay to publish" policy does not apply just to the government but also to the nonprofit sector. The Citizen Public Security Council in Baja California under Alberto Capella Ibarra's leadership frequently paid for positive press coverage. The continuation of this practice corresponds with a lack of professionalism and a tendency for overworked reporters to mix up even some of the most basic elements of a news story. As a result of organized crime intimidation, continued dependence on the government for revenues, lack of investigative journalism, and lapses in professionalism, the media has generally failed to provide citizens with the information that they need to be able to effectively monitor, evaluate, and hold their public officials accountable.

Conclusion

The police and Mexican society are trapped in a vicious cycle whereby ineffectiveness and corruption fuel distrust, which leads to low levels of compliance, coproduction, and support—furthering ineffectiveness and corruption. Ending the vicious cycle will require changes by both citizens and the police; however, the solution to this collective action problem is not clear. On the one hand, experiences in Tijuana, Mexicali, and Chihuahua provide examples of civil society-promoted compliance, coproduction, and support, and, to a lesser extent, accountability. On the other hand, civil society's impact is dependent on the discretion of governing officials. This establishes a conceptual dead end: how can civil society hold officials accountable if its effectiveness is dependent on those very leaders?

The mutually beneficial solution to this dilemma is that civil society encourages compliance, coproduction, and support in exchange for institutionalized opportunities to hold the police accountable. Of course, police and city leaders would prefer compliance, coproduction, and support without strings attached, and members of civil society would prefer opportunities for accountability regardless of support. The evidence suggests that in both Mexicali and Chihuahua, civil society and police/city leaders did arrive over time at such a cooperative solution. In Chihuahua, for example, the primary role of the committee was to support the police. The incoming police chief in 2004 was initially skeptical toward the committee and had several conflicts with the committee's leadership. Nonetheless, over the five years of his tenure as police chief, a mutually beneficial relationship emerged. This, in fact, is indicative of one of the clear conclusions of the collective action literature. When individuals interact regularly, they can develop the trust and reciprocity needed to overcome collective action problems (Axelrod 1984). Unfortunately however, in the Mexican municipal context, this solution is only temporary because the players in the game change every three years. As a result, each new administration has to become convinced of the importance of civic engagement. Again, the problem returns to the lack of continuity in personnel and policies as explored in Chapter 3. This is the unfortunate irony: on the one hand, it is hoped that civil society can help maintain good programs and policies across administrations; however, on the other hand, it appears that civil society is also vulnerable to the very same lack of continuity.

The most promising way out of this dilemma is suggested by the Mexicali DARE experience. The potential loss of civil society financial resources might preserve civil society influence across administrations. Complementary strategies include strengthening civil society capacity and improving the formal rules. While these factors were found to be secondary to the informal discretion of political leaders, they are still relevant. There is an active civil society in each of the four cities; however, Mexico generally lacks the philanthropic foundations that proved to be important in the U.S. case. Citizen committee leaders also recognize that many citizen counselors lose interest over time or participate on the committees for the wrong reasons. Improvements to the formal rules could also help solve the dilemma. True, governing authorities in Hermosillo circumvented the spirit of the law when they appointed a government official to be the citizen council's representative on the Honor and Justice Board; however, rather than conclude that the statute is irrelevant, it would be far more productive to close the legal loophole that allowed for the appointment. Regardless of the mechanism, however, the important conclusion is that greater accountability to citizens and civil society represents the most promising means to overcome the vicious cycle currently reinforcing police corruption and ineffectiveness.

7   The Federal Government
and Local Reform

The *Michoacanazo*

Police forces need effective oversight to not only discourage misconduct and promote professionalism but to ensure that reform initiatives continue beyond individual administrations. This oversight could come from citizens; however, the previous chapter showed that neither the vote nor more direct means have provided sufficient tools to hold the police accountable. Oversight could also come from checks and balances in municipal government; however, Chapter 3 provided evidence that such mechanisms were not functioning effectively. Given this lack of vertical accountability (between citizens and public officials) and a lack of horizontal accountability (between the executive and city council), this chapter considers what role the federal government can play in providing sufficient carrots and sticks for reform.

In the state of Michoacán on May 26, 2009, military and federal authorities arrested ten mayors, a judge, and nineteen state government officials, including an advisor to the governor who had previously served as the secretary of public security, an advisor to the state attorney general who was a former deputy attorney general, and the head of the state police academy who was also a former secretary of public security (De la Luz González and Gómez 2009). The officials were arrested for alleged ties to the organized criminal group known as La Familia (the Family), a unique criminal organization that mixed crime with a religious cult, claimed to be working for the benefit of the people of Michoacán, and even employed public relations officers. La Familia had a strong presence throughout the state and was believed to have de facto replaced the government in many of the state's municipalities. As such, the arrests were hailed by many as a welcomed effort to reestablish the government's territorial control in a state that had been overwhelmed by a violent criminal group. Federal officials contended in interviews that the action had put mayors, governors, and political candidates throughout the country on notice that they too would be brought to justice if they collaborated with organized crime.

But the Calderón administration received more condemnation than praise for the arrests. Michoacán, Calderón's home state, was governed by the opposition PRD party (Partido de la Revolución Democrática) under the governorship of Leonel Godoy Rangel. Although the federal government stated that Godoy was not a target of its investigations, he was nonetheless uninformed of the raid, which involved federal officials entering into and making arrests in the state capital building. Godoy condemned the arrests as a violation of the state's autonomy, and the opposition PRI and PRD parties both denounced the action as motivated by mid-term elections, which were a mere five weeks away. The dispute took center stage at a meeting of the National Public Security Council and inhibited the body from advancing on important issues of public security.[1] As one editorialist pointed out, the partisan fight had managed to hide "how dangerous, grave, and threatening it is for everyone—citizens, parties, governments, candidates, mayors, and the base of the government, the municipality—that parties and governments have been penetrated by drug trafficking in strategic areas" (Alemán 2009).

The incident highlights three important points. First, given the failure of local-level horizontal and vertical accountability mechanisms, the federal government offers a potential means to ensure the accountability of local authorities. The federal government has information-gathering abilities, expertise, resources, and legal faculties that everyday citizens, civil society, and city council members lack. However, the incident also reveals the dangers of the federal government as a check on the municipality. On the one hand, if the Calderón administration acted *without* partisan intentions, then the incident shows how opposition party actors can use partisan politics and allegations of political motivations to politicize and undermine efforts to make state and municipal governments accountable. On the other hand, if the federal government *did* act with partisan intentions, then it raises questions about who the federal government is accountable to and if it can be expected to act in the interest of citizens. Finally, the incident also reveals the limitations of federal executive action. Over the course of the next two years, all but one of the arrestees was exonerated by the courts.

The Promise and Problem of Accountability to the Federal Government

This chapter explores a series of policies implemented by the Calderón administration to promote police reform at the municipal level, including a substantial subsidy program (SUBSEMUN), whose largess is conditioned on adopting reforms. In many respects, use of the power of the purse to promote local reform is the ideal role for a national-level government in a federal system (Shah 2003). This is particularly the case given that local officials have largely failed to reduce corruption, abuse, and ineffectiveness on their own. This chapter, therefore, considers if the carrot of federal funding and accountability to the federal government can realign the incentives for more meaningful local reform.

Accountability to the federal government, however, creates two challenges. First, local accountability to the federal government implies a new principal-agent problem. As with any principal-agent problem, the federal government must overcome the information asymmetries between it and numerous local governments to effectively constrain, monitor, evaluate, and supervise municipal spending and actions. It is an open question as to whether the federal government has the capacity to both do its own job and oversee that of the municipalities. If the federal government is unable to do so, local governments could misuse federal funds through embezzling, growing the size of the local bureaucracy, or steering contracts toward favored providers at inflated rates. When the conditions are policy oriented, municipalities might only "simulate" reform to obtain the needed resources. For example, municipalities might create new formal rules and policies required by the federal government while continuing to adhere to the old informal rules. In addition, the ability to obtain funds from the federal government might discourage local officials from increasing their own tax base (Giugale and Webb 2000).

Second, accountability to the federal government might replace rather than complement accountability to citizens. If vertical accountability mechanisms are functioning effectively at the federal level, this is not necessarily cause for concern. However, if citizens have a hard time holding the federal government accountable, then federal officials will be able to use their leverage over the municipalities to pursue objectives not necessarily in the interest of the public. In fact, this was largely the case during the many decades of one-party rule when local governments were informally subordinated to the federal government and citizens had only limited mechanisms to control either (Rodriguez 1997). It is also what critics of the Calderón administration allege occurred in Michoacán.

There are several ways in which federal authorities could misuse their leverage over subnational governments. In cases the world over, federal authorities have abused their control over the budget for electoral advantage, targeting funding to either political supporters (Cox and McCubbins 1986) or to swing voters (Lindbeck and Weibull 1987). Mexico has a long history of targeted federal government spending. Perhaps the most analyzed case involved former president Carlos Salinas de Gortari's Solidarity Program (PRONASOL), which used local development grants to build and shore up political support for the PRI (Cornelius, Craig, and Fox 1994). While such abuses appear far less common today, it is not unusual to hear municipal officials complain that state and federal monies are still politically manipulated. Like their local counterparts, federal officials could also push contracts toward favored contractors. Furthermore, policy conditions could steer municipal law enforcement activities toward federal rather than local priorities. Less pernicious but no less problematic, federal authorities might erroneously promote one-size-fits-all reforms and policies that are neither tailored nor suited to the local environment.

Given the need for local officials to be held accountable, but given the challenges of federal government monitoring and the risks of federal abuse, conditional fiscal transfers will be most effective if they strengthen local-level vertical and horizontal accountability. While federal officials will have a difficult time monitoring hundreds of municipalities, by providing access to information and expanding opportunities for local oversight, federally promoted efforts could achieve a greater measure of success.

The Zedillo and Fox Administrations

As discussed in Chapter 1, police reform in Mexico did not become a priority until the administration of Ernesto Zedillo Ponce de León (1994–2000). While much of Zedillo's efforts focused on the federal level—purging the Federal Judicial Police and establishing the Federal Preventive Police—the administration recognized the need to strengthen local police forces and improve coordination among the many different departments. Toward that end, it oversaw the creation of the National Public Security System (Sistema Nacional de Seguridad Pública—SNSP) to set and oversee national-level public security policy. The SNSP includes the National Public Security Council, made up of state and national police and political leaders, and state and local councils, made up of federal, state, and municipal leaders.[2] At the close of the administration, the Mexican Congress set up a large Public Security Support Fund (Fondo de Aportaciones para la Seguridad Pública – FASP) to support states and their municipalities in improving public security, including development of emergency call and dispatching centers under a unified 066 number (equivalent to the U.S. 911), creation of national crime and police databases, and training and infrastructure improvements.

In its first annual report, the Fox administration at least rhetorically recognized the need to promote police professionalism at the municipal level:

> The new administration considers the standardization of the country's preventive police to be a strategic priority, with the goal of providing the population a preventive police force unified in their training, presentation, and technical capacity, that is guaranteed to protect society and its property through the standardization of profiles, legal norms, and parameters offering a minimum quality of preparation, training, and police equipment across the three levels of government. (Fox Quesada 2001, 593)

To achieve this objective, the Fox administration grew the annual FASP to half a billion dollars to help augment state and municipal police budgets. The money was transferred to the state governments based on population, crime rates, prison population, and advances toward meeting national goals. The states were required to match a percentage, oversee its use in the state, and pass on a portion to the municipalities. Table 7.1 offers a breakdown of the fund's diverse uses for the final year of the Fox administration, including monies for professionalization, equipment, national telecommunications network, infrastructure, and evaluation.

While desperately needed, the FASP funding did not produce radical changes in municipal police departments. States found it too tempting to use the windfall of money to strengthen their own public security capacity rather than pass the money on to the municipalities. Chihuahua, Baja California, and Sonora all created new elite state police forces during this time, leaving the municipalities largely to fend for themselves.[3]

TABLE 7.1. 2006 Fox administration FASP funding to support state and municipal public security efforts (in thousands of U.S. dollars)

Topic	Federal transfer	State match	Total
Professionalization	$34,897	$17,533	$52,430
Equipment	$46,784	$16,234	$63,018
Nat'l telecom network, emergency call centers	$76,214	$10,326	$86,540
National Information Center	$16,621	$2,598	$19,219
Public Vehicle Registry	$3,739	$585	$4,324
Public Security infrastructure	$51,026	$7,671	$58,697
Coordination mechanisms	$72,214	$21,539	$93,753
Fighting drug dealing	$75,728	$22,892	$98,620
Joint operations	$0	$10,112	$10,112
Community participation	$0	$8,478	$8,478
Continuity and evaluation	$7,525	$4,110	$11,635
Unspent at publishing of report	$30,469	$10,146	$40,615
Total	$415,217	$132,224	$547,441

NOTE: Pesos converted to dollars at a four-year average of 12.04 pesos to the dollar.
SOURCE: Data from Fox Quesada (2006).

The administration did develop some initiatives to work more closely with the municipalities. The Preventive Police Standardization Program sought to create model criteria for future police development, and a pilot initiative called the Planning and Police Control System was developed in a few municipalities to improve local-level operations and internal supervision. Neither of these efforts, however, had sufficient political impetus to move beyond a pilot stage.

The Calderón Administration, SUBSEMUN, and the National System

By the time Felipe Calderón came into office in late 2006, public security had become the top political issue, and both Calderón and the head of public security, Genaro García Luna, recognized their dependence on the municipalities. Federal police made up only a fraction of the country's police force (6.5 percent in 2007) (Zepeda Lecuona 2009), and a campaign against elaborate organized criminal networks required local manpower and local knowledge. Moreover, because many local forces had fallen prey to organized crime's threats and bribes, the administration's war with these organizations was severely handicapped by corrupted municipal and state law enforcement personnel. Far more so than its predecessors, the administration accepted that strengthening local law enforcement had to be a central element in a successful long-term fight against organized crime.

Given the scope of the problem, many within the Calderón administration initially hoped to nationalize the country's police forces. A national force would, at least in theory, offer the administration a number of advantages: it would unify command, standardize procedures, facilitate implementation of needed professionalization and anti-corruption policies, and permit the rotation of officers feared to be compromised or under death threats. Many officials and commentators took as their model the Colombian National Police, which was able to clean its own house in the 1990s and subsequently dismantle the Cali drug cartel. However, such parallels had their limitations, and the proposed centralization, which would have implied major constitutional changes and undermined state and municipal sovereignty, never gained sufficient political traction (Sabet 2010).

Unable to centralize command, the Calderón administration instead used the "power of the purse" to incentivize changes at the municipal level. In 2008, the administration began the Municipal Public Security Subsidy (Subsidio de Seguridad Pública Municipal—SUBSEMUN), worth a total of close to $300 million (in addition to half-a-billion dollars provided through the FASP). Under the 2008 SUBSEMUN program, 150 of the largest and most crime-plagued municipalities were offered a large subsidy that substantially raised local police budgets. The program was expanded to 206 municipalities in 2009, and the budget increased to $344 million.[4] In order to obtain the funds, however, selected municipalities had to comply with a series of formal requirements, including:

- Matching 30 percent of the funds and dedicating these monies to police remuneration.
- Using the funds exclusively for improving communication technology, equipment purchases, infrastructure improvements, and police professionalization (i.e., not for operational and administrative expenses).
- Connecting to a shared system of national databases known as Platform Mexico (Plataforma México), adopting standardized police reports, and uploading information to a national crime database and a national registry of police.

- Developing model police units of one hundred officers who would undergo written and practical testing in seven basic areas of policing and who would submit themselves to "confidence control" procedures entailing psychological and intelligence testing, drug testing, medical examination, asset declarations and background checks, and polygraph (lie detector) testing
- Adopting a form of police civil service that determines criteria for selection, training, promotion, and discipline known as the Sistema Integral de Desarrollo Policial (Comprehensive System for Police Development – SIDEPOL).
- Adopting a national police operations manual, implementing new patrolling policies, standardizing police uniforms and vehicles, and participating in joint operations.

As this list suggests, the requirements reflected a fairly comprehensive and ambitious approach to police reform. The main tool to ensure compliance was the carrot of funding and the threat that funds could be cut off if municipalities failed to comply. In a sense, the conditions and reporting requirements made the municipalities accountable to the federal government, and federal funds gave the Calderón administration leverage that citizens had not been able to obtain with their own tax dollars.

In addition to funding these reform initiatives, the administration also sought to build a consensus around them. As discussed in the previous chapter, the tragic death of the fourteen-year-old Fernando Martí and subsequent civil society upraising led to the signing of the National Agreement on Security, Justice, and Lawfulness, which included commitments to many of the reforms that the federal government had already been pushing. The Martí tragedy allowed the federal government to, on the one hand, respond to civil society anger and, on the other hand, push the states and municipalities to commit to its reform agenda.

Finally, the administration enshrined the reform proposals into law. By shepherding a new General Law for the National Public Security System through the Mexican Congress in 2008 (published in 2009), the administration made much of the reform agenda legally binding as a "national" rather than federal initiative. Mexico's legal system is unique in that, in addition to municipal, state, and federal jurisprudince, there is also a fourth: national or constitutional legislation (SCJN 1999). The National Public Security System and its governing General Law represent a manifestation of this additional layer. As such, both the General Law and the decisions made by the National Public Security Council are legally binding for all three levels of government.[5]

In summary, by 2009 the Calderón administration had articulated a reform agenda for the municipalities, enshrined that agenda into law, built a consensus around it, funded the agenda's new mandates, and (at least in theory) shifted it from a federal policy to a national policy. Could this be enough to overcome the enormous obstacles to reform? In the following sections, I explore four different aspects of this national reform effort and the policy design and implementation challenges they have confronted thus far; these include (1) equipment purchasing, (2) Platform Mexico, (3) vetting processes, and (4) police professionalization.

The Subsidy and Equipment Purchasing

Without question, the federal subsidy represented a significant increase in local police budgets. In 2008, Tijuana, Mexicali, and Chihuahua were each provided the maximum amount of $8.6 million, while Hermosillo received $6.8 million. Although the maximum would rise again in 2010, in 2009, it was reduced to $7.9 million, which was collected by Tijuana, Mexicali, and Chihuahua, and Hermosillo received $5.9 million (Arredondo Sánchez Lira 2010). As shown in Table 7.2, SUBSEMUN money increased police budgets by between 5 percent and 35 percent in reporting municipalities. Budgets that had long been primarily dedicated to salaries now included needed investments in infrastructure, equipment, and professionalization. According to official statistics, of the $7.2 million Hermosillo received in 2010, it matched $2.2 million to improve police remuneration, increasing the public security budget by a total of 45.5 percent. The municipality reported spending the money on training, evaluation of commanding officers, cadet training, arms, uniforms, bulletproof bests, radios, pickup trucks, patrol cars, motorcycles, equipment for the SWAT team, computers, printers, digital cameras, scanners, license plate reading technology, fingerprinting equipment, GPS systems for vehicles, secure radios, and improvements to the buildings and infrastructure. Table 7.3 shows the total equipment purchases made across the 150 SUBSEMUN municipalities in 2008. From the point of view of Mexico's cash-starved, large and medium-sized municipalities, the subsidy was an unequivocal success. Of particular importance were the almost twenty-two thousand bulletproof

TABLE 7.2. Reported police budgets

	2008 budget	2008 federal money from SUBSEMUN	Federal subsides as a percent of other 2008 budgetary sources	Total 2008 spending per police officer
Guadalajara	$43,875,200	$8,647,653	24.55%	$13,832
Monterrey	$23,941,579	$4,323,719	22.04%	$29,704
Mérida	$4,620,575	$1,729,531	59.82%	$14,810
México DF	$461,606,485	$23,884,505	5.46%	$12,872
Chihuahua	$34,734,550	$8,639,960	33.11%	$30,522
Cuernavaca	$14,601,852	$747,689	5.40%	$14,425
Hermosillo	$28,465,366	$6,769,089	34.82%	$26,603

NOTE: Several cities did not provide adequate budgetary information. San Luis Potosí and Torreón provided information that appeared to be inaccurate and was excluded. There is some difficulty in comparing police budgets, as different departments include different line items in their budgets, potentially inflating or deflating a given department's budget. There are also slight rounding differences. Pesos converted to dollars at a four- year average of 12.04 pesos to the dollar.

SOURCE: Information provided by police departments in response to the author's Police Professionalism Survey administered in early 2009.

TABLE 7.3. Total 2008 SUBSEMUN equipment purchases nationwide

	Quantity	Cost	Percent
Pickup trucks	1,355	$42,751,107	24.6%
Bulletproof vests	21,991	$25,742,915	14.8%
Patrol cars	1,076	$25,450,485	14.6%
Uniforms	47,082	$18,938,638	10.9%
Tactical group equipment (SWAT)	127	$15,393,691	8.8%
Radio base	142	$12,273,717	7.0%
Radios	8,822	$12,019,011	6.9%
Motorcycles	1,248	$11,318,763	6.5%
Assault rifle ammunition	445,334	$7,076,714	4.1%
Hand guns	8,341	$1,485,342	.9%
Assault rifles	3,342	$1,415,225	.8%
Hand gun ammunition	1,516,517	$222,405	.1%
Total		$174,088,013	100.00%

NOTE: Pesos converted to dollars at a four-year average of 12.04 pesos to the dollar.

SOURCE: Data from SSP (2009).

vests and the more than 3,300 assault rifles, which would allow officers to better protect themselves from organized crime. The subsidy also allowed for the purchase of previously out-of-reach big ticket items, such as encrypted radios (another protection from organized crime), mobile command units, and license plate reading technology.

Despite the success of the program, there are inevitable challenges inherent in moving such large quantities of money. Many of these are what Chapter 2 referred to as benign implementation challenges, which can be overcome with time, effort, and human and financial resources. In the first year of the program, many municipalities failed to turn in quarterly financial reports, and the federal government lacked the capacity to effectively monitor purchasing in all 150 municipalities. In other cases, divergent interests between the federal government and the municipalities produced coordination problems. For example, municipalities were required to match 30 percent of the federal funds to improve police remuneration. Although the research cities technically complied, they did not use the money to increase salaries per se, but instead paid the money out through bonuses, compensation, awards, benefits, and other non-ordinary payments. Once raised, salaries could not be easily lowered, and municipalities did not want to commit themselves to new expenses if the permanence of the federal subsidy was not guaranteed.

The federal government, as the principal, was able to prevent most potential agency abuses of subsidy monies through ex ante controls. Rather than give the municipalities the money as block grants, the federal government provided very specific guidelines for equipment purchasing. For example, municipalities were not allowed to use subsidy funds to cover administrative and operational expenses, heading off inflation of the bureaucracy. Prior to the negotiation of the agreement, selected cities were required to facilitate a federal diagnostic study of the police force, which helped the federal government overcome information asymmetries about local needs. Based on this diagnostic study, the federal government played a key role in determining local purchases. If it was determined that a municipal department needed one hundred patrol cars, the federal government delineated the specifications of the cars and estimated the costs accordingly. A detailed agreement between the governments afforded cities very limited discretion in how the money could be spent. Furthermore, the municipalities had quarterly reporting requirements, and federal auditors were enlisted to confirm municipal purchases. Consequently, there was a robust system in place to ensure that the "agent" did not deviate from the interest of the "principal." This is not to say the problems did not occur. SUBSEMUN money is supposed to be added to already-existing public security funding; however, a high-level officer in one department reported that most of the non-SUBSEMUN funding in the city's public security budget was unofficially being diverted to other uses. There seemed to be some support for this assertion, in that after three years of federal subsidy money, the department's ratio of vehicles per ten officers (between 1.9 and 2.2) did not improve and was on the low end of the range of surveyed departments in 2008, which were presented in Chapter 2 and ranged from 1.3 to 6.8 vehicles per officer.

Federal intervention into municipal spending also risks purchases not being suited to local needs. Improvements to radio communications are illustrative of the potential problem. As discussed in Chapter 4, organized crime (or anyone with an inexpensive receiver) is able to listen in and even broadcast over standard police radio frequencies. In order to better protect police communications, the federal government promoted the adoption of encrypted radio transmitters, offering yet another means to reduce the ability of organized crime to threaten police forces. However, encrypted radios are an expensive specialty good without a proven track record, and with far less market competition than, say, police vehicles. While more than one company produces such radios, the Spanish company Matra became the preferred choice of the federal government. Confronting a monopoly, municipalities complained that Matra's prices were extremely high, not just for the equipment, but for mandatory maintenance packages many years into the future. Numerous interviewees across the research sites raised unsolicited concerns about the Matra radio purchases. The problem is reminiscent of the video camera dilemma in Tijuana discussed in Chapter 2, where cameras fell into disuse because of an exorbitant maintenance contract. The Matra radios run the same risk.[6] In fact, interviews suggest that many municipalities have purchased goods that they know they will not be able to use, reasoning that it is more important to keep the federal government happy and the flow of "free money" uninhibited than to obtain the best value for that money. One department had storage shelves full of PDAs that they were not using but had purchased because of federal insistence.

Federal purchasing guidelines have confronted other problems. Recognizing the unfortunate tradition of redesigning the image of the police force every three years (which was discussed in Chapter 3), the federal government has pressured municipalities to adopt a new style of police vehicle, badge, uniform, logo, etc. In theory, the proposal is an attempt to standardize and institutionalize the image of the police throughout all of Mexico. The Hermosillo case, however, is illustrative of how a perhaps well-intended federal policy only exacerbated the problem at the local level. Under the *panista* María Dolores del Río administration, Hermosillo's police vehicles were blue, but, as discussed earlier, blue is the color of the PAN party and generally opposed by PRI admin-istrations. When the *priísta* Ernesto Gándara Camou administration came into office, the city painted the vehicles orange. Gándara Camou argued that orange was the color of Hermosillo and a sustainable compromise between PRI and PAN governments. The *panista* Javier Gándara Magaña administra-tion continued the orange trend (although it redesigned the coloring and re-painted the vehicles of specialty units several different colors). Enter the fed-eral government, which required that dozens of vehicles purchased by the city with federal monies in 2010 be painted blue with the federally designed police logos. The city complied but responded to the federal mandate by passing a new city law requiring that all *future* police vehicles be orange. The product is police vehicles of every different color in Hermosillo. Rather than set a new standard, the Calderón administration just became one more player in the constant redesigning of the police force, leaving municipalities to wonder what colors the next administration would require.

This discussion suggests that through numerous ex ante controls the fed-eral government has reduced the opportunities for local misuse of funds. This is not to say that abuses have not occurred at the local level; however, the op-portunities have been limited by the policy design. The federal congress also limited the ability of the federal administration to politically target the funds: municipal eligibility was determined through a formula based on the average number of crimes over a nine-year period, the average number of homicides over that same period, and population.[7] Clearly, the subsidy has provided an important injection of resources, and it has offered police better tools to per-form their job, a key element of professionalization. Moreover, assault rifles, bulletproof vests, and encrypted radios reduce (although certainly do not eliminate) the threat posed by organized crime. It is, however, important to note that citizens and civil society have not been provided with an oversight role in supervising SUBSEMUN spending. Despite the limitations of federal oversight and the risk of misused or poorly used funds, the details of SUBSE-MUN purchasing are not made public, ostensibly due to security concerns. For all its enormous benefits and positive design features, the subsidy missed an opportunity to strengthen local vertical accountability.

Platform Mexico

One of the main criticisms of the police is the lack of coordination among dif-ferent departments. Unable to create a national police force, García Luna and the Calderón administration pushed to fully implement the improved communication and information system initiated by Zedillo and Fox. The result, Mexico Platform (Plataforma México), is a high-tech system connecting all the country's police departments through several different databases, including a crime database, or Unified Criminal Information System (Sistema Único de Información Criminal – SUIC) and a registry of the country's police officers, or Kardex.

Both SUBSEMUN criteria and National Public Security Council policy require departments to adopt a standardized police report form and upload crime data into the SUIC. In this way, the license plate and vehicle identification number of a car stolen in one state will be available to police in another. Platform Mexico also contains a registry of police personnel, which had become a priority because corrupt, ineffective, or abusive police were being fired from one department only to find work in a different municipality (Arteaga Botello and López Rivera 1998). In theory, if all police firings are entered into the database, then this practice could be ended. In addition to basic information about officers, the registry also has the capacity to include officers' merits and demerits, professional development, and DNA, voice, and writing samples.

Creation of the two databases might appear to be common sense, but implementing them has been challenging. Previous efforts by the Zedillo and Fox administrations in this regard were hindered by divergent categorizations for crime reporting and insufficient capacity to upload information, which typically existed only in hard copy. Because recordkeeping has been largely non-digitalized, and because there is constant turnover in police departments, the records of even basic personnel information are often poor. To offer one extreme example, confronting a situation of poorly maintained personnel files, the Ramos administration in Tijuana decided to temporarily suspend direct deposit of paychecks and required officers to sign for and pick up their checks in person. After several weeks, around two hundred individuals on the payroll had still not reported to pick up their checks, raising suspicions that at least a portion of these were receiving unjustified salaries (Salinas 2008a). As a result of this disorganization, uploading the required information at times requires a major (albeit necessary) reform of information management.

While Calderón administration documentation contends that the Mexican states and SUBSEMUN municipalities were close to 100 percent compliance with the police registry and uniform police report,[8] interviews suggested that challenges continue. In their March 2009 and August 2009 analysis of the implementation of the National Agreement for Security, Justice, and Legality, a collection of citizens' groups gave the government a rating of "low" (on a scale of low, medium, and high) for its efforts to interconnect "the systems and protocols of Platform Mexico for the registry, access, and analysis of substantive information" (MUCD 2009a; MUCD 2009b).

Some of the obstacles confronting Plataforma México are benign implementation challenges. Even when the databases are in use, they are not necessarily exploited to their potential. As one SSP official put it in 2009, "While everyone has it [Plataforma México] and is connected, there is a difference between having it and using it." For example, while in theory an officer's file should contain any merits, demerits, courses taken, DNA, writing and voice samples, etc., interviews suggest that in practice, uploaded information is very basic. This applies to police reports as well, as local police are often unaccustomed to filling out detailed police reports. As a result, even where the standardized form was adopted, only the most basic fields were completed.

As with equipment purchasing, however, some implementation challenges are more complex. Because of the wealth of knowledge and sensitive information contained in the Plataforma México databases, federal authorities strictly control use. To obtain access, municipalities are to form an analysis unit, whose members are to undergo rigorous vetting and, upon selection, detailed training. Personal at different levels of security clearance are then to be able to access different levels of data through the system. With a limited pool of users, the system is in theory able to track users' activity and detect potential security breaches. Nonetheless, the need to preserve confidentiality has fostered a perception that the federal government is more interested in obtaining access to local-level crime data than to providing local authorities with information. The case of Chihuahua is illustrative.

Chihuahua was one of several municipalities that had implemented a geographically referenced crime analysis system, whereby neighborhood-level crime data was collected in real time and analyzed on a weekly basis. Local commanders were provided with weekly reports to help inform their decision making. For several years, Chihuahua even used a New York-style CompStat system where commanders were held to account for increases in crime in their districts. As such, Chihuahua had many years of experience electronically inputting crime reports and analyzing crime data. In theory, Plataforma México could allow for the same type of data analysis, but local interviewees complained that even cleared individuals could do little more than conduct individual searches to, for example, determine if a detainee had a previous criminal offense in another state. Even the head of Chihuahua's statistical analysis unit was unable to access the very data that Chihuahua was inputting into the system. Consequently, Chihuahuan police personnel complained that they were uploading their data to Plataforma México and then uploading it a second time to their own databases.

Because of problems accessing the system, as of late 2010, in both Hermosillo and Chihuahua, police cadet names were run through the police registry only *after* their cadet training. Consequently, ex-officers were accepted as cadets, provided months of training at great expense to the municipalities, and then not admitted to the police force when their previous employment was discovered. As a result of all these factors, use of the system has lagged behind expectations. Despite the enormous potential, several officials interviewed viewed Plataforma México as something designed to benefit the federal government rather than their own department.

Vetting

The process of vetting, or trust or confidence control tests, as they are referred to in Mexico (*control de confianza*), has been the cornerstone of the Calderón administration's effort to clean up Mexico's local police forces. Municipal police agencies that received the federal subsidy were asked to form model units of one hundred and to send candidates for a multiday examination. In addition to a written exam in basic police knowledge and practical examinations in seven areas of policing, police also had to pass medical tests, a psychological evaluation, drug testing for five drugs, a lie detector test, and a socioeconomic study.[9] Tests were initially conducted by the federal government; however, this authority passed to the states, which were to be accredited by a national center by the beginning of 2012.[10] By the beginning of 2013, all police nationwide were to have successfully passed confidence control tests and to be certified by a state evaluation center.

Although official certification would take time, testing began immediately. Municipal presidents and police chiefs were provided with a list of tested officers divided into those who were recommended, those who were not recommended, and those who were not recommended with risk. No additional information was provided. In the beginning, non-recommended officers were to be excluded only from the model units, but starting in 2009, municipalities reported pressure from the Calderón administration to fire any officers who failed to pass the tests.

In the first year of operation, the administration reported that thousands of municipal police were subjected to integrity control tests.[11] Most major departments had some experience with the different tests; however, the socioeconomic study, verifying asset declarations with house visits and interviews with family members, colleagues, and neighbors, was typically not done in great depth, and the lie detector test was entirely new for all but a handful of municipalities. Former personnel from the federal intelligence agency (CISEN) took the lead in the expansion. CISEN had developed specialized skills in comprehensive integrity control tests over the previous decade and a half, and they had helped replicate the testing in other government agencies and even in other countries. Such a rapid, nationwide expansion, however, was entirely new. While admirable for its sheer size and ambition, expansion of a complex test over a short period of time was bound to confront implementation challenges. Conducting polygraph tests, for example, is a skill that takes years of experience, training, professional development, and mentorship. Lacking such human resources, the Calderón administration had to rapidly train hundreds of polygraphists. Those close to the process report a number of irregularities, including preliminary interviews conducted in groups rather than individually, tests run by inexperienced and overworked polygraphists, and exams squeezed into extremely shortened time intervals. The result has been inaccurate and unreliable tests.

There are, however, more fundamental policy *design* problems. Of course, trust control tests could be an enormously important tool for improving police forces. In some cases, they have successfully identified ties to criminal groups and led eventually to successful prosecutions. In addition, fear of the test led some corrupt officers to defect. Interview respondents generally were supportive of using test results to screen applicants to the department and to disqualify aspirants for positions of leadership. In addition, several interviewees felt that the tests should help raise red flags for investigation. Nonetheless, there is no test that can accurately and consistently distinguish between a good, honest officer and a corrupt cop, regardless of the quality of the examiner. Despite the promise of lie detector tests, research has found that they produce unreliable results, can be fooled, and are highly dependent on the interviewer (Honts and Perry 1992). As a result, most judicial systems, including Mexico's, do not permit lie detector tests to be submitted as evidence in court proceedings.

Rather than recognize these weaknesses, however, the Calderón administration has made the confidence control testing the basis for its anticorruption strategy. The administration took three important measures to avoid the legal repercussions of an unreliable test. First, the administration altered the burden of proof. According to the General National Public Security System Law, a failed trust test is not so much a reason to be fired; rather, a positive test is required to stay on the force. Second, as discussed in Chapter 4, the Calderón administration successfully promoted a constitutional amendment that prohibits officers from reinstatement after dismissal. As such, officers let go from the force for failing to meet the trust control requirement can be awarded a severance by the courts, but the courts cannot reinstate the officer. Third, and most Kafkaesque, the results of the test are integral, confidential, and cannot be appealed. *Integral* means that the evaluation centers combine all the information from the socioeconomic tests, the polygraph tests, the psychological tests, etc. and emit one final ruling. Little is known about what criteria are used or even who makes this determination. Officers who fail the test are not able to find out why they failed, and they have no means by which to appeal the results. Federal officials report in interviews that these measures were designed to prevent organize crime from learning about and fooling the test; however, they also have the effect of covering over any flaws in the testing process.

In late 2008, following a request from the Mexican Congress, the administration released data on how many exams had been conducted and what percent of officers were recommended for service. The results of 26,165 separate tests were not encouraging. Nationwide, only 30.1 percent of the police tested were recommended, 61.6 percent were not recommended, and 8.3 percent either did not finish the testing or the tests were still in progress. Of the three states examined here, only Baja California had a substantial number of police tested; shockingly only 3.9 percent of tested officers were recommended. One research municipality reported in 2010 that only 142 of 600 (23.7 percent) had passed. Of those who failed, ninety-two were considered a risk.

Throughout the research sites, interviewees reported a high degree of skepticism toward the tests. Critics pointed to high-profile cases where the vetting process failed to identify or result in the firing of corrupt officers. For example, Víctor Gerardo Garay Cadena, former interim head of the Federal Preventive Police, had been subject to integrity control tests on three different occasions prior to being arrested for collaborating with the Beltran Leyva brothers (El Financiero 2008). Lorena González Hernández, a federal police officer who participated in the kidnapping of Fernando Martí (whose death led to marches protesting insecurity), had also been subject to integrity control tests (Medellín 2008b). Interviewees pointed to similar cases at the local level, such as a district commander in Tijuana who was recommended but later confessed to collusion with organized crime (*Zeta* 2009e).

Police leaders across the research sites reported that good officers whom they fully trusted failed the tests and officers that they were confident were corrupt were recommended. One skeptical chief went so far as to only send officers he was confident were either completely honest or completely corrupt. The results came back contradictory. In Baja California, both the state and the federal government operated separate trust control tests. Municipal police leaders reported that some officers passed the state tests and failed the federal tests while others failed the state tests and passed the federal tests. As one official complained, "SIEDO [federal police] took away two officers to Mexico City for organized crime ties. The two had passed their exams, but personnel with a good record in the department, without complaints, and with good parents and wives failed." Leaders also expressed particular frustration that they were not provided with any additional information but simply told to fire the officers. From their point of view, they were hesitant to ignore the policing history of an officer in favor of an unreliable test from federal authorities.

One police chief, who personally did not believe that the results were reliable, admitted to acquiescing and firing a percentage to appease the federal government.[12] To compensate for what he regarded as an injustice, he worked behind the scenes to place some of these officers into other municipal jobs. Other cities tried to hold firm against federal pressure. Despite reforms at the federal level, state law in Sonora had still not been normed to the federal legislation and still provided strict labor protections. As such, it was still technically illegal to fire officers for failing the tests at the time that federal authorities were pressuring municipal leaders to do so. As one interviewee opposed to the tests stated, "In the beginning it makes you angry—to feel so powerless. You say that you can't do it because of the law and they tell you, 'Do it.' But you can't; there are state laws that say that you can't."

If police leaders felt that there was a degree of arbitrariness in the tests, this sentiment was even stronger among officers interviewed. As one of many officers stated:

> I don't think that the results are very reliable. I had a partner, who I learned a great deal from, and we worked together. He was an honest officer, but he came out bad [on the test]. He was a good police officer but they fired him. In

the polygraph test there is a lot of pressure. They kept asking me the same three questions. [When you fail] they don't tell you where you failed. They need to give you an explanation if they fire you.

Partially as a consequence of the opacity of the process, several officers interviewed viewed the tests as an excuse for the police chief and operational commanders to fire people whom they did not like. This claim is not so unbelievable when police chiefs themselves admit that they are firing police to appease federal officials. One of the primary arguments for a robust accountability mechanism is that a commitment to fire and punish police involved in misconduct sends a strong message to remaining members of the force. In the case of confidence control tests, however, this message has been diluted by a sense that the firings are arbitrary and are not the product of legitimate misconduct. Instead officers doubt that many of their fired colleagues were involved in misconduct and do not trust that those who remain on the force are not infiltrated by organized crime.

Proponents interviewed at the federal level accepted that some good cops might be caught up with the bad, and some interviewees recognized that the process should be amended, but they also feared that such draconian methods were necessary given the failure of local accountability mechanisms. From a policy perspective, federal officials cannot ensure that internal affairs departments and Honor and Justice Commissions are functioning effectively, but they can oversee the integrity control tests. While perhaps this view is understandable, there appears to be no shortcuts. Integrity control tests are an enormously important advance; however, given their unreliability, they should serve as a complement to investigative mechanisms, not as a replacement for them. As one police chief commented, "Yes, it's an indicator and sign, but it is not 100% conclusive nor convincing." Unfortunately, as Chapter 4 demonstrated, local accountability mechanisms are still unwilling to tackle corruption. Having placed its bet on confidence control testing, federal pressure has to date not helped strengthen these local tools. It should also be mentioned that confidence control tests ignore the rotten barrel. While police officials proudly announce large-scale firings of officers and commanders, such actions do little good if their shoes are filled by new recruits and new commanders who, facing the same perverse incentives, also become corrupted.

Police Civil Service—SIDEPOL

Perhaps the most ambitious aspect of federally promoted police reform is a package of initiatives designed to create a police civil service, dignify policing, and construct a well-trained and well-educated police force. As part of the New Police Model (Nuevo Modelo Policial), the National Public Security Council approved the Comprehensive Police Development System (Sistema Integral del Desarrollo Policial - SIDEPOL) in early 2009. The program lays out a police career path entailing mandates and guidelines for recruitment, selection, cadet training, ongoing in-service training, promotion, and dismissal or retirement.

Selection is to be based on a similar vetting process to that discussed above. If candidates are certified by the state trust control center, then they become eligible to join the force. Once on the force, SIDEPOL proposes that officers will continue to take courses and training, which will become requirements for moving up a new set of standardized ranks, ranging from Police, to Officer, to Inspector, to Commissioner, with incremental steps in between. As reflected in Table 7.4, moving up each step in the ranking requires meeting certain education standards in addition to other criteria. By the time a police officer has risen from Police to Third Police, he or she will have a vocational high school degree, by the rank of First Police a technical degree, and by the rank of Sub-Inspector a college degree (SSP 2009c). Officers who repeatedly fail to meet the requirements to rise up through the ranks are to be let go.

If implemented, the program would certainly lead to a better-trained and educated police force in an environment where most police currently only have a junior high school education. This would likely increase the sense of professionalism within the police and lead to a superior service to the community. More important, SIDEPOL would help build a solid police institution less susceptible to the capriciousness and short-term political time horizons of city mayors. The creation of a promotion system based on measurable phenomenon means that city and police leaders would have a harder time assigning ranks to friends, colleagues, and political clients who fail to meet these core qualifications.

It is still too early to determine how the program, which is outlined in new federal legislation, clarified by the SNSP, and slowly being incorporated into state and municipal legislation, will manifest itself in practice.[13] The effort confronts a number of implementation challenges. At the most basic level,

TABLE 7.4. Ranks and new educational requirements under SIDEPOL

Rank	Years required before promotion	Role	Level of education
Commissioner General	.	Direction	
Commissioner Chief	2		
Commissioner	2		
Inspector General	2	Planning and Coordination	Specialization and advanced study
Inspector Chief	2		
Inspector	2		
Assistant Inspector	2		
Official	3	Supervision, interaction	University degree
Assistant Official	3		
First Police	3	Operation and execution	Technical degree
Second Police	3		Vocational high school degree
Third Police	3		
TBL:Police	3		

NOTE: Other official publications provide different categorical divisions and even slightly different ranks. For example, one places subinspector as part of the officer group and distinguishs between first and second officer.
SOURCE: Information from *Sistema Integral de Desarrollo Policial*. 2009. Mexico City: Secretaría de Seguridad Pública.

Mexico lacks the police-training capacity and educational infrastructure to be able to offer such coursework in the short or medium term. In theory, the federal government had hoped to address this problem through a technological solution. As part of the SUBSEMUN criteria for 2009, police departments were required to build a virtual classroom that could be used for distance learning; however, there is as of yet insufficient bandwidth for such methods. Although most would agree that the training and education program represents a necessary long-term investment in departments' human resources, as Chapter 2 illustrates, police and city leaders have been reluctant to reduce officers hours for far less demanding training purposes, much less for such an ambitious program. To date, the educational plan laid out by SIDEPOL is an aspirational goal rather than a realistic one; nonetheless, the Chihuahua City experience suggests that a comprehensive educational program is possible. By working with local educational institutions and civil society, a police chief committed to education was able to achieve many of the objectives of SIDEPOL.

The more fundamental obstacle, however, will be insulating the promotion process from patronage-based promotion criteria. As discussed in Chapter 3, municipal and police leaders have successfully resisted surrendering their discretion to name their subordinates despite local legal reform efforts. Federal officials contend that municipalities will have to comply with SIDE-POL if they want continued access to SUBSEMUN resources. The 2011 SUBSE-MUN rules indicate that funding can be cut for failure to comply with the new police model, along with twenty-seven other requirements (Diario Oficial de la Federación 2011). In the first three years of the program, however, funds were only cut off for financial reasons, and in most of the cases, because municipalities lacked the capacity to spend subsidy money consistent with federal guidelines.

Conclusion

In many ways, federal efforts, which include legal reforms, a large subsidy, and a pacted national consensus, offer an unprecedented opportunity for local level reform. The federal subsidy has allowed municipalities to make long-needed investments in equipment and infrastructure: resources that will allow police to better carry out their mission and protect themselves from organized crime. Through ex ante controls, the Calderón administration has reduced the opportunity for local abuse of funds; through a distribution formula, the Mexican Congress has limted opportunity for partisan manipulation of resources, and matching fund conditions compel a financial commitment on the part of the municipalties. Plataforma México represents the culmination of efforts across three federal administrations. In contrast to 1994, Mexico now has 066 call centers servicing almost the entire country and a networked system of databases, with increasingly reliable information. Confidence control tests, while problematic in their current application, offer a new tool for desperately needed accountability. Finally SIDEPOL, although far from implementation, at least offers a clearly articulated plan to improve the professionalism of the police by dramatically reforming police training and the process for determining promotions.

In theory, a rigorous monitoring and enforcement regime could compel local leaders to fully implement SIDEPOL and other policy requirements; however, federal leaders have understandably focused their oversight efforts on monitoring the use of federal funds rather than the more complex policy requirements. Many observers are, however, understandably ambivalent about strict federal enforcement because of the risk that the federal government will misuse its leverage over the municipalities and/or enforce the implementation of policies unsuited to local environments. The potential for political manipulation of SUBSEMUN funding has been reduced by a funding formula; nonetheless, difficulty in accessing Plataforma México data, only limited discretion in expensive purchases such as encrypted radios, and the lack of information accompanying trust control measures suggest that reform efforts have not always been designed to empower local decision makers. In addition, several of the required policies appear unsuited to the cities in which they are to be implemented. All of the research sites ignored a federal requirement that police patrol in groups of three: a requirement that all four departments felt was unrealistic. More advanced departments like Chihuahua worry that they will have to backtrack on local innovations to comply with federal requirements.

For federally driven reform to be successful, therefore, it must achieve two contradictory goals: it must allow for local level decision making while enforcing rules and ensuring accountability. Overcoming this contradiction likely requires using federal reform efforts to strengthen horizontal and vertical accountability mechanisms at the local level. By making information publically available and involving citizen councils and observatories in oversight of reform efforts, citizens, rather than the federal government, will be in a better position to hold their local leaders accountable.

8 Looking Forward

Still Faced with Two Realities

In Chapter 1, I argued that there were two realities within Mexican policing. On the one hand, police leaders can point to a host of reform efforts, new policies, firings of corrupt cops, and arrests of important criminals, suggesting that the police are undergoing a major transformation. Throughout the course of this book, I have explored numerous efforts to improve selection criteria, training programs, salaries and benefits, promotion procedures, administrative and operational procedures, and accountability mechanisms. Furthermore, a major federal commitment to local police reform beginning in 2008 suggests that Mexico's police forces are undergoing profound change. There is a danger in failing to recognize how far municipal police in Mexico have come.

On the other hand, the average citizen certainly could not be blamed for thinking that the police have never been more corrupt and untrustworthy. Despite numerous reform initiatives, Mexico's security crisis has progressively worsened, and organized crime continues to operate with impunity. Every week seems to bring new revelations of police involvement in criminal organizations, and day-to-day corruption to forgive traffic tickets and avoid infractions continues unabated. It is hard to contest the commonly held fear of many observers that the numerous reform efforts in Mexico's municipal police are mere simulations designed to appease a frustrated electorate.

I refer to this as "the two realities" because paradoxically, both perspectives are correct. To make sense of this seeming contradiction, it is necessary to understand that police reform is made up of a basket of reform policies. Police and city leaders have made significant advances on some of these policies. Despite a series of ongoing implementation problems, it is clear that on balance there has been positive change in the following areas:

- Selection criteria: Even prior to new federal requirements, some municipalities had already begun to require a high-school level of education and to apply drug, knowledge, medical, and psychological testing along with background checks. More robust confidence control tests required by new legislation will serve to further strengthen these filters.

- Training for cadets and in-service officers: In contrast to the past, incoming police receive cadet training, and many departments now require annual in-service training. Several departments offer additional educational opportunities, and numerous police interviewed are pursuing undergraduate and graduate degrees.

- Equipment purchases: With the help of a large federal subsidy beginning in 2008, municipalities invested heavily in police infrastructure, equipment, and technology. The four research sites all have geographically referenced crime maps, GPS tracking of new police vehicles, standardized handguns and assault rifles, bulletproof vests, and cameras throughout the city, among other technological improvements.

- Operational and administrative procedures: While a traditionally under-prioritized arena, Chihuahua gained international notoriety by obtaining certification from the U.S.-based Commission on Accreditation for Law Enforcement Agencies (CALEA). In light of Chihuahua's success, many large municipalities, including Mexicali, have followed suit.

- Salary and benefits: Although salaries and benefits still pale in comparison with U.S. police officers, police in Mexico's large cities earn far more than they used to, with salaries rising as high has $1,200 a month in Tijuana. Police in these locations also have access to better benefits.

Of course, these improvements are not without their shortcomings. As I discussed throughout the book, they have confronted and continue to confront considerable challenges of policy design, implementation, and, most important, institutionalization. Successful efforts to develop selection criteria and training by one administration could be and have been rolled back by subsequent administrations guided by a "limited-discretion" vision of policing that erroneously (in my view) recommends limiting police authority and increasing the size of the force. In addition, it is important to note that this study has focused on Mexico's large municipalities. Evidence suggests that progress has been far slower and more uneven in police forces operating in Mexico's medium and small cities and towns.

Even in the large cities, however, and even when the design, implementation, and institutionalization challenges have been largely overcome, advances in the above areas have been insufficient to produce an honest, effective police force protective of individual rights. In many respects, the above areas of improvement are the lower-hanging fruit of police reform. City officials, police leaders, mid-level commanders, and line-level officers do not stand to lose from investing federal dollars in purchasing better equipment. And yet, city officials and police leaders might be negatively affected (at least in the short term) by a dramatic reduction in their discretion to dole out rank and command. In addition, those who benefit from corruption, including corrupt officers and organized crime, can be expected to resist efforts to develop robust accountability mechanisms and oversight. Because of the enormous collective action problems inherent in building merit-based promotion and robust accountability mechanisms, these reforms have been largely left pending.

However, it would be a mistake to conclude that these two areas of reform have been entirely ignored. Municipalities have passed regulations detailing merit-based promotion and established a myriad of agencies to address misconduct. Nonetheless, these formal policies and laws are outweighed by informal rules of clientelism and tolerance toward corruption. In practice, police chiefs rarely outlast a given administration, and leadership changes produce turnover in the upper- and mid-level command structure. Commanders interviewed reported seeing their fortunes rise and fall (along with their paychecks) with changes in administration. Furthermore, Honor and Justice Commissions, internal affairs units, citizen outreach offices, and human rights commissions barely scratch the surface of misconduct, do not focus on the rotten barrel, and avoid responsibility for organized crime infiltration. Given the legacy of corruption, inadequate system of carrots to reward professional policing with promotion, and the absence of sticks to punish police misconduct, well-trained, well-equipped, and well-paid officers still lack sufficient incentives for honest, effective policing respectful of individual rights.

Federal efforts have sought to alter this status quo. In theory, the proposed police civil service (SIDEPOL) should replace the informal rules of clientelism; however, municipalities are only in the very early stages of implementation, and, if history is any guide, SIDEPOL confronts serious challenges. In addition, recognizing the limited capacity to gather evidence and build criminal cases against corrupt officers, the federal government has focused national policy on integrity control tests. While confidence control has led to dramatic firings, police and police leaders doubt the veracity of the tests and worry that innocent police are being fired while infiltrated officers remain on the force.

Fundamentally, few actors at any level of government seem willing to confront the risks of crossing organized crime or even taking on day-to-day bribe payments. The addressing of informal rules of patronage and corruption tolerance remain the hardest fruit to reach on the tree of reform. Arguably, Lt. Colonel Julián Leyzaola's tenure heading the Tijuana police represents one possible exception to the tendency to shy away from addressing corruption and organized crime infiltration. Absent institutionalized accountability mechanisms, Leyzaola was accused of going to the opposite extreme and torturing police officers believed to have links to organized crime. Leyzaola's controversial "success" in Tijuana has been the topic of both an international and national debate, causing one profiler to ask, "Leyzaola: Hero, Villain, or Both?" (Alvarado 2010). Regardless of the answer, Leyzaola himself recognized the need for stronger institutions and less arbitrary processes. Summarizing the fundamental problem that underlies this research, Leyzaola stated:

> Tijuana is a three year old child. It will never pass three years. It starts growing, after a year it begins to walk, and when it begins to walk well, to speak, it is cut short, and it is born again. No one has had sufficient consciousness, the institutional orientation necessary, to give continuity to programs, to give continuity to development. Everyone wants to be the patron saint of the city. Everyone wants to be it. And no one has achieved it, because they don't have any idea of what an institution really is. (Alvarado 2010)

But if the Formal Rules Don't Work . . . ?

The inability to apply the formal rules ostensibly governing the police creates a serious policy dilemma. How does one reform a policy if policies are ignored or worked around? How does one ensure that policies continue in future administrations, when the discretion of the executive is more powerful than the laws and institutions of governance? It is not that policy design is not important; it certainly is. In the area of accountability, internal affairs units fail by design: existing accountability mechanisms respond to citizen complaints and focus on individual incidents; they are not designed to address the institutional incentives that give rise to corruption (the rotten barrel). Nonetheless, policy design and the formal rules are only half of the story in an environment where such rules conflict with a long history of day-to-day behavior supported by culture, habit, and custom.

Reformers have two possible and complementary responses to this dilemma: they can attempt to persuade a critical mass of police officers, officials, and citizens of the desirability of new rules (i.e., reform the informal rules) or they can aggressively enforce the new rules (i.e., supersede the informal rules). There is an ongoing debate on the relative importance of culture and enforcement in understanding corruption. As discussed in Chapter 5, Fisman and Miguel's (2007) innovative research suggests that effective enforcement can override contradictory informal rules, but enforcement is only a temporary solution in an environment of constant turnover.

Alternatively, enforcement might be achieved through greater external oversight. As discussed throughout this book, the executive, city council, citizens, civil society, and federal government all offer potential avenues for police oversight. As is natural in a representative democracy, many have turned to the mayor for a solution to the police. Unchecked by a strong institution, civil service rules, or an independent city council, municipal presidents are able to quickly adopt new reform initiatives. As this research has shown, however, the authority of the executive has served as more of a curse than a blessing. Given the overwhelming discretion of the municipal executive, the continuity of reform efforts depends not on laws or society, but on the subsequent mayor. As three years is not enough time to confront the many implementation challenges and/or alter the informal rules within the police, advances are dependent on political champions, and risk falling apart once their champion leaves office. In short, executive control is part of the problem rather than part of the solution.

In theory, the city council could oversee the executive, the police, and the correct application of municipal regulations. In fact, the city council does have the power to pass municipal legislation, solicit information from the police, and obligate the police chief to provide public testimony. However, electoral rules tend to grant mayors a loyal supermajority on the council, and empirically, the councils have not played a meaningful oversight role.

Notwithstanding the possibility of internal drivers of reform from frustrated police and city officials, oversight and demand for reform continuity could and should come directly from citizens. Without question citizens are angry at the status quo, dissatisfied with the police, and frustrated by police misconduct and abuse. Moreover, while administrations come and go, citizens remain. Unfortunately, the short time horizons created by elections and rules of no reelection have likely exacerbated the problem, fomenting dramatic policy reform proposals but producing little meaningful change. The limitations of elections, however, do not preclude and, in fact, highlight the need for greater direct accountability mechanisms. Powerful public commissions investigating police misconduct and citizen review boards have been important tools in the U.S. experience for more direct citizen oversight; however, these methods have not been tried in the Mexican context. Instead, Mexico has preferred citizen public security councils with very limited oversight authority, inviting criticism of yet another simulation. While one can point to successful councils, such as Baja California's state council in the mid-2000s, citizen oversight, like police reform in general, appears to depend more on the support of the executive than on the formal laws or the strength of civil society. To date, proposed "citizen observatories," which are to monitor and collect reliable data on both the process and impact of policing strategies, have not emerged as significant actors. Nonetheless, such tools have proven successful in other Latin American countries, and offer a potential mechanism to overcome information asymmetries between the citizens and the police.

Instead of strengthening vertical accountability mechanisms between citizens and their police, Mexico is moving in a direction of greater accountability to the federal government. The federal government's ability to turn on or off the flow of needed funds to local governments could significantly alter the incentives at the local level. Without question the SUBSEMUN program has been a transformative boom to municipal police departments, and ex ante controls and financial oversight have reduced opportunities for local abuses. Federal government intervention has led to the firing of thousands of officers and could lead to a police civil service; however, perceptions of organized crime infiltration and corruption continue apace, and SIDEPOL implementation is only in its early phases. Moreover, accountability to the federal government requires that federal officials overcome the huge logistical challenge to overseeing the country's many municipal forces. While it is relatively easy for the federal government to confirm that a city has amended its municipal regulations to match federal criteria, it is far more difficult to monitor if those regulations are put in practice. This inability to detect "simulations" could be overcome, however, if federal initiatives strengthen local horizontal and vertical accountability mechanisms. Public information developed and analyzed by citizen observatories with data on both police outcomes and police reform processes offers an important avenue for future reform.

The police have changed in significant and measurable ways since the mid-1990s; however, many public officials still fail to appreciate problems produced by discontinuity, tend to underestimate the strength of informal rules, resist strengthening accountability mechanisms, are unwilling to investigate the deaths of assassinated officers, and turn a blind eye to day-to-day corruption. Unfortunately, rather than focus on overcoming these many challenges to reform, since 2009 the primary public discussion has focused on a proposed dramatic restructuring of the local police into unified state police forces.

Policía Única: Radical Reform?

Given the continued problems of police abuse, corruption, and ineffectiveness, in September 2009 the federal Secretary of Public Security Genaro García Luna went before the Mexican Congress and promoted the consolidation of the municipal police under state control: a proposal that would become known as the *mando único* or *policía única* (unitary command or unitary police). The primary argument in favor of a unified state police is the failure of the current system and the strong sense that radical change is needed. Proponents argue that a unified police force would solve the severe coordination problems that have plagued Mexico's response to the security crisis. Admittedly, the cross-jurisdictional conflict has at times been shocking, including several incidents of actual confrontations between different police forces (Tapia 2009b). Concern over the bureaucratic infighting among Mexican police led Davis (2008) to provocatively argue that:

> Mexico's deepening democracy has overly complicated the difficult task of police reform by creating an environment of obsessive partisan competition, which, combined with a democratization-led decentralization of the state and an attendant fragmentation of its coercive and administrative apparatus,

exacerbates intrastate and bureaucratic conflicts so as to prevent the government from reforming the police sufficiently to guarantee public security and citizen trust (60).

In his study of police reform in Latin America, Ungar (2011) also concludes that decentralization has led to an unnecessary proliferation and fractionalization of policing in federal systems like Mexico, Brazil, and Venezuela. By contrast, proponents of unification point to the two success stories of police reform in the region: Chile (Candina 2006) and Colombia (de Francisco Z. 2006), which are centralized, military-oriented national police forces organized under the ministry of defense. Finally, proponents also contend that unification could facilitate the implementation of SIDEPOL, the integration of Plataforma México, and the effectiveness of other federal initiatives. Rather than oversee compliance among over two thousand police forces, the federal government would have a much easier time holding thirty-one states and the Federal District accountable.

In March, 2010 the proposal picked up political momentum when the National Conference of Governors (CONAGO) gave its unanimous approval (El Universal 2010a). Since that time, the measure has earned many supporters but also some detractors. Although the unified police model was championed by the Calderón administration, ideologically the president's PAN party has always been an advocate of decentralization, and, as such, some party militants broke ranks with the president. The country's various municipal associations also lined up against the proposal, along with a number of important mayors.

There are several different visions of what the unified police will or could mean. The initial Calderón proposal envisioned unification of the state investigative, state preventive, and municipal departments into one police force in each of Mexico's thirty-one states and the Federal District. In theory, municipalities could maintain their own force if they met very strict criteria, although their chief would be appointed and could be removed by the governor. Alternative proposals envision only merging the municipal and state preventive police or consolidating the country's small and medium police forces while preserving the big-city police.

On the one hand, the conclusions of this study support dissolving the municipal police. Chapter 3 argued that three-year municipal administrations with weak horizontal accountability mechanisms, concentration of authority in the mayor's office, no-reelection, and a patronage-based appointment system made it extremely difficult to implement and institutionalize reform efforts. This would suggest that the municipalities are unfit to handle public security, and that policing authority would be better placed in the hands of the states.

On the other hand, there are a several problems with this conclusion. Most of the formal and informal rules that exist at the municipal level also exist at the state level. States confront the same formal rules of no-reelection, and the same mix of formal and informal rules that place power in the hands of the executive, limit checks and balances, and allow for patronage appointments deep into the bureaucracy. Appointments at the state level, like those at the municipal level, continue to prioritize personal trust over ability and knowledge. For example, despite (or perhaps because of) the security crisis raging throughout the country, upon arrival into office in 2009, the new governor of Sonora, Guillermo Padres Elías, appointed as his top public security cabinet minister a trusted friend who publically admitted having no knowledge of or experience in public security issues. Padres Elías's predecessor, Eduardo Bours Castelo, had also prioritized personal trust over proven ability and even the law. Midway through his administration, he appointed to the position an inexperienced political operative who did not even meet the state's minimum thirty-year age requirement for the position.

One also confronts the same allegations of corruption, abuse, and ineffectiveness at the state level as at the municipal level. According to a study among prison inmates, a suspect is more likely to be asked for a bribe by state investigative police than by the local preventive police (Azaola and Bergman 2007). Even if corruption is perceived to be greatest at the municipal level, it is likely due to the fact that local officers have the most contact with the population and the most opportunities for corruption. In other words, police misconduct is driven by the nature of contact, not by the level of government.

To some extent, the primary difference between governance at the state and municipal level is that state administrations last six years as opposed to the three years of municipal administrations. While this would give state administrations three additional years to implement reforms, such initiatives would still confront the problem of institutionalization. For decades, the Sonoran ministerial police was known as the Judicial Police (Policía Judicial). Under the Bours administration (2003–09) they became the Ministerial Police (Policía Ministerial), and under the Padres Elías administration (2009–13) they were renamed the Investigative Police (Agencia Estatal de Investigaciones).

Even at the federal level, there is a tendency to reinvent public security policy in each administration. The de la Madrid administration (1982–88) dissolved the Federal Security Directorate, Zedillo (1994–2000) purged the judicial police and created the Federal Preventive Police, Fox (2000–06) dissolved the judicial police and created the AFI, and Calderón (2006–12) created the Federal Police and undermined the AFI. Even though the AFI had been the flagship public security reform of the Fox administration, six years after its creation, the attorney general's office reported that over two thousand of its officers had been under investigation and 10 percent of the force fired (Otero 2006). Herein lays one of the great paradoxes of police reform in Mexico. Seemingly dramatic changes, such as dissolving one police force and creating an entirely new one, might in practice amount to very little actual reform of how policing is done.

The real problem is not decentralization per se, but politics—and the way decentralization interacts with the informal rules of Mexican politics. Davis (2008), in her above-mentioned critique of interjurisdictional conflict in Mexico, is not as critical of decentralization as she is of the tendency of elected officials to attempt to centralize power within their realm of authority for their own political ambitions. The tendency to constantly reinvent the police is another manifestation of the vicious cycle that exists between citizens and officials. Deeply unsatisfied, citizens demand change, and elected officials continue to provide them with "change"—new police leaders, new policies, and new police forces—but the informal rules are unaffected, and meaningful institutional change remains elusive. Rather than produce meaningful reform, the demand for change has the unintended effect of concentrating authority in the executive, undermining the police as an institution, and actually exacerbating the problems of the police. Ungar (2011), who is critical of the fractionalization of police forces, recognizes this vicious cycle when he writes:

> Indeed, the impediments to citizen security reform spring from the same processes that create it. Politically, governments are often so pressured by panicked societies to deliver short-term results that they discard ministers and policies at a rate often directly proportionate to their inabilities to face down the entrenched agencies with the most to lose from reform but with the greatest ability to block it. (21)

Unfortunately, even the problem of coordination would probably not be resolved by a unified police. While the plan would in theory address coordination between the states and the municipalities, this is not the crux of Mexico's coordination problem. The real dilemma lies between the federal police and state police forces. Homicides are state crimes, for which state authorities have primary responsibility. Organized crime and the use of weapons solely authorized for the military, (e.g. assault rifles), however, are federal crimes. In theory, an organized crime-related homicide committed with an assault rifle should overlap jurisdictions; instead, however, it falls through a large hole. In Chihuahua and many other states, state authorities conduct only the most cursory investigations, concluding that killings are out of their jurisdiction. Federal authorities protest that the states still have responsibility for investigating what is clearly a homicide, and, from a practical point of view, they note that they lack the capacity to investigate the country's thousands of annual organized crime-related killings, which make up the majority of homicides. A newspaper report likened trying to determine the results of police investigations to a game of ping-pong where the responsibility bounces between the state and federal attorney generals' offices (Veledíaz 2009). The real problem is that state investigators fear organized crime retributions, and, in fact, many investigators have been killed in the line of duty, particularly in Chihuahua. The result has been impunity. Worse yet, several years of organized crime-related killings have failed to produce a sustainable consensus between state administrations and federal authorities. Even the cases of assassinated police officers fall into this black hole (Yáñez Romero 2009).

Opponents of the unified police proposal also worry that state-led police will not be responsive to the needs of local communities. The ideological premise behind three decades of decentralization in Mexico was that government closer to the public will be more responsive to citizens and act based on local knowledge and local needs. Research from the United States suggests that solutions to neighborhood-based crime problems require local knowledge and often neighborhood-specific strategies (Ostrom and Whitaker 1999). There are also worries that municipalities not of the same political party as the governor will receive worse service than politically aligned municipalities, one of the factors that led to the proliferation of municipal police in the first place.

Is there a preferred structure for the police? A comparison of Argentina with Mexico suggests that change is driven by the "need to do something" rather than to transition to the ideal structure. Even as Mexico attempts to consolidate police functions and centralize its police forces, reformers in

Argentina in the 1990s and 2000s sought to do the exact opposite (Eaton 2008). Although the two success stories of the region, the Chilean Carabineros and the Colombian National Police, are both centralized, most of the region's countries have national police forces with far less success. Furthermore, it is important to note that reformers in Chile and Colombia had the difficult enough task of reforming their police forces without the additional challenge of building entirely new agencies. While the logic of starting with a clean slate is appealing, the slate is never entirely clean as reformers quickly realize they need the experience and manpower of existing officers and police leaders.

More to the point, however, establishment of new agencies implies a series of unintended complications. The impact of the elimination of the Federal Preventive Police (PFP) on the Federal Police's disciplinary regime is illustrative. Like most police in the country, the PFP had an Honor and Justice Commission to rule on disciplinary cases. The passage of the new law eliminated the Commission upon publication in June 2009, but the Commission was not replaced with a new Federal Police Development Council until almost a year later when implementing legislation was passed in May 2010. During the intervening eleven months, as many as 1,300 new disciplinary cases were filed, yet no disciplinary action was possible until the Council was fully constituted and operational procedures in place to handle the cases (Sabet and Olson forthcoming). Even once the Council was created, cases were not brought before the Council because it was designed to include high level operational officers, who did not have the time to dedicate to the arduous task of hearing disciplinary cases. As a result, it was not until April 2011, almost two years later, with the creation of technical committees that the disciplinary regime began to function (Sabet and Olson). At a time when the Calderón administration was promising to fight corruption, the creation of a new police force severely hampered its efforts.

While there is no magic police structure, and while there are dangers in recreating police forces, there are, however, lessons that can be learned from the region. Successful reform in the United States, Colombia, and Chile had two elements in common. First, in all three cases, a police civil service had already been established; in Colombia and Chile, removing the police from the grip of patronage required subsuming it under the defense ministries, and in the United States, it required a widespread progressive social movement. In other words, reform leaders already had a relatively merit-based command structure in place to implement reforms. Second, in all three cases, reform was driven by professionals within the police but under considerable external pressure. In the Chilean case, the Carabineros leadership reoriented the traditionally isolated police force toward an ambitious community policing approach after the fall of the Pinochet regime partially to head off attempts to bring the Carabineros under the civilian leadership of the Interior Ministry (Dammert 2006). In Colombia, reform was led by a popular general in the midst of numerous organized crime-related scandals (Llorente 2006). In other words, in all three cases there was relative insulation from partisan politics but some degree of accountability to the political system and society at large.

In addition to consolidation, another popular proposal has been militarization of Mexico's police forces, and as discussed in Chapter 2, many municipal and state forces are now led by current and former military officers. Again, the organization of the Colombian and Chilean police under the ministries of defense has supported this push. However, attempts throughout the region to militarize the police in Brazil, Venezuela, Peru, and even Mexico (during the 1990s) have led to a lack of responsiveness to community needs and to severe human rights violations. In Brazil the National Human Right Movement's Database on Criminal Violence counts 7,835 killings at the hands of police officers from 1994–2001, the vast majority by civilian-controlled-but-militarized preventive police known as Military Police (Ahnen 2007).[1] As a result, even as Mexico perpetuates the limited-discretion approach to reform and seeks to militarize its police forces, Brazil has opted to confront its growing organized crime problem by *demilitarizing* and employing a community policing strategy that has shown some initial successes (Husain 2009).

There are lessons to be learned from the region's success stories, but it is not clear that the lessons are centralization and militarization. It is uncertain if unification will eventually occur or not. In response to the insecurity, some states have moved forward with consolidation plans even absent the necessary constitutional reforms.[2] The lessons of this analysis, however, are that the unified police proposal represents a likely "continuation" of existing approaches to reform that ignore persistent informal rules and threaten to further politicize policing at the cost of building strong institutions.

The Problem of Outcomes

One of the primary reasons that the consolidation proposal has garnered so much support is a perception that no progress has been made in Mexico's municipal departments. Rather than recognize the advances of the first "reality," citizens are confronted squarely by continued police corruption and ever-increasing insecurity. The Chihuahua case illustrates a major challenge for promoting reform in Mexico. The department has advanced further and more quickly than its peer departments. Its police are better trained, have higher education levels, possess more and better equipment, are more likely to be promoted based on merit, and follow stricter operational and administrative procedures, and yet Chihuahua City has become one of the country's most dangerous cities racked by organized crime-related violence. It is hard to view the department as a model when it has failed to provide the results that its citizens expect. While the department has won national and international attention and praise, its own citizens are more skeptical.

This has set the stage for the advances in Chihuahua to be rolled back. Reformist civilian police chiefs have been replaced by retired military officers, who have shifted the department's focus and reduced their support for some reform initiatives. More important, the city's incoming *priísta* mayor Marco Ádan Quezada (2010–13) stated his support for the dissolution of the municipal force and its incorporation into the state police. Chihuahua would not be the first reform project to be derailed because it failed to have a positive effect on crime (Tulchin and Golding 2003). In addition to the pendulum swings in Argentina discussed in Chapter 3, Amaya (2006) profiles how an ambitious rights-based reform agenda in El Salvador was rolled back in the 1990s following a dramatic increase in crime.

Police and police leaders in Chihuahua offer several different responses for why a more professional police force has failed to correspond with a more secure city, including a tremendous organized crime challenge, limited authority, and dependence on the larger criminal justice system. The organized crime conflict between the Juárez and Sinaloa organizations is an external factor that would be a fundamental challenge to even the most professional and best-trained police force. The violence has led to the killings of dozens of Chihuahua police officers, including several of the agency's top leaders. In response, the department has had to modify its operations: police officers frequently work in teams, only respond to crime calls in groups, and at times wait for the federal police to arrive first. All of this has slowed their response time considerably and reduced their effectiveness.

Pointing to arrest statistics, Chihuahuan police officials argue that they are performing well within their jurisdiction and contend that the security failings can be blamed on state and federal officials. Echoing municipal offi-cials throughout the country, Chihuahuan police leaders note their lack of jurisdiction over organized crime-related activities. While the law is clear on this point, many municipal leaders and police chiefs narrowly limit their mandate and leave much of the real police work to the state and federal gov-ernment. While *effective* prevention (i.e., not just physical dissuasion) is per-haps more important than reaction, it seems strange that the majority of the country's police are able to claim that they only have an auxiliary role in ad-dressing the security crisis. Such a constrained interpretation of municipal responsibilities is a reflection of the continued dominance of the limited-discretion paradigm: if the police cannot be trusted, then it is better to limit their authority. The result, however, is that the majority of the country's police forces are not playing a proactive role in addressing local crime concerns.

Even prior to the promotion of unified local police forces, Genaro García Luna and the Calderón administration recognized that local law enforcement authority needed to be expanded. In fact, according to interviews with federal officials, one of the rationales behind standardizing the colors and appearance of police vehicles and uniforms was to inhibit the ability of organized crime to distinguish between local and federal police. More substantively, the admin-istration successfully expanded local police responsibilities in the area of local drug sales and investigation. Because Mexico was historically more of a traf-ficking than a consumption country, all drug-related offenses were previously categorized as federal offenses. Intelligence about a location selling illegal drugs had, therefore, produced a dilemma for local police. According to the law, the municipal police were required to report the matter to the federal authorities, who were to obtain the necessary warrants and make subsequent arrests. However, without there being the manpower, geographic coverage, capacity, or bureaucratic flexibility to quickly process the necessary warrants, no fed-eral action typically occurred. One municipal officer reported a case where he and his unit waited a week for a federal response while guarding a house sus-pected to contain illegal drugs before they called off the operation. Arguably this was less of a problem when local consumption was low; however, drug use surveys suggest that drug use is on the rise, particularly in the country's north, and particularly for highly addictive, low-cost drugs such as methamphet-amines (CONADIC 2003; CONADIC 2009).

As discussed earlier, the failure of the system provided sufficient cover for municipal police to justify a lack of action while accepting bribes to allow the drug selling operation to continue. By ignoring local drug sales, however, law enforcement was ignoring a crime problem that was helping to fuel organized crime-related violence. Interviews suggest that local police not in collusion with drug sellers had three response options. First, they could tolerate the illegal activity and claim that they did not have jurisdiction. Second, they could conduct an illegal search and shut down the operation. Although the detainees would eventually be released by a judge, municipal authorities could at least claim that they had broken up the operation and were doing something to solve the problem.[3] Third, they could target the consumers. Interviewees reported that agencies would place an undercover officer near a *tiendita*, or drug dealing location, who would radio intelligence to uniformed officers. Nearby officers would then search indicated subjects and make arrests. Of course, local police with limited authority were not legally allowed to conduct undercover operations, so the intelligence provided by the agent would not find its way into the police report.

The Fox and Calderón administrations attempted to solve this problem and combine local knowledge and federal jurisdiction through mixed local and federal units. Police in Chihuahua reported that these units, which generally consisted of a large convoy of uniformed military and federal, state, and municipal police, did not produce significant results and were eventually abandoned. Officers contended that by the time their convoy arrived, dealers had long since dispersed.[4] Failed enforcement is evident in regular reporting of the open sale of drugs as chronicled in local newspapers.[5] Inadequate enforcement efforts have produced a frustrated citizenry that does not understand or accept why blatant neighborhood drug dealing continues despite reports and complaints. Responding to this problem, in April 2009 the Mexican Congress passed legislative reforms legalizing small amounts of drug possession for consumption, empowering local authorities with jurisdiction over local drug sales, and permitting the police to operate undercover.

A similar expansion of authority is occurring in investigations and intelligence gathering. In recent decades, policies based on the limited-discretion paradigm sought to reduce opportunities for police abuse by preventing municipal police from participating in investigations or collecting evidence— tasks that were reserved for the state investigative police operating under orders of the public minister. However, much as the federal government lacks the capacity to respond to all federal offenses, state investigative police lack the capacity to conduct all necessary investigative activities. Municipal officers reported that they would at times wait at a crime scene for hours until the investigative police arrived. As one officer complained, "rain would wash evidence away, and we were not allowed to touch anything." Consequently, recent reform allows for the creation of analysis and investigative units within municipal police forces to be staffed by college graduates who have passed integrity control tests and received specialized training.

Response to this expansion of police authority has generally been slow, although the reforms do not fully go into effect until 2012 when state authorities are obligated to have aligned their public security legislation with the General National Public Security System Law. Only in Tijuana, as discussed in Chapter 4, have the municipal police aggressively combated local drug sales, working in close collaboration with the military and state and federal officials. The strategy has not been without risks. In 2009, Teodoro García Simental's organization began to randomly kill police officers, announcing that it would continue to do so until Leyzaola stepped down. *Zeta* (2009f) reported that García Simental's actions were a direct response to the municipal police forces' pressure on local drug sales. Despite the tragic police killings, the Tijuana police force won considerable praise for their successful enforcement actions, and, as discussed in Chapter 4, by 2010 Tijuana had emerged, somewhat surprisingly, as the poster child of an anti-organized crime strategy (Finnegan 2010). It is not clear, however, how much of Tijuana's response was due to the 2009 reform legislation and how much was due to Leyzaola's personality. As discussed in Chapter 4, critics allege that the Tijuana police has, in fact, relied heavily on extralegal measures (Alvarado 2010; Finnegan). In addition, ad hoc subordination of Leyzaola to then-regional military commander Alfonso Duarte Mujica in an experiment with flexible unified command often blurred the distinction between the police and the military (Alvarado).

As of 2010, other municipalities did not report dramatic changes in their approach to local drug sales, although they had begun to take a more active role in investigations. Chihuahua's police, acting based on orders from public ministers, regularly collected crime scene evidence. Chihuahua also reported an investigative unit of twenty-eight officers primarily focused on gathering intelligence on the city's youth gangs and on stolen cars. Hermosillo's officers had not yet begun to collect evidence; however, because of a 1999 agreement with the state's attorney general's office, for several years they had been working under the orders of state public ministers to carry out judicial warrants, a rare example of successful coordination combining state authority with local police knowledge. Still the city's investigative unit only included eight officers with joint responsibility for investigations and responding to car theft. The Mexicali police's authority increased with the commencement of judicial reform implementation in January 2010. Officers underwent a forty-hour training course in preparation for the transition and are now allowed to collect crime scene evidence. Municipal police are also permitted to receive formal crime denunciations, or *denunicas,* directly from citizens. In the past, even if the municipal police responded to a crime, citizens had to personally go to the state attorney general's office to file a formal report.

It is still too early to evaluate such changes, but they appear to offer a necessary corrective to the limited-discretion approach. To be sure, the paradigm emerged because of a long history of police abuses, and there is some fear that an expansion or re-expansion of police authority will correspond with increases in such abuse. While there is some legitimacy to this concern, it reinforces the false dichotomy that has developed between the protection of individual rights and improving security (Ungar 2011). In recent years, human rights organizations have successfully argued that crime can be reduced more effectively by respecting individual rights and earning citizen trust (Brewer 2007). In similar fashion, giving the police the tools to address crime problems does not have to imply an increase in human rights violations. Certain expansions of authority should be avoided, but not all. For example, police authority should not seek to circumvent the courts and due process. This has been the case in numerous countries where *mano dura,* or iron-fisted policing measures were enacted because of perceived problems in the judicial system. Until the late 1990s Chile's Carabineros and Venezuela's police had the authority to make arrests solely based on physical appearances (Ungar). Instead, greater police authority operating within clear operational procedures and improved accountability mechanisms offers the best means to both solve crime problems and protect individual rights. Although this analysis has focused on the process of police reform, successful reform processes must also produce results.

Of course, in order for the police to be successful, the courts and penitentiary system must also be successful. While this analysis has focused solely on police reform, as Ungar (2011) notes, improvements to the police also depend on improvements to the larger criminal justice system. Perhaps not surprisingly, Chihuahua's municipal police blame much of their own impotence on the state justice system.

The Promise and Challenge of Judicial Reform

In addition to the reforms occurring in the police, Mexico is also in the process of transitioning its judicial system to a fully accusatorial system. Under the traditional system, law enforcement, prosecutors, and courts have not adequately guaranteed rights to the accused, and many critics allege that suspects have been de facto presumed guilty and must prove their innocence (Lara Klahr 2008). Most convictions continue to be primarily based on confessions rather than actual evidence, with critics worrying that the confessions are the products of torture or forced confessions (IRCT 2006). There is relatively limited access to bail, and defendants, even those accused of minor offenses, are frequently held in pretrial detention that might last months or over a year before their case goes before a judge (Shirk 2010). Even then, many defendants do not even get a day in court, as the verdict is often based on the judge's review of the written documentation rather than an oral trial. As a result, judicial reforms include new oral adversarial procedures, alternative sentencing and dispute resolution mechanisms, and greater protection for the rights of the accused, including the presumption of innocence, due process protections, access to legal defense, and opportunities for bail (Shirk). The reforms set a higher bar for police and prosecutors as convictions require evidence that goes beyond confessions. Errors and illegalities committed by either the police or the prosecution might be sufficient cause for a case to be thrown out. Advocates hope that this higher bar will create greater incentives for police professionalization. If police and investigators want their arrests to lead to prosecution, they will need to ensure that they follow the letter of the law, respect procedure, properly fill out paperwork, and work in collaboration with state prosecutors.[6]

Judicial reform had been a priority of the Fox administration; however, faced with PRI opposition, the administration was unable to get the proposed reforms through the Mexican Congress. With financial and technical support from the U.S. Agency for International Development, many states began to pursue their own reforms. Chihuahua state was the poster child of these efforts, embarking on a far quicker and far more ambitious reform agenda then other pioneering states. After several years of preparation, in 2007 the new system went into effect in Chihuahua City, and the reforms have been gradually expanded throughout the state. Rather than lead to dramatic improvements in policing and justice in Chihuahua, however, the reforms have corresponded temporally with the country's worst organized crime-related violence. The timing could not have been worse. At the same time that citizens were demanding draconian measures to stop the violence, the state was improving its protections for the accused. Although experts generally agreed that the judicial reform has not been a cause of violence and impunity in the state, the temporal correlation has made the reforms enormously unpopular.

Few dislike the judicial reforms more than the municipal preventive police. Under the old system, arrests had consequences, but under the new system, instead of being sent to preventive detention, arrestees are often released on bail. Others are able to escape punishment through alternatives to the courts. The most unpopular measure among the preventive police is a process known as *reparación de daños*, or reparation of damages, an effort to unclog the overwhelmed justice system and focus on repairing the damages suffered by crime victims. For example, if an individual's car is stolen, an important response of the justice system should be to restore that individual's car and/or see that the victim is financially compensated. Under reparation of damages, if the suspect can agree to repair the harm done by the crime and the victim consents, then the former is permitted to go free. Because the suspect is not formally found guilty by a court of law, however, the detainee emerges from the process without a criminal record. As a result, municipal police report that there are no additional consequences if they arrest the same individual for the same crime the following week. The police department maintains a book of press clippings reporting theses "*reincidencias*," or individuals arrested multiple times for the same crimes. Unfortunately, there is not a strong U.S.-style parole officer system to keep tabs on suspects released through such mechanisms. The police also contend that the new system has allowed cases against suspects to be thrown out based on minor procedural matters that they do not view as justifiable. From the police point of view, the justice system is failing. In interview after interview, officers report that they are doing their job better than ever before and that citizens erroneously blame them for the failure to reduce crime.[7]

State reformers defend their record, however. They contend that they have modified the reform to address problems that have arisen, pointing to "113 modifications to the Criminal Code" since the reform went into effect (Hernández 2010). They argue that if the reform has fallen short, it is because it is yet another victim of organized crime. State officials report that ninety-eight trained police, investigators, public ministers, and forensic experts were killed by organized crime between 2008 and July 2010, even as the number of homicide cases overwhelmed the system (Hernández). Most knowledgeable observers interviewed for this study support the judicial reform but feel that it has been improperly implemented and insufficiently modified. Even the strongest detractors do not favor a full return to the old system.

Regardless, the recent failings in Chihuahua have not only had a negative impact on justice in the state, they have slowed the entire process of judicial reform nationwide. Rather than raise the bar for greater professionalism within the police and the justice system, the Chihuahua reforms have engendered a counterreform backlash. Federal legislation passed in 2008 states that the new judicial system be operational nationwide by 2016, and yet, the federal government has made few strides toward realizing this mandate (Ramos 2010). At a recent public conference on the topic, high-level federal and state officials expressed their skepticism toward moving forward (Ramos).

Conclusion

The future is uncertain for Mexico's municipal police forces specifically and Mexican law enforcement more generally. The challenges remain enormous and risk being obscured by dramatic plans of restructuring and the need to show results to a public desperate for security. It is important to recognize the advances that reformers have achieved in Mexico, but it is also necessary to acknowledge continued corruption, ineffectiveness, and abuse. Officers like José Luis Montoya in Mexicali are still waiting for the day when there is, as New York City's whistle-blower Frank Serpico said, "an atmosphere in which the dishonest officer fears the honest one, and not the other way around" (Knapp Commission 1972, 51). It is easy to become discouraged in an environment where reform almost always seems to fall short of producing meaningful change, and where the lives of good officers are senselessly taken by an organized crime syndicate asserting its dominance.

This analysis has sought to answer why police reform in Mexico has failed to produce meaningful institutional change. Unfortunately, the answer to this question has been complex, entailing multiple variables interacting with one another, which does not make for parsimonious political theory. However, if the problem of police reform in Mexico could be reduced to a couple of key variables, there would be a larger number of success stories among the country's numerous departments. This analysis has shown that the police are but one institutional actor in a complex policy arena, and that they are very much dependent on the current executive in office, highly susceptible to organized crime's threats and bribes, and generally distrusted and unsupported by citizens.

By the nature of the endeavor—explaining a lack of success—the analysis is pessimistic, and yet there is room for optimism and opportunity for change. Local and federal officials have laid a foundation by addressing the lower-hanging fruit of reform. Reformers will have an easier time overcoming rank-and-file resistance to robust accountability mechanisms given improved salaries, benefits, professional training, and the equipment officers need to do their job. Furthermore, a reform agenda has been enshrined in the constitution, passed into law, and agreed to in the consensus-based National Agreement for Security, Justice, and Lawfulness. Finally, citizens are angry, concerned, and engaged in the policy arena. Although there is a concern among many observers that change is simply not possible, it is important to note that Mexico has in recent years witnessed dramatic transformations in elections, human rights, and access to information. In short, change is possible. The results of this analysis suggest the following keys to building onto existing reform efforts.

- Formal policies are not enough: reform policies have to be designed with the informal rules in mind and implemented with a focus on changing informal rules.
- Partial reform is not enough: reform has to move beyond the low-hanging fruit of reform and include the positive incentives of a merit- based promotion system and the sticks of effective accountability mechanisms.
- Advances during a given administration are not enough: incoming executives must face pressure to continue successful policies. Public evaluations would help fill the information gap and make it harder to discontinue effective personnel and policies.
- Mayoral discretion and dramatic new policies are a large part of the problem, not the solution: vertical and horizontal accountability mechanisms need to be strengthened. Change will require long-term, persistent muddling through.
- Reform must address the threat of organized crime: the logic of the bullet or the bribe can only be overcome by protecting threatened police and prioritizing investigations of police killings.

- Corruption is the problem, perhaps even more so than ineffectiveness: police need citizens to be effective, but tolerance of petty corruption perpetuates a vicious cycle of citizen distrust. And the police need citizen support if they are to be effective.

- Accountability to the federal government can help, but it is also difficult to achieve and potentially problematic: federal requirements should strengthen local vertical and horizontal accountability mechanisms.

Advocacy of "muddling through" and an emphasis on informal rules perhaps provides an unclear path through which to pursue reform. It would be far easier to recommend a specific formal law that had somehow been neglected. Nonetheless, "muddling through" suggests that there have been positive changes already and that the way forward is to build on them. This is a far more encouraging conclusion that one that states that everything needs to be scrapped and an entirely new police force created. "Informal rules" cannot be amended through a legislative process, but institutional learning is possible. Mexico's police, citizens, and political leaders are not doomed to continue making the same mistakes. Through research, policy evaluation, debate, and reflection, it might be far more expedient to rewrite the informal rules than to alter the constitution in every administration.

Reference Matter

Appendix A

TABLE A-1. Generalized summary of design, implementation, and institutionalization problems

	Generalized policy design problems prior to 2008	Generalized policy implementation problems	Generalized policy institutionalization problems	Long-term policy challenge	Potential opportunities for change
Selection criteria and recruitment	—Failure to use a complete mix of available selection criteria	—Criteria are ignored or relaxed to expand the size of the force —Perfunctory implementation of otherwise time intensive selection criteria	—New administrations relax previously rigid criteria to expand the force	—Small pool of desirable candidates absent recruitment drives, good pay and benefits, and a better police image —Political pressure to increase the size of the force	—LGSNSP requires confidence control certification —CALEA accreditation requires certain selection standards
Training	—Earlier policies did not require cadet training —Few legal limitations on shortening cadet training —Some policies did not mandate regular in-service training	—Training shortened to graduate cadets sooner and keep more active officers on the streets —Training quality inhibited by uncertified instructors and uncertified institutions	—New administrations cut training to put more police on the street. —Inability to develop a long-term training program in three years.	—Legacy of poor training —Political pressure to fully exploit total manpower	—SNSP is certifying instructors and SIDEPOL will eventually require regular training —CALEA accreditation requires certain training standards
Salary and benefits	—Low wages, limited benefits, limited pension, little access to credit. —No police civil service —No police unions	—Salaries and pensions kept low to avoid future financial obligations	—Difficult to develop a long-term system of regular increases to pay and benefits given administration changes.	—Improving salary and benefits requires increasing municipal revenues.	—Municipal matching funds to SUBSEMUN go to incentives for officers, and the federal government is promoting a police civil service —Civil society provided benefits

Operational procedures	—Procedures were often not formalized or published in manuals	—When developed, procedural manuals and instruction were not made available to police —Requires effective supervision	—Procedures change with administrations —Certifications allowed to lapse with administration changes	—Informal rule granting commanders discretion.	—SNSP has developed a procedural manual and is pushing adoption —Procedures are at the heart of CALEA certification
Equipment	—Rare to have policies for the regular purchase of equipment at minimum quality and quantity standards	—Failure to provide maintenance to equipment	—Expectation that equipment need not outlast the administration. —Rebranding every three years	—Long-term equipment purchase and maintenance requires larger budgets.	—SUBSEMUN money has allowed for major purchases using minimum standards —CALEA requires minimum equipment standards —Financial support from business/philanthropic community
Promotion	—Formal policies contain loopholes that allow for avoidance —No police civil service	—Regular evaluations are often not conducted —Political and police leaders decline to surrender discretion in appointments despite the law	—Leadership turnover throughout the bureaucracy at the change of administration	—Informal rule of discretion in appointment	—The federal government is promoting a police civil service —Citizen oversight of promotion process in Chihuahua
Accountability mechanisms	—Current mechanisms are reactive and not preventive, proactive, or focused on systemic concerns. —Focus on administrative rather than penal violations.	—Internal affairs departments are understaffed, narrowly interpret their mandate, lack independence, and do not address corruption	—Independence and resources are subject to a given administration.	—Informal tolerance of corruption	—The federal government requires police to undergo integrity tests

Appendix B

TABLE A-2. Variables in the LAPOP AmericasBarometer study

Concept	Operationalization
Bribe solicitation	Do you think that given the way things are now that at times it is justifiable to pay a bribe? Yes (1) / No (0)
Bribe solicited	Has a police officer ask you for a bribe in the last year? Yes (1) / No (0)
Confidence in justice system	Combined score based on confidence in the justice system, the attorney general's office, and the police: low (1) – high (7)
Break law for security	To capture criminals do you think that the authorities should always respect the law or on occasions they can act outside the law. Respect (1) / Act outside (0)
Tolerance of patronage	An unemployed person is the in-law of an important politician, and this person uses this advantage to get a public job. Do you think what the politician did . . . is corrupt and should be punished (1) / It is corrupt but justifiable (2) / It is not corrupt (3).
Drugs in the neighborhood	In your neighborhood, have you seen anyone selling drugs in the last 12 months? Yes (1) / No (0)
Education (5 categories)	Education in five categories: No formal (0); primary (1); secondary (2); high school/vocational (3); University or higher (4)
Gender	Male (1) / Female (2)
Income (11 categories)	Monthly household income in 11 categories from none (0) to $13,500 pesos (10)

(continued)

TABLE A-2. (*continued*)

Concept	Operationalization
Religious (5 categories)	How often do you attend religious services? More than once a week (1) / Once a week (2) / Once a month (3) / One or two times a year (4) / Never or almost never (5).
Age (5 categories)	18–24 (1), 25–34 (2), 34–44 (3), 45–65 (4), over 65 (5)
Size of community (4 categories)	Mexico City (1), big (2), medium (3), small (4), rural (5)
Northern states	North (1); Central, Western-Central, Southern (0)
Southern states	South (1); Northern, Western-Central, Central (0)
Central states	Central (1); Northern, Western-Central, Southern (0)

SOURCE: Data from the AmericasBarometer by the Latin American Public Opinion Project (LAPOP), www.LapopSurveys.org.

Appendix C

TABLE A-3. Variables in the ICESI study

Concept	Operationalization
Satisfaction	Evaluation of the local preventive police, 1–10, where 1 is poor and 10 is excellent
Bribe	Has a local preventive police officer solicited a bribe from you?, 0/1, where 0 is no and 1 is yes.
Sociotropic perception	Do you think the city is insecure?, 0/1, where 0 is insecure and 1 is safe.
Egocentric perception	In 2008 was your life affected by crime?, 1–3, where 1 is a lot, 2 is a little, and 3 is not at all.
Egocentric objective	Were you a victim of crime (cumulative based on pre-2008, 2008, and 2009)?, 0/1, where 0 is no and 1 is yes.
Temporal perceptive	Has crime in 2008 in your city increased, decreased, or stayed the same?, 1-3, where 1 is increased, 2 is stayed the same, and 3 is decreased.
Media exposure	Do you watch, read or hear news the news a lot, a little, or not at all?, 0/1, where 0 is a lot and 1 is little or not at all.
Proxy for ideological view on security	Do you support the operations carried out by the federal government against organized crime?, 0/1 where 0 is no and 1 is yes.
Confidence in institutions	Average confidence in legislators, the public ministry, the judicial system, and political parties, 0–4, where 0 is poor and 4 is excellent.
Education	Education recoded, 1–3, where 1 is primary school, 2 is secondary school or high school, and 3 is greater than high school.

(*continued*)

TABLE A-3. *(continued)*

Concept	Operationalization
Income	Income, 1–5, where 1 is low and 5 is high.
Gender	Gender, 0/1, where 1 is female and 0 is male.
Age	Age, 1–4, where 1 is 18–24, 2 is 25–44, 3 is 45–64, and 4 is 65 and older.

SOURCE: Data from ICESI-ENSI6 Urbana.

Notes

1. Two Realities

1. Zepeda uses data from June 2007, when there were an estimated 368,315 police in the country. If the sources of data are accurate, this suggests that there has been an 11 percent increase in the number of police in Mexico over a two-year period. Ungar (2011) cites a higher standard of 350 police for 100,000 inhabitants.

2. Based on the Latin American Public Opinion Project's 2010 unweighted dataset. This percentage is consistent with the results of the 2006 survey, 23 percent; however, it is higher than the findings of the 2008 survey, 18.5 percent.

3. Mexico's overall homicide rate increased dramatically in 2009 and 2010 after several years of decline; however, at an estimated 14.36 per 100,000 inhabitants in 2009, it still remained below those of Brazil, Colombia, Honduras, and Venezuela (México Evalúa 2010).

4. For more information on kidnappings in Mexico see MUCD (2009c).

5. For more on these deployments see Brewer (2008) and SSP (2009a).

6. The most commonly cited cases of corruption in the military include General Jesús Gutiérrez Rebollo, who served the interests of the Juárez organization while running Mexico's anti-drug program and the Zetas, originally an armed enforcement wing of the Gulf organization, which was formed by former members of an elite Mexican anti-drug unit. For more recent cases see Reyez (2009). The military also suffered from an enormous desertion rate, fueling speculation that former military officers might be using their training and knowledge in support of the cartels. During the Fox administration (2000–06), there were 123,218 desertions from the military (Moloeznik 2009).

7. See also Meyer (2010).

8. For example, a driver was chased down and arrested for refusing to stop at a makeshift police checkpoint that he feared was part of a robbery attempt (PDHBC 2004). In another case, a woman ordered by police late at night to step out of her car refused to do so until a family member arrived. She was subsequently forcibly and illegally detained, jailed for driving under the influence of alcohol despite a negative test, and held overnight in a cell with male detainees (CEDHSON 2005).

9. *Professionalism* is something of a catchall term that means different things to different people. I understand a professional to be someone who has adopted the formal goals of his or her occupation as part of his or her own personal goals. This does not imply that self-interest has been replaced by altruism, but that professionalism offers individuals the best means to realize more basic personal goals.

10. These broad brushstrokes are conceptually and theoretically problematic. The causes of corruption are not necessarily the same causes of human rights abuses. In fact, even different types of corruption might have different causes. Furthermore, police effectiveness and protection of individual rights are at times presented as conflicting objectives. Many citizens would gladly allow the rights of others to be infringed to increase their own security. Nonetheless, there is a strong correlation among corruption, ineffectiveness, and abuses across Mexico's police departments, and all three undoubtedly contribute to a loss of citizen trust. Rather than delve into the details of the causes and consequences of particular behaviors, this study hopes to speak more broadly to the general factors that have undermined Mexico's professional development.

11. For a critique of such approaches, see Paternoster (1987).

12. Other scholars are more specific. For example, Ostrom, Gardner, and Walker (1994) tell us that the rules of the game dictate what actions are permitted, obligatory, or forbidden and the appropriate sanctions for violating rules. The authors conceptualize an arena where individuals interact, and they argue that the nature of the game among these individuals is affected by distinct rules affecting position, boundaries, authority, aggregation, scope, information, and payoffs.

2. Troubled Reforms

1. For example, the assassination of Alfredo Yáñez Piñón, coordinator of Michoacan's state preventive police, provoked speculation that he was killed for investigating corruption within the department (Milenio 2010).

2. The city's academy was closed in 2009, and department personnel are trained at the state academy.

3. Quoted in White and Escobar (2008).

4. By contrast, according to the Law Enforcement Management and Administrative Statistics database of U.S. departments with between 500 and 2,500 sworn officers, 97.8 percent use background checks and 76.1 percent use lie detector tests (DOJ 2003).

5. This is a global problem not specific to Mexico. In Washington D.C. for example, in response to growing crime, in 1989 the department was authorized to hire 1,800

officers. To expedite the process, background checks could be postponed. Much like in Mexico, critics alleged that the absence of background checks drew criminals into the force (Carlson 1993). Similar complaints have been made about the U.S. Border Patrol's expansion.

6. For example, every formal recommendation from Sonora's state human rights commission in response to a rights violation reviewed for this study included a specific recommendation for increased police training in human rights.

7. While the predominant obstacle to arms training was the limited-discretion paradigm, the highly regulated nature of bullets and arms in Mexico (all of which must be purchased from the military) presented an additional implementation challenge to such courses.

8. While not the focus of this research, many departments in Mexico's rural low-income communities pay even less. Using date from the National Survey of Household Income and Expenses, Asch, Burger and Fu (2011) estimate that police in the bottom quartile only earn $300 a month.

9. For an effort to quantify the effect of pay on the quality of military recruits see Asch, Hosek and Warner (2007). See Asch, Burger, and Fu (2011) for a discussion of how variations in pay scales can impact incentives.

10. At the time, salaries in the seven municipalities ranged from $560–800. Subsequently, it appears that several of Monterrey's municipalities reneged on this agreement.

11. On top of the base salary, officers in Hermosillo can see additional compensation, including $54 as a standard amount, $224 as a stimulus, $20 in credit, $42 for punctuality, between $42–457 for a leadership post, between $7–159 for years of service, and between $24–132 if trained by the state academy or certified.

12. As the survey was conducted at the end of 2008, some of these purchases might have been made with federal subsidy money.

3. A Problem of Municipal Governance

1. Some material from this chapter was previously published in Sabet (2009).

2. For a more detailed discussion of the municipality in early Mexican history, see Selee (2010).

3. While not adjusted for population changes, the growth in employment has clearly outpaced that of population.

4. Mexican municipalities often have city centers, as is the case of the four municipalities examined here; however, they are more comparable geographically to a U.S. county.

5. An unwillingness to raise taxes can be found even at the federal level. In 2008, 33.76 percent of federal revenue came from oil revenues.

6. It should be mentioned that an open-list system has been criticized by Weyland (1996) and others of inadvertently hampering representation and party discipline in Brazil.

7. The five exceptions include Durango, Guanajuato, Morelos, Tlaxcala, and Veracruz. If there is a three-party race, the winning mayor is not guaranteed a majority (Guillén López 2006).

8. By some accounts, the council is not designed to be a check on the mayor's authority. Merino (2006b) points out that the *cabildo* was originally designed to be a "cuerpo colegiado," or collegial governing body rather than a system of checks and balances. Historically, however, voters elected the councilmen and women, who then elected among themselves a municipal president.

9. Encuesta Nacional de Gobiernos Municipales. 2004. Secretaría de Desarrollo Social. These numbers exclude other forms of employment that make up a small percentage of municipal employees.

10. See Rose-Ackerman for a discussion of short time horizons outside of the Mexican context.

11. While the study was meant to be a census, only 1,324 municipalities provided information on the tenure of the director of public security and only thirty-two cities with over two hundred thousand inhabitants responded.

12. Instead, the new administration promoted what it called a Citizen Evaluation of Public Security Institutions and Policies. Unfortunately, there did not appear to be much substance behind this initiative.

13. Of course, this is not to say that Chihuahua's promotion process was entirely merit based. As demonstrated by the above-mentioned survey of 250 officers, as of 2006 there was still considerable dissatisfaction with the process.

14. See for example Moreno (2010).

15. See for example Guerrero (2010).

4. Organized Crime, the Police, and Accountability

1. Some material from this chapter was previously published in Daniel M. Sabet, "Confrontation, Collusion, and Tolerance: The Relationship Between Organized Crime and Law Enforcement in Tijuana," *Mexican Law Review* 2, no. 2 (2010): 3–29.

2. In total, allegations were made against thirty public officials. Unpublished research by the Trans-Border Institute as of May 2010 found that seven of the officers had been fired, one resigned, and three were arrested. Three additional allegations had been confirmed. Five were murdered, including one of the fired officers. Six more were under investigation or had been investigated. In three cases no action was taken, and in three additional cases insufficient information was provided to accurately identify the suspected officers.

3. These three divergent strategies are outlined in Bailey and Taylor (2009).

4. There are divergent accounts of this division. Ricardo Ravelo (2006) writes that Rafael Aguilar Guajardo was given rights to Ciudad Juárez, Chihuahua, and Nuevo Laredo; Héctor Luis Palma Salazar was given Nogales and Hermosillo; Jesús Labra was given Tijuana; Ismael Zambada García was given Sinaloa; and Joaquín Guzmán Loera was given Mexicali and San Luis Rio Colorado. Jesus Blancornelas (2002) offers

a different division, whereby Joaquin Guzmán Loera received Tecate; Hector Palma received San Luis Río Colorado; and Rafael Chao received Mexicali.

5. In the early 1990s, rivals not only killed the family of Sinaloa-based trafficker Hector Palma but sent him his wife's head. Ravelo attributes this killing to the Arellano Félix family; Astorga and Shirk (2010) attribute the crime to Félix Gallardo.

6. For more extended accounts of the violence in Nuevo Laredo, see Payan (2006b) and Ravelo (2006). Observers disagree on the reasons for the challenge. It was perhaps the product of a perceived weakness in the Gulf organization, whose leader Osiel Cárdenas Guillén had been directing operations from his jail cell since his arrest in 2003. Another potential motivation pointed out by Ravelo (2006) was the killing of Guzman Loera's brother Arturo in prison, allegedly on the orders of Cárdenas and Benjamín Arellano Félix. For another perspective, Luciano Campos Garza (2009) contends that the Gulf organization-affiliated Zetas had been threatening Guzmán's interests in Nuevo León since 2003.

7. The Zetas would gradually become independent of the Gulf organization until their violent split in 2010.

8. As with all organized-crime conflict, there is disagreement about the origin. Some view the conflict as a personal dispute between Guzmán Loera and Vicente Carrillo Fuentes, whose brother Rodolfo was believed to have been killed by Guzmán Loera in 2004 (Ravelo 2006). Others argue that Carrillo Fuentes was charging his Sinaloa partners too much to traffic drugs through Ciudad Juárez.

9. This hierarchically reinforced corruption would not necessarily operate in the same way in all countries. A strong civil service, a more autonomous police force, or alternative procedures for the appointment of the chief of police might produce an honest police force serving under a corrupt mayor; however, as discussed in the previous chapter, these features are absent from Mexican municipal governance. It is also possible for a mayor or police chief to collude with organized crime while taking steps to confront corruption in the lower ranks.

10. For details of collusive corruption in Tijuana, see Blancornelas (2002). This historical section draws heavily on Blancornelas's work.

11. There is disagreement on the role that Labra played in the AFO. Fernández Menéndez (2002) portrays Labra as the true head of the organization, but most accounts, including that of Blancornelas, view Labra as a sort of *consiglieri*, or chief advisor. He was arrested in 2000, eventually extradited to the United States, and pled guilty in U.S. court in 2009.

12. The Ibarra killing left a number of questions, as his body was found with a briefcase of cash.

13. By mid-March, the head of the Tijuana police acknowledged in an interview that there had been fourteen ATM robberies in the first two-and-a-half months of 2008 (Ovalle and Andrade 2008).

14. Following the reprisals from the ATM robbery, some officers began illegally using tape to cover over the patrol numbers and license plate numbers identifying their vehicles (Ovalle 2008b).

15. Of course, the failure to publish such stories is by no means assurance that there are no collusive ties. It should also be mentioned that ten commanders did test positive in random drug testing.

16. Data comes from a 2008 Police Professionalization Survey conducted by the author.

17. For example, of around 1,200 judicial police fired in Zedillos's1996 purge, 234 were reinstated by the courts (Uildriks 2010).

18. Faith in the much-celebrated firings has also been undermined by admissions that the city wanted to reduce the size of the department for financial reasons. Police interviewed pointed to colleagues who were fired for small administrative violations rather than involvement in organized crime. In their defense, the department leadership notes that some corrupt officers were fired on lesser charges because of the difficulty in building a case against officers for more serious charges.

19. Mauricio López Alvarado (2009) offers an important case to illustrate the power of the rank and file over the police leadership. In Guadalajara in the early 2000s, a new chief sought to draw his operational leadership from the community rather than the distrusted police force. He held a competitive application process and submitted candidates through a rigorous training program. Upon coming into their positions, however, the new leadership's commands were simply ignored by the rank and file. It is further alleged that the officers actually encouraged crime in order to discredit the reform initiative. With rising crime rates, the new city was forced to capitulate and the operational leaders were removed from their positions.

5. Citizens and Their Police

1. The extent of the problem can be seen even within the police department, where one investigative report found that the very police officers charged with enforcing registration laws were not compliant, with many driving personal cars without plates or with U.S. plates (Ramírez 2008c)

2. The "dark statistic" or *cifra negra* is actually higher than 79 percent as it includes an additional 6 percent of crime that was reported but did not result in the creation of a case file.

3. Measures of association are small; however, the significance of the central variable is consistent regardless of what variables are included in the model.

4. The egocentric/sociotropic division is most commonly used in economic evaluations. See for example Anderson and Guillory (1997).

5. More detailed information on variable operationalization is available in Appendix C.

6. Tests for multicollinearity find no such problems.

7. The analysis produces a low pseudo R^2, and, although such R^2s are common in studies attempting to explain confidence in institutions, it does raise the possibility of omitted variable bias and certainly suggests that there are other factors that could be

included in future research. For example, Sampson and Jeglum Bartusch (1998) were able to explain a greater amount of variation in police confidence using hierarchical linear modeling to explore both neighborhood and individual level impacts in a study of 343 Chicago neighborhoods. Other researchers have delved more deeply into issues of procedural justice and interaction with the police (Tyler 2004). In addition, it is important to recognize that the survey responses analyzed are limited to individuals who report being aware of the municipal and transit police, producing a drop of between 14.8 percent and 47.9 percent of the survey respondents in the municipal samples. This increases internal validity (people cannot reliably evaluate a police force they are unfamiliar with), but it does limit generalization to the whole community and possibly introduces sampling bias.

6. Civil Society and the Police

1. See for discussion Hodgkinson and Foley (2003).

2. The author formerly worked with the Culture of Lawfulness Project, an initiative of the National Strategy Information Center that works with police, schools, government officials, and media on promoting a culture of lawfulness in Mexico.

3. U.S. pressure following the killing of DEA agent Enrique Camarena was also an important factor in the DFS's dissolution (Astorga and Shirk 2010).

4. A review of the literature in Mexico only yielded a handful of documented attempts at citizen oversight (Mendoza 2007).

5. Data from the Latin American Public Opinion Project. *AmericasBarometro.* 2008.

6. While state authorities in Sonora and Chihuahua have also experimented with state- level citizen councils, at the time of the research they were not active in the policy arena.

7. Prior to 2007, there were citizen committees that existed to facilitate the development of each administration's three-year development plan.

8. I did not find evidence that the committees played a particularly strong role in promoting compliance, although there are some examples, such as Hábitos Buenos, or Good Habits, in Chihuahua City. The organization develops and implements educational programs designed to help participants see the benefits of good habits and develop internalized norms ensuring these behaviors.

9. In addition to traditional public funding, the council is funded by an interesting mechanism to increase local financial support for the police. Businesses in the state agreed to an additional tax that goes into a trust for public security, education, and infrastructure investments.

10. See for example CCSP (2005).

11. See for example Valdez Gutiérrez (2008). In its annual report, Mexicali presents data on only six public security indicators with only simple comparisons with the previous year. All the graphs show dramatic improvements, leaving the reader wondering

if the previous year had been a statistical anomaly or if the administration chose to exclude indicators that did not show positive change.

12. See also Arzaluz Lozano (2004).

13. In interviews, many members of Tijuana's civil society felt that Capella Ibarra had been successful co-opted by the Ramos administration. Rather than continue to serve as a needed critical voice from the outside, Capella was now on the inside. Untrained for the job and unable to stop the city's crime wave, Capella was removed from office after less than one year of service.

14. The text of the editorial is reproduced in La Jornada (2010).

15. Newspapers in the first three cities provide online access to all of their new stories. Research assistants and I reviewed thousands of articles systematically over a one-year period and then less systematically over an additional two-year period. Unfortunately, in Chihuahua none of the papers offer a good online library of news articles, and, as a result, the news in this city was explored through keyword searches on the newspapers' websites.

7. The Federal Government and Local Reform

1. Of the mayors arrested, five were PRI, two were PAN, and three were PRD. Critics of the arrests argue that Godoy himself had upon taking office in early 2008 alerted military and federal officials as to the infiltration of certain municipalities and question why the federal response took so long, was not done in coordination with the governor, and was carried out only in the run up to the election. Critics point to arrests in the PAN-governed state of Morelos, where the federal government did coordinate its actions with the governor. By late 2010, all but one of the suspects had been absolved by the federal courts.

2. For a more detailed discussion on initial development of the SNSP, see Macías and Castillo (2002).

3. See for example Cepeda (2007).

4. In 2009, the program was expanded to 206 cities (including fifteen territorial demarcations of the Federal District).

5. In fact, while this chapter discusses accountability to the federal government, legally speaking, it is the SNSP that oversees the SUBSEMUN program.

6. Municipalities also reported implementation problems with the radios, which are dependent on adequate transmission towers. In Tijuana, for example, officers reported that radios in the hilly terrained parts of the city did not pick up the frequencies.

7. Because the criteria used gross crime numbers rather than crime rates normed to the size of the population, the formula favors high-population cities over small cities and/or towns with high crime rates. In 2009, this formula was amended to favor tourist destinations, border cities, and large suburban areas. (Arredondo Sánchez Lira 2010).

8. As of September 2009, the SSP reported that 474,500 police were in the registry, which they estimated as 93 percent of total active personnel. However, the percentage

should also include former personnel. SSP reports that over a one-year period there were over 1.8 million searches conducted on the registry (SSP 2009b). See also SNSP (2010a).

9. These exams were typically conducted at one of the country's five federal regional academies. The examiners for technical police skills were municipal and state police certified by the national academy, and the polygraph technicians were typically graduates from a program run by the country's intelligence agency (CISEN). Police leaders were brought to Mexico City for evaluations conducted by the federal Public Security Secretariat.

10. As of this writing, five states' integrity control test centers had been accredited, including Baja California's.

11. Exact numbers are difficult to determine, as the initial information presented counted the number of specific tests administered (e.g., psychological, toxicological) rather than the number of officers tested. The administration reported that 26,165 tests were conducted among state and municipal police forces.

12. Some municipalities have fired all police who fail the test. Reynosa, Tamaulipas, fired 527 police (more than half of the department) over a two-year-period (El Universal 2010c).

13. At the time of this writing, twenty-five states had brought their legislation in line with the SIDEPOL requirements.

8. Looking Forward

1. See Birbeck and Gabaldón (2009) for more on Venezuelan militarization.

2. Because the constitution gives municipalities responsibility for public security, creating a unified police force requires a constitutional amendment. Although constitutional changes are common in Mexico, the October 2010 decision of the PRD caucus to reject the proposal prevented its passage (Michel and Gómez 2010). Many states nonetheless attempted to proceed with consolidation on their own. Coahuila, Durango, and Chihuahua all unified their attorney general's office and secretariat of public security into a Fiscalía General, or prosecutor's office. Each of these states has also expressed an intention to absorb the municipal police. To solve the legal challenges, two of Durango's municipalities have voluntarily ceded their policing responsibilities to the state, a strategy that has also been followed in Aguascalientes and Hidalgo (El Universal 2010b). While proponents of the unified police have celebrated these efforts, absent the constitutional reform, such arrangements depend on the support of the municipal administration in office.

3. This approach was actively promoted at a conference of police chiefs attended by the author in 2006.

4. More recently, police in Hermosillo, working undercover with federal authorities, reported a more positive experience.

5. For an example see Salinas (2008b).

6. Statements made at the conference Criminal Justice Reform in Mexico: Orientation for Human Rights NGOs and Civil Society. Washington D.C.: November 10, 2008.

7. Others argue that cases are thrown out because municipal police fail to follow proper procedure or fill out forms properly. Unlike in Baja California, local preventive police did not receive formal training ahead of the transition to a fully accusatorial system.

References

[ACCM] American Chamber of Commerce of Mexico. 2009. *Encuesta de Hábitos de Consumo de Productos Pirata y Falsificados en México.* Mexico City: American Chamber of Commerce of Mexico.

Ahnen, Ronald E. 2007. "The Politics of Police Violence in Democratic Brazil." *Latin American Politics and Society.* 49(1):141–64.

Alemán, Ricardo. 2009. "Itinerario Político: El Falso Debate." *El Universal,* May 3.

Amaya, Edgardo Alberto. 2006. "Security Policies in El Salvador." *Public Security and Police Reform in the Americas,* edited by John Bailey and Lucía Dammert. Pittsburg: University of Pittsburg Press.

Almond, Gabriel A., and Sidney Verba. 1963. *The Civic Culture: Political Attitudes and Democracy in Five Nations.* Princeton, NJ: Princeton University Press.

Alvarado, Ignacio. 2010. "Leyzaola: Héroe, villano, ¿o ambos?" *El Universal,* November 8.

Anderson, Christopher J., and Christine A. Guillory. 1997. "Political Institutions and Satisfaction with Democracy: A Cross-National Analysis of Consensus and Majoritarian Systems." *American Political Science Review* 91(1):66–81.

Andrade, Luis Gerardo. 2008a. "Cumplen amenaza; balean comandancia." *Frontera,* April 10

———. 2008b. "Atrapan en bautizo 60 'narcos' y 2 jefes." *Frontera:* June 23.

———. 2008c. "'Levantan' a policía por 'chueco': SSPM." *Frontera,* January 1.

———. 2008d. "Pasó 'narcopolicía' test de confianza." *Frontera,* June 24.

Anteo, Mario. 2007. "Mordida moderna." *El Norte,* January 14.

Aponte Polito, Sergio. 2008. "Carta íntegra del general Aponte Polito." *Frontera,* April 23.

Arellano Gault, David, and Juan Pablo Guerrero Amparán. 2003. "Stalled Administrative Reforms of the Mexican State." In *Reinventing Leviathan: The Politics of*

Administrative Reform in Developing Countries, edited by Ben Ross Schneider and Blanca Heredia. Boulder, CO: Lynne Rienner.

Arias, Patricia, and Liza Zúñiga. 2008. *Control, Disciplina, y Responsabilidad Policial: Desafíos doctrinarios e institucionales en América Latina.* Santiago: Flacso-Chile.

Arnold, R. Douglas. 1992. *The Logic of Congressional Action.* New Haven, CT: Yale University Press.

Arredondo Sánchez Lira, Jaime. 2010. *El Subsidio Municipal para la Seguridad Pública: Análisis de la Fórmula de Elegibilidad.* Unpublished thesis, Instituto Tecnológico Autónoma de México.

Arreola Ayala, Alvaro. 1985. "Elecciones Municipales." In *Las Elecciones en México,* edited by Pablo González Casanova. Mexico City: Siglo XXI Editores.

Arteaga Botello, Nelson, and Adrián López Rivera. 1998. *Policía y corrupción: El caso de un municipio en México.* Mexico City: Plaza & Valdés.

Arzaluz Lozano, Socorro. 2004. "Experiencias de participación ciudadana en municipios metropolitanos del Estado de México y Nuevo León." In *Participación ciudadana y políticas sociales en el ámbito local,* edited by Alicia Ziccardi. Mexico City: Universidad Nacional Autonomo de Mexico.

Asch, Beth, Nicholas Burger, and Mary Fu. 2011. *Mitigating Corruption in the Mexican Security Forces: The Role of Institutions, Incentives, and Personnel Management.* Washington, DC: Rand.

Asch, Beth, James Hosek, and John Warner. 2007. "New Economics of Manpower in the Post-Cold War Era." In *Handbook of Defense Economics,* edited by Todd Sandler and Keith Hartley. 2:1075–1138

Astorga, Luis. 2000. "Organized Crime and the Organization of Crime." In *Organized Crime and Democratic Governability: Mexico and the U.S. Mexican Borderlands,* edited by John Bailey and Roy Godson. Pittsburgh: University of Pittsburgh Press.

———. 2005. *El Siglo de las Drogas: El narcotráfico, del Porfiriato al nuevo milenio.* Mexico City: Plaza Jánes.

———. 2007. *Seguridad, traficantes, y militares: El poder y la sombra.* Mexico City: Tusquets.

Astorga, Luis, and David A. Shirk. 2010. "Drug Trafficking Organizations and Counter-Drug Strategies in the U.S.-Mexican Context." In *Shared Responsibility: U.S.-Mexico Policy Options for Confronting Organized Crime,* edited by Eric L. Olson, David A. Shirk, and Andrew Selee. Washington, DC: Woodrow Wilson International Center for Scholars.

Avilés, Carlos. 2005. "Dotan a los municipios de mayor autonomía." *El Universal,* June 1.

Avilés, Carlos, and Elly Castillo. 2010. "Poder Judicial defiende a juez del 'michoacanazo.'" *El Universal,* October 6.

Axelrod, Robert. 1984. *The Evolution of Cooperation.* New York: Basic Books.

Ayuntamiento de Chihuahua. 2010. "Exhorta DSPM hacer buen uso del 060 para evitar movilizaciones en falso," news release, April 5, Ayuntamiento de Chihuahua, April 5.

Ayuntamiento de Tijuana. 2004. Reglamento de la Secretaría de Seguridad Pública. *Periódico Oficial del Estado de Baja California* 121(16): April 9.

Azaola, Elena. 2009. "The Weaknesses of Public Security Forces in Mexico City." In *Police and Public Security in Mexico,* edited by Robert A. Donnelly and David A. Shirk. San Diego, CA: University Readers.

Azaola Garrido, Elena, and Marcelo Bergman. 2007. "The Mexican Prison System." In *Reforming the Administration of Justice in Mexico,* edited by Wayne A. Cornelius and David Shirk. Notre Dame, IN: University of Notre Dame Press.

Azaola Garrido, Elena, and Miguel Ángel Ruíz Torres. 2009. *Investigadores de papel: Poder y derechos humanos entre la Policía Judicial de la Ciudad de México.* Mexico City: Fontamara.

Bachrach, Peter and Morton S. Baratz. 1970. *Power and Poverty: Theory and Practice.* New York: Oxford University Press.

Bailey, John and Roy Godson, eds. 2000. *Organized Crime and Democratic Governability: Mexico and the U.S. Mexican Borderlands.* Pittsburgh: University of Pittsburgh Press.

Bailey, John, and Pablo Paras. 2006. "Perceptions and Attitudes About Corruption and Democracy in Mexico." *Mexican Studies/Estudios Mexicanos.* 22(1):57–81.

Bailey, John, and Matthew M. Taylor. 2009. "Evade, Corrupt, or Confront? Organized Crime and the State in Mexico and Brazil." *Journal of Politics in Latin America* 2: 3–29.

Bayley, David. 1990. *Patterns of Policing: A Comparative International Analysis.* New Brunswick, NJ: Rutgers University Press.

Baumgartner, Frank R., and Bryan D. Jones. 1991. "Agenda Dynamics and Policy Subsystems." *Journal of Politics* 53(4):1044–74.

————.1993. *Agendas and Instability in American Politics.* Chicago: University of Chicago Press.

Bayley, David. 1985. *Patterns of Policing: A Comparative International Analysis.* New Brunswick, NJ: Rutgers University Press.

Becker, Gary S. 1968. "Crime and Punishment: An Economic Approach." *Journal of Political Economy* 76(2):169–217.

Benavides, Carlos. 2008. "Penetraron los Beltrán a PGR desde 1997: EU." *El Universal,* August 23.

Bieck, William, and Tim Oettmeier. 1998. *The Houston Police Department: Integrating Investigative Operations Through Neighborhood Oriented Policing.* Washington, DC: Police Executive Research Forum.

Birkbeck, Chirstopher and Luis Gerardo Gabaldón. 2009. "Venezuela: Policing as an Exercise in Authority." In *Policing Developing Democracies,* edited by Mercedes S. Hinton and Tim Newburn. New York: Routledge.

Blake, Charles H. 2009. "Public Attitudes Toward Corruption." In *Corruption and Democracy in Latin America,* edited by Charles H. Blake and Stephen D. Morris. Pittsburgh: University of Pittsburgh Press.

Blancornelas, Jesús. 2002. *El Cártel: Los Arellano Félix: La mafia más poderosa en la historía de América Latina.* Mexico City: Plaza & Janés México

Blumstein, A., J. Cohen, and D. Nagin. 1978. *Deterrence and Incapacitation: Estimating the Effects of Criminal Sanctions on Crime Rates.* Washington, DC: National Academy of Sciences.

Brewer, Stephanie E. 2008. *Human Rights Under Siege: Public Security and Criminal Justice in Mexico.* Mexico City: Centro de Derechos Humanos Miguel Agustín Pro Juárez.

Brockhaus, R. 1980. "Risk Taking Propensity of Entrepreneurs." *Academic Management Journal* 23(3):509–13.

Burns, Pamela, and Dale K. Sechrest. 1992. "Police Corruption: The Miami Case." *Criminal Justice and Behavior* 19(3):294–313.

Búrquez, Francisco. 2001. *Primer Informe de Gobierno.* Hermosillo: H. Ayuntamiento de Hermosillo.

Calderón Hinojosa, Felipe. 2009. *Tercer Informe de Gobierno.* Mexico City: Presidencia de la Republica.

Camarena, Kriztian. 2008. "Opera 'El Chapo' en TJ." *Frontera,* November 13.

Camp, Roderic Ai. 2010. "Armed Forces and Drugs, Public Perceptions and Institutional Challenges." In *Shared Responsibility: U.S.-Mexico Policy Options for Confronting Organized Crime,* edited by Eric L. Olson, David A. Shirk, and Andrew Selee. Washington, DC: Woodrow Wilson International Center for Scholars.

Campos Garza, Luciano. 2009. "Nuevo León: De Poder a Poder." *Proceso.* Edición Especial 25.

Candina, Azun. 2006. "The Institutional Identity of the Carabineros de Chile." In *Public Security and Police Reform in the Americas,* edited by John Bailey and Lucía Dammert. Pittsburg: University of Pittsburg Press.

Carlson, Tucker. 1993. "D.C. Blues: The Rapsheet on the Washington Police." *Policy Review* 63:26–33

Carothers, Thomas. 1999. *Aiding Democracy Abroad: The Learning Curve.* Washington, DC: Carnegie Endowment for International Peace.

Castro Salinas, Consuelo. 2001. "Mexico." In *El tercer sector Iberoamericano: Fundaciones, asociaciones, y ONG's,* edited by J.L. Piñar Mañas and R. Sánchez Rivera. Valencia: Tirant lo Blanch.

[CBDH] Centro Binacional de Derechos Humanos. 2008. *Migrantes repatriados: Arresto y detención arbitraria.* Tijuana: Centro Binacional de Derechos Humanos.

[CBP] Customs and Border Protection. 2009. "Calexico CBP Officers Seize 3 Tons of Marijuana with Cargo Shipment," news release, November 29, U.S. Customs and Border Protection.

[CCSP] Consejo Ciudadano de Seguridad Pública. 2005. *Evaluación de las Instituciones de Seguridad Pública.* Mexicali: Consejo Ciudadano de Seguridad Pública.

[CEDHSON] Comisión Estatal de Derechos Humanos de Sonora. 2005. *Recomendación No. 09/2005.* Hermosillo: Comisión Estatal de Derechos Humanos de Sonora.

——. 2007a. *Recomendación No. 05/2007.* Hermosillo: Comisión Estatal de Derechos Humanos de Sonora.

——. 2007b. *Recomendación No. 07/2007.* Hermosillo: Comisión Estatal de Derechos Humanos de Sonora.

Cedillo, Juan. 2007. "Designan nuevo secretario de gobierno en Nuevo León." *El Universal,* July 5.

[CEMEFI] Centro Mexicano para la Filantropía. 1996. "Understanding Mexican Philanthropy." In *Changing Structure of Mexico: Political, Social, and Economic Prospects,* edited by L. Randall. Armonk, NY: M. E. Sharpe.

Cepeda, Cesar. 2007. "Relegan seguridad municipal." *El Norte,* February 4.

Chaiken, J., P. Greenwood, and J. Petersilia. 1977. "The Criminal Investigation Process: A Summary Report." *Policy Analysis* 3:187–217.

Chu, Ted, and Alejandro Delgado. 2009. "Used Vehicle Imports Impact on New Vehicle Sales: The Mexican Case." *Análisis Económico* 24(55):347–64

[CISALVA] Instituto de Investigación y Desarrollo en Prevención de Violencia y Promoción de Convivencia Social. 2008. *Guía Metodológica para la Replicación de Observatorios Municipales de Violencia.* Cali: Centro Editorial CATORSE SCS.

[CISEN] Centro de Investigación y Seguridad Nacional. 2009. *CISEN: 20 años de historia: Testimonios.* Mexico City: Centro de Investigación y Seguridad Nacional.

Cisneros M., Jorge. 2008. "Crímenes que cambiaron instituciones." *El Universal,* August 17.

[CNDH] Comisión Nacional de Derechos Humanos. 2004. *Informe especial de la Comisión Nacional de los Derechos Humanos relativo a los hechos de violencia sescritazos en la Ciudad de Guadalajara, Jalisco, el 28 de mayo de 2004.* Mexico City: Comisión Nacional de Derechos Humanos.

——. 2006. *Recomendación 38/2006 sobre el caso de los hechos de violencia suscitados los días 3 y 4 de mayo de 2006 en los municipios de Texcoco y San Salvador Atenco, Estado de México.* Mexico City: Comisión Nacional de Derechos Humanos.

[CONADIC] Consejo Nacional Contra las Adicciones. 2003. *Encuesta Nacional de Adicciones 2002.* Mexico City: Consejo Nacional Contra las Adicciones.

——. 2009. Encuesta Nacional de Adicciones 2008. Mexico City: Consejo Nacional Contra las Adicciones

Contreras, Cristina. 2008. "Acusan a jefe policiaco." *El Imparcial* (Hermosillo), June 4.

Cordero, Manuel. 2008. "Balean a policía y amenazan a otras." *La Voz de la Frontera,* March 22.

Cornelius, Wayne A., Ann L. Craig, and Jonathan Fox, eds. 1994. *Transforming State-Society Relations: The National Solidarity Strategy.* La Jolla, CA: Center for U.S.-Mexican Studies.

Correia, Mark, Michael Reisig and Nicholas Lovrich. 1996. "Public perceptions of state police: An analysis of individual-level and contextual variables." *Journal of Criminal Justice.* 24:17–28.

Cosgrove, Colleen, and Mary Ann Wycoff. 1997. *Investigations in the Community Context.* Washington, DC: Police Executive Research Forum.

Cox, Gary W., and Matthew McCubbins. 1986. "Electoral Politics as a Redistributive Game." *Journal of Politics* 48(2):370–89.

Craig, Ann L., and Wayne A. Cornelius. 1980. "Political Culture in Mexico: Continuities and Revisionist Interpretations." In *The Civic Culture Revisited,* edited by Gabriel A. Almond and Sidney Verba. Boston: Sage.

Cruz, Guillermo, and Rolando Herrera. 2011. "Ejecutómetro 2010. Anticipan expertos que podrían aumentar los hechos de violencia." *La Reforma,* January 1.

Dammert, Lucía. 2005. "Violencia criminal y seguridad ciudadana en Chile." Santiago, Chile: Naciones Unidas.

———. 2006. "From Public Security to Citizen Security in Chile." In *Public Security and Police Reform in the Americas,* edited by John Bailey and Lucía Dammert. Pittsburgh: University of Pittsburgh Press.

Davis, Diane E. 2008. "Undermining the Rule of Law: Democratization and the Dark Side of Police Reform in Mexico." *Latin American Politics and Society.* 48(1):55–86.

Davis, Gina, and Elinor Ostrom. 1991. "A Public Economy Approach to Education: Choice and Coproduction." *International Political Science Review* 12(4):313–35.

de Francisco Z., Gonzalo. 2006. "Armed Conflict and Public Security in Colombia." In *Public Security and Police Reform in the Americas*, edited by John Bailey and Lucía Dammert. Pittsburg: University of Pittsburg Press.

de Mesquita Neto, Paulo. 2006. "Paths toward Police and Judicial Reform in Latin America." In *Toward a Society under Law: Citizens and their Police in Latin America*, edited by Joseph S. Tulchin and Meg Ruthenburg. Washington, DC: Woodrow Wilson Center Press.

De la Luz González, María, and Francisco Gómez. 2009. "Histórico: PGR pega al gobierno de Michoacán." *El Universal,* May 27.

Dean, Deby. 1980. "Citizen Ratings of the Police: The Difference Contact Makes." *Law & Policy Quarterly* 2:462.

del Valle Martínez, Antonio. 2004. *La Transicón Democrática en los Cuerpos de Seguridad Pública: Participaci'on Ciudadana y Derechos Humanos.* Mexico City: Gernika.

Dellasoppa, Emilio Enrique, and Zoraia Saint'Clair Branco. 2006. "Brazil's Public Security Plans." In *Public Security and Police Reform in the Americas,* edited by John Bailey and Lucía Dammert. Pittsburg: University of Pittsburg Press.

Diamond, Larry, and Richard Gunther, eds. 2001. *Political Parties and Democracy.* Baltimore: Johns Hopkins University Press.

Diario del Desierto. 2007. Responde estado en el discurso, faltan los hechos… Caborca. *Diario del Desierto,* March 8.

Diario Oficial de la Federación. 2005. "Ley General que Establece Las Bases de Coordinación del Sistema Nacional de Seguridad Pública." *Diario Oficial de la Federación*, December 11.

———. 2011. "Reglas para el otorgamiento del subsidio a los municipios." *Diario Oficial de la Federación*, January 28.

Díaz Ochoa, Jaime. 2004. *Tercer informe de gobierno.* Mexicali: H. Ayuntamiento de Mexicali.

Díaz, Gloria Leticia. 2009. "En Tijuana, Guerra sucia contra denunciantes." *Proceso:* Nov. 16.

Dibble, Sandra. 2011. "Tijuana officers accused of organized crime ties released." *San Diego Union Tribune,* April 17.

[DOJ] U.S. Department of Justice, Bureau of Justice Statistics. Law Enforcement Management and Administrative Statistics. 2003. *Sample Survey of Law Enforcement Agencies.* CPSR04411-v1. Washington, DC: U.S. Department of Justice.

Drummond, D.S. 1976. *Police Culture.* Thousand Oaks, CA: Sage Press.

Duverger, Maurice. 1954. *Political Parties: Their Organization and Activity in the Modern State.* London: Methuen.

El Imparcial. 2008a. "Enemigo natural de delincuentes." *El Imparcial,* March 8.

———. 2008b. "Paga Miranda Multa." *El Imparcial,* April 23.

———. 2008c. "Crecen las renuncias de policías." *El Imparcial,* July 22.

El Milenio. 2010. "Sospechan que asesinato de director de policía en Morelia fue cometido por miembros de la corporación." *El Milenio,* October 24.

Eaton, Kent. 2008. "Paradoxes of Police Reform: Federalism, Parties, and Civil Society in Argentina's Public Security Crisis." *Latin American Research Review.* 43(3):5–32.

Elorduy Walther, Eugenio. 1998. *Tercer Informe de Gobierno.* Mexicali: H. Ayuntamiento de Mexicali.

El Universal. 2006. "A dose of culture fights police corruption." *El Universal,* October 23.

———. 2008a. "Policías de Tabasco, en nómina del narco." *El Universal,* August 26.

———. 2008b. "Se enfrenta federales y municipales en Torreón." *El Universal,* September 9.

———. 2009. "12 Golpes a la Libertad de Expresión." *El Universal:* http://www.eluni versal.com.mx/graficos/graficosanimados09/EU_periodistas/.

———. 2010a. "Conago avala crear policía única en cada estado." *El Universal,* March 23.

———. 2010b. "Mapa Interactivo: Policía Única." *El Universal,* October 18.

———. 2010c. "Reynosa cesa a 572 policías en dos años." Mexico City. *El Universal,* November 8.

Elster, Jon. 1986. *Rational Choice: Readings in Social and Political Theory.* New York: New York University Press.

Escalante Gonzalbo, Fernando. 2009. *La homicida en México entre 1990 y 2007: Aproximación estadística.* Mexico City: El Colegio de Mexico.

Escalante Gonzalbo, Fernando. 2011. "Homicidios 2008–2009. La muerte tiene permiso." *Nexos,* January 1.

Fagen, Richard R., and William S. Tuohy. 1972. *Politics and Privilege in a Mexican City.* Stanford, CA: Stanford University Press.

Fernández Menéndez, Jorge. 2002. *El Otro Poder.* Mexico City: Aguilar.

Financiero, El. 2008. "Dictan formal prisión a ex mandos de la PFP." *El Financiero* (Mexico City), Dec. 11.

Finnegan, William. 2010. "In the Name of the Law." *New Yorker,* October 18.

Fisman, Raymond, and Edward Miguel. 2007. "Corruption, Norms, and Legal Enforcement: Evidence from Diplomatic Parking Tickets." *Journal of Political Economy* 115(6):1020–48.

Fogelson, Robert M. 1977. *The Big-City Police.* Cambridge, MA: Harvard University Press.

Foster, Vivienne. 1996. *Policy Issues for the Water and Sanitation Sectors.* No. IFM96-101. Washington, DC: Inter-American Development Bank.

Fox Quesada, Vicente. 2001. *Primer Informe de Gobierno.* Mexico City: Presidencia de la República.

———. 2005. *Quinto Informe de Gobierno.* Mexico City: Presidencia de la República.

Freeman, J. Leiper. 1965. *The Political Process.* New York: Random House.

Friedman, George. 2010. "Mexico and the Failed State Revisited." *Geopolitical Intelligence Report,* April 6.

Fuentes, Claudio A. 2006. "Advocacy Networks and Police Reform: Assessing their Impact." In *Toward a Society under Law: Citizens and their Police in Latin America,* edited by Joseph S. Tulchin and Meg Ruthenburg. Washington DC: Woodrow Wilson Center Press.

Fuss, Charles M. 1996. *Sea of Grass: The Maritime Drug War: 1970–1990.* Annapolis, MD: Naval Institute Press

Galán, Marcelo. 2011. "Militares, a cargo de la seguridad en 17 entidades." *El Universal,* February 28.

Gandaría, Manríque. 2007a. "Se han integrado 16 mil soldados del Ejército a la PFP." *El Sol de México,* May 22.

———. 2007b. "Reduce SSP a 3 meses el tiempo de capacitación para policías." *El Sol de México,* May 23.

———. 2008. "Rechazan creación de Observatorio Ciudadano para la Seguridad Pública." *El Sol de México,* September 3.

García del Castillo, Rodolfo. 2006. La profesionalización en México: El caso de los gobiernos locales. In *La Gestión Profesional de los Municipios en México: Diagnóstico, oportunidades y desafíos,* edited by Mauricio Merino. Mexico City: Centro de Investigación y Docencia Económicas.

Garza, Ramón Alberto. 2009. "Mauricio y su pacto con los Beltrán Leyva." *Indígo* 134, June 11.

Geddes, Barbara. 1996. *Politician's Dilemma: Building State Capacity in Latin America.* Berkeley: University of California Press.

Giugale, Marcelo M., and Steven B. Webb, eds. 2000. *Achievements and Challenges of Fiscal Decentralization: Lessons from Mexico.* Washington, DC: The World Bank.

Godoy Molina, Fernando. 2007. "Perfil psicológico del policía municipal de Hermosillo, Sonora." Master's thesis, Universidad de Sonora.

Gómez, Francisco. 2008. "60 policías en 'narconómina' de Tabasco." *El Universal,* September 11.

———. 2009. "Piratería, el otro frente del narco." *El Universal,* March 1.

Gómez, María Idalia, and Darío Fritz. 2005. *Con la muerte en el bolsillo: Seis desafora-das historias del narcotráfico.* Mexico City: Planeta.

Gómez-Cespedes, Alejandra. 1999. "The Federal Law Enforcement Agencies: An Ob-stacle in the Fight against Organized Crime in Mexico." *Journal of Contemporary Criminal Justice* 15(4):352–69.

González, Guadalupe, Susan Minushkin, and Robert Y. Shapiro, eds. 2004. *México y el Mundo: Mexican Public Opinion.* Mexico City: Centro de Investigación y Do-cencia Económicas.

González G., Jose. 1983. *Lo negro del Negro Durazo: La biografía criminal de Durazo, escrita por su Jefe de Ayudantes.* Mexico City: Editorial Posada.

Granados Chapa, Miguel Ángel. 2010. "'Zeta' periodismo de la adversidad." *Reforma,* April 18.

Grant, Heath, and Karen J. Terry. 2005. *Law Enforcement in the 21st Century.* Boston: Pearsons.

Grindle, Merilee S. 2007. *Going Local: Decentralization, Democratization, and the Promise of Good Government.* Princeton, NJ: Princeton University Press.

Guerrero Gutiérrez, Eduardo. 2009. "Las Tres Guerras: Violencia y narcotráfico en México." *Nexos:* September 1.

Guerrero, Claudia. 2010. "Apura Senado reforma política." *Reforma,* April 19.

Guillén López, Tonatiuh. 1996. *Gobiernos Municipales en México: Entre la Modern-ización y la Tradición Política.* Mexico City: El Colegio de la Frontera Norte, Miguel Angel Porrua Grupo Editorial.

———. 2006. Democracia Representativa y Participativa en los Municipios de México: Procesos en Tensión. In *Democracia y Ciudadanía: Participación Ciudadana y De-liberación Pública en Gobiernos Locales Mexicanos,* edited by Andrew W. Selee and Leticia Santín del Río. Washington, DC: Woodrow Wilson International Center.

Guillén López, Tonatiuh, Pilar López Fernández, and Pablo Rojo Calzada. 2006. *Mu-nicipio y buen gobierno: Experiencias del ímpetu local en México.* Mexico City: Centro de Investigación y Docencia Económicas.

Gutiérrez, Óscar. 2006. "A Dose of Culture Fights Police Corruption." *El Universal,* October 23.

———. 2009. Mujeres policías contra corrupción. *El Universal,* January 4.

Hayek, F. A. 1948. *Individualism and Economic Order.* Chicago: University of Chicago Press.

Hernández, Anabel. 2008. "Intocable y solapado." *Proceso* 1672, November 16.

Hernández, Evangelina. 2010. "Narcoguerra rebase a la reforma judicial." *El Universal,* July 19.

Herrera, Rolando. 2010. "Acelera narco ejecuciones." *Reforma.* January 1.

Hinds, Lyn. 2009. "Public Satisfaction with Police: The Influence of General Attitudes and Police-Citizen Encounters." *International Journal of Police Science and Man-agement* 11(1):54–66.

Hodgkinson, Virginia A., and Michael W. Foley, eds. 2003. *The Civil Society Reader.* Lebanon, NH: University Press of New England.

Honts, Charles R., and Mary V. Perry. 1992. "Polygraph Admissibility: Changes and Challenges." *Law and Human Behavior* 16(3):357–79.

Hughes, Sallie. 2006. *Newsrooms in Conflict: Journalism and the Democratization of Mexico.* Pittsburgh: University of Pittsburgh Press.

Huntington, Samuel. 1968. *Political Order in Changing Societies.* New Haven, CT: Yale University Press.

Husain, Saima. 2009. "On the Long Road to Demilitarization and the Professionalization of the Police in Brazil." In *Policing Insecurity: Police Reform, Security, and Human Rights in Latin America,* edited by Niels Uildriks. Lanham, MD: Lexington Books.

[ICESI] Instituto Ciudadano de Estudios sobre la Inseguridad. 2009. Sexta encuesta nacional sobre inseguridad. http://www.icesi.org.mx/documentos/encuestas/encuestasNacionales/ENSI-6.pdf. Instituto Ciudadano de Estudios sobre la Inseguridad.

———. 2010. *Análisis de la ENSI-6/2009: Victimización, Incidencia y Cifra Negra en México.* Mexico City: Instituto Ciudadano de Estudios sobre la Inseguridad. .

[IRCT] International Rehabilitation Council for Torture Victims. 2006. *Country Assessment Report: Mexico.* Copenhagen: International Rehabilitation Council for Torture Victims.

Johnston, Michael, ed. 2005. *Civil Society and Corruption: Mobilizing for Reform.* Lanham, MD: University Press of America.

Kelling, George L., and Mark H. Moore. 1988. "The Evolving Strategy of Policing." *Perspectives on Policing* 4.

Kerner Commission. 1968. Report of the National Advisory Commission on Civil Disorders. Washington, DC: U.S. Government Printing Office.

Kingdon, John W. 1995. *Agendas, Alternatives, and Public Policies.* New York: Harper Collins.

Kleinig, John. 1996. *The Ethics of Policing.* New York: Cambridge University Press.

Klitgaard, Robert. 1988. *Controlling Corruption.* Berkeley: University of California Press.

[Knapp Commission.] Commission to Investigate Allegations of Police Corruption and the City's Anti-Corruption Procedures. 1972. *Knapp Commission Report on Police Corruption.* New York: George Braziller.

Kohlberg, Lawrence. 1981. *Essays on Moral Development, Vol. 1: The Philosophy of Moral Development.* San Francisco: Harper & Row.

Kutnjak Ivkovic, Sanja. 2005. *Fallen Blue Knights: Controlling Police Corruption.* New York: Oxford University Press.

La Frontera. 2008a. "Hacen policías a mecánicos 'patrunegocio.'" *La Frontera,* March 19.

———. 2008b. "Guerra de 'narcos' deja a 13 muertos," *La Frontera,* April 27.

———. 2008c. "Vinculan a agentesa crimen organizado." *La Frontera,* November 12.

La Jornada. 2010. "'Ustedes son, en estos momentos, las autoridades de facto en esta ciudad.' Diario de Juárez a narco." *La Jornada,* September 19.

Lai, Alan. 2000. "A Quiet Revolution: The Hong Kong Experience." *Trends in Organized Crime* 5(3):79–86.

Lara Klahr, Marco. 2008. *Prisión sin condena*. Mexico City: Debate, Random House Mondadori.

Lauría, Carlos, Mike O'Connor, Monica Campbell, and José Barbeito. 2010. *Silence or Death in Mexico's Press: Crime, Violence, and Corruption Are Destroying the Country's Journalism*. New York: Committee to Protect Journalists.

Laveaga, Gerardo. 1999. *La Cultura de la Legalidad*. Mexico City: Universidad Nacional Autónoma de México.

La Voz de la Frontera, La. 2009. "Juan Galván gana premio México de Periodismo 2009." *La Voz de la Frontera*, June 16.

Lawson, Chappell. 2002. *Building the Fourth Estate: Democratization and the Rise of the Free Press in Mexico*. Berkeley: University of California Press.

Leff, Nathaniel. 1964. "Economic Development Through Bureaucratic Corruption." *American Behavioral Scientist* 8(3):8–24.

Lindbeck, Assar, and Jorgen Weibull. 1987. "Balanced-Budget Redistribution as the Outcome of Political Competition." *Public Choice* 52: 273–97.

Lipsky, Michael. 1980. *Street-Level Bureaucracy: Dilemmas of the Individual in Public Services*. New York: Russell Sage Foundation.

Llorente, María Victoria. 2006. "Demilitarization in a War Zone." In *Public Security and Police Reform in the Americas,* edited by John Bailey and Lucía Dammert. Pittsburgh: University of Pittsburgh Press.

López Alvarado, Mauricio. 2009. El des-control de la autoridad en la organización policial preventiva mexicana. Presented at La seguridad entre lo local y lo global: los entornos latinoamericanos. Mexico City, June 12.

López Portillo Vargas, Ernesto. 2002. "The Police in Mexico: Political Functions and Needed Reforms." In *Transnational Crime and Public Security*, edited by J. Bailey and J. Chabat. La Jolla, CA: Center for U.S.-Mexican Studies.

López-Montiel, Angel Gustavo. 2000. "The Military, Political Power, and Police Relations in Mexico City." *Latin American Perspectives* 27(2):79–94.

Macaulay, Fiona. 2002. "Problems of Police Oversight in Brazil." Working Paper Series CBS-33-02. University of Oxford Centre for Brazilian Studies.

Macías, Vivianna, and Fernando Castillo. 2002. "Mexico's National Public Security System: Perspectives for the New Millennium." In *Transnational Crime and Public Security*, edited by John Bailey and Jorge Chabat. La Jolla, CA: Center for U.S.-Mexican Studies.

Mainwaring, Scott. 1999. "Multipartism, Robust Federalism, and Presidentialism in Brazil." In *Presidentialism and Democracy in Latin America*, edited by Scott Mainwaring and Mathew Soberg Shugart, 55–109. New York: Cambridge University Press.

Mantzavinos, C., Douglass C. North, and Syed Shariq. 2004. "Learning, Institutions, and Economic Performance." *Perspectives on Politics* 2(1):75–84.

Manzetti, Luigi, and Carole J. Wilson. 2009. "Why Do Corrupt Governments Maintain Public Support?" In *Corruption and Democracy in Latin America*, edited by Charles H. Blake and Stephen D. Morris. Pittsburgh: University of Pittsburgh Press.

Marosi, Richard. 2009. "One Mexico border city is quiet, maybe too quiet." *Los Angeles Times:* Sept. 16.

Marshall, Claire. 2005. "Gang Wars Plague Mexican Drugs Hub." *BBC News*, August 18.

Martínez Assad, Carlos ed. 1985. *Municipios en Conflicto.* Mexico D.F.: Universidad Autónoma Nacional de México.

Martínez de Murguía, Beatriz. 1999. *La policía en México: Orden social o criminalidad?* Mexico City: Planeta.

Martínez Mercado, Fernando, Alejandra Mohor Bellalta, and Ximena Tocornal Montt. 2008. "Elementos Introductorios: Hacia una concepción de la responsabilización policial." In *Responsabilidad Policial en Democracia: Una propuesta para América Latina,* edited by Ernesto López Portillo Vargas and Hugo Frühling E. Mexico City : Instituto para la Seguridad y la Democracia, AC Centros de Estudios en Seguridad Ciudadana.

Mastrokski, Stephen D., Jeffrey B. Snipes, and Anne E. Supina. 1996. "Compliance on Demand: The Public's Responses to Specific Police Requests." *Journal of Crime and Delinquency* 33:269–305.

McCluskey, John D. 2003. *Police Requests for Compliance: Coercive and Procedurally Just Tactics.* New York: JFB Scholarly Publishing.

McKinley, James C. 2007. "Mexico's New President Sends Thousands of Federal Officers to Fight Drug Cartels." *New York Times:* Jan. 6.

Meagher, Patrick. 2004. "Anti-Corruption Agencies: A Review of Experience." Working Paper 04/02: Columbia, MD: Center for Institutional Reform and the Informal Sector.

Medellín, Jorge Alejandro. 2008a. "Narco pagaba hasta $10 mil a policías." *El Universal*, September 10.

———. 2008b. "Plagiaria de Martí es agente federal." *El Universal* (Mexico City), Sept. 10, 2008

Mendoza, Antia. 2007. "Supervisión de la policía por sociedad civil en México ¿Transición hacia la reforma policial democrática?" Mexico City: Instituto para la Seguridad y la Democracia.

Mendoza, Antia, and Juan Salgado. 2009. *Una visión del futuro . . . hacia la seguridad ciudadana: La Policía Municipal de Chihuahua.* Mexico City: Instituto para la Seguridad y la Democracia A.C.

Mendoza Mora, Carlos. 2009. "El Costo de la Inseguridad en México." Mexico City: Instituto Ciudadano de Estudios sobre la Inseguridad.

Merino, Mauricio. 2006a. "La importancia de las rutinas: Marco teórico para una investigación sobre la gestión pública municipal en México." In *Democracia y Ciudadanía: Participación Ciudadana y Deliberación Pública en Gobiernos Locales Mexicanos,* edited by Andrew W. Selee and Leticia Santín del Río. Washington, DC: Woodrow Wilson International Center for Scholars.

———. "La Profesionalización Municipal." In *La Gestión Profesional de los Municipios en México: Diagnóstico, oportunidades y desafíos,* edited by Mauricio Merino. Mexico City: Centro de Investigación y Docencia Económicas:

Merlos, Andrea. 2007. "Nueve mil ejecutados en sexenio foxista, reportan." *El Universal*, January 2.

México Evalúa. 2010. *Índice de inseguridad ciudadana y violencia.* México D.F.: México Evalúa.

Meyer, Maureen. 2010. *Abuso y miedo en Ciudad Juárez.* Washington, DC: Washington Office on Latin America.

Michel, Elena, and Ricardo Gómez. 2010. "PRD niega apoyo a ley de mando único." *El Universal*, October 28.

Miller, Gary J. 1993. *Managerial Dilemmas: The Political Economy of Hierarchy.* New York: Cambridge University Press.

Mockus, Antanas. n.d.. *Bogotá: Acción y Pedogógica y Gobierno.* Unpublished manuscript.

[Mollen Commission], New York City Commission to Investigate Allegations of Police Corruption and the Anti-Corruption Procedures of the Police Department. 1994. *Commission Report.* New York.

Moloeznik, Marcos Pablo. 2009. "The Militarization of Public Security and the Role of the Military in Mexico." In *Police and Public Security in Mexico,* edited by Robert A. Donnelly and David A. Shirk. San Diego, CA: University Readers.

Moloeznik, Marcos Pablo, David A. Shirk, and María Eugenia Suárez de Garay. 2009. *Justiciabarómetro: Reporte Global: Resultados de la encuesta de la policía preventiva de la Zona Metropolitana de Guadalajara.* San Diego, CA: Justice in Mexico Project.

———. 2011. *Justiciabarómetro: Reporte Final: Diagnóstico Integral de la Policía Municipal de Ciudad Juárez.* San Diego, CA: Justice in Mexico Project.

Moncada, Eduardo. 2009. "Toward Democratic Policing in Colombia: Institutional Accountability through Lateral Reform." *Comparative Politics.* 41(4):431–49.

Montoya, José Luis. 2005. Personal correspondence with Sr. Kevin LaChapelle. June 14.

Moore, Molly. 2000. "Mexicans Stunned by Killing of Police Chief; Attack in Tijuana Follows Tough Talk by President." *Washington Post,* February 28.

Moreno, Alejandro. 2010. "Encuesta/Reforma." *Reforma,* March 14.

Morosi, Richard. 2009. "One Mexico Border City Is Quiet, Maybe Too Quiet." *Los Angeles Times,* September 16.

Morris, Stephen D. 1991. *Corruption and Politics in Contemporary Mexico.* Tuscaloosa: University of Alabama Press.

[MUCD] México Unido Contra la Delincuencia. 2009a. *Evaluación del Acuerdo Nacional por la Seguridad la Justicia y la Legalidad: Segundo Informe de Seguimiento. México Unido Contra la Delincuencia.* Accessed June 22. http://www.evaluaciona cuerdonacional.org.mx/

———. 2009b. *Seguimiento al Acuerdo Nacional por la Seguridad, la Justicia, y la Legalidad: Un Año.* Mexico City: México Unido Contra la Delincuencia.

———. 2009c. *Secuestro 2009: Informe.* Mexico City: México Unido Contra la Delincuencia.

———. 2010. *Encuesta Nacional sobre la Percepción de Seguridad Ciudadana en México*. Mexico City: México Unido Contra la Delincuencia.

Murillo, Yadira. 2008. "Suman 11 secuestradores detenidos; 2 son policías." *Frontera*, July 17.

Nájera Ruíz, Tonatiuh, ed. 2006. "Diagnóstico Interno de Cultura Laboral." Chihuahua City, Mexico: Instituto Tecnológico y de Estudios Superiores de Monterrey and the Comité Ciudadano de Seguridad Pública Municipal.

Naval, Claire. 2006. *Irregularities, Abuses of Power, and Ill-Treatment in the Federal District: The Relation Between Police Officers and Ministerio Público Agents, and the Population*. Mexico City: Fundar, Centro de Análisis e Investigación A.C.

Naylor, R. T. 2004. *Wages of Crime: Black Markets, Illegal Finance, and the Underworld Economy*. Ithaca, NY: Cornell University Press.

Norte, El. 2007. "Operación Conjunta Tijuana: Grafico animado." *El Norte*, February 2.

———.2008. "Da NL primer paso: Sube sueldo a Policía. Monterrey." *El Norte*, August 28.

North, Douglass C. 1990. *Institutions, Institutional Change and Economic Performance*. New York: Cambridge University Press.

O'Neil, Shannon. 2009. "The Real War in Mexico." *Foreign Affairs* 88(4): 63–77.

Olken, Benjamin. 2005. "Monitoring Corruption: Evidence from a Field Experiment in Indonesia." NBER Working Paper No. 11753.

Olson, Mancur. 1993. "Dictatorship, Democracy, and Development." *American Political Science Review* 87(3):567–76.

Orlando, Leoluca. 2001. *Fighting the Mafia and Renewing Sicilian Culture*. San Francisco: Encounter Books.

Ostrom, Elinor, Roy Gardner, and James Walker. 1994. *Rules, Games, and Common-Pool Resources*. Ann Arbor: University of Michigan Press.

Ostrom, Elinor, Larry Schroeder, and Susan Wynne. 1993. *Institutional Incentives and Sustainable Development: Infrastructure Policies in Perspective*. Boulder, CO: Westview Press.

Ostrom, Elinor, and Gordon P. Whitaker. 1999. "Does Local Community Control of Police Make a Difference?" In *Polycentricity and Local Public Economies: Readings from the Workshop in Political Theory and Policy Analysis*, edited by Michael D. McGinnis. Ann Arbor: University of Michigan Press.

Otero, Sivia. 2006. "AFI 'celebra' aniversario permeada por corrupción." *El Universal*, November 2.

———. 2008. "Hampa 'pega' más a policías locales." *El Universal*, April 14.

Ovalle, Fausto. 2008a. "Persiguen y matan policías a asaltante." *Frontera*, January 15.

———. 2008b. "Tapan placas de patrullas los policías." *Frontera*, March 27.

Ovalle, Fausto, and Luis G. Andrade. 2008. "Bandas 'secuestran' ahora a cajeros." *La Frontera*, March 19.

Ovalle, Fausto, and Manuel Villegas. 2008. "Vive Tijuana una jornada sangriente." *Frontera*, January 16.

Padilla Delgado, Hector. 2000. "Democracia y gobernabilidad en una experiencia local: El caso de Ciudad Juárez visto desde la perspectiva de la clase política." In *Transición democrática y gobernabilidad: México y América Latina*, edited by

J. Labatista, M. del Campo, A. Camou, and N. Lujan Ponce. Mexico City: Plaza y Valdes.

Parás, Pablo, and Ken Coleman. 2006. *The Political Culture of Democracy in Mexico: 2006.* Mexico City: Latin American Public Opinion Project.

Paternoster, Raymond. 1987. "The Deterrent Effect of the Perceived Certainty and Severity of Punishment: A Review of Evidence and Issues." *Justice Quarterly* 4:173–217.

Payan, Tony. 2006a. *The Three U.S.-Mexico Border Wars: Drugs, Immigration, and Homeland Security.* Westport, CT: Praeger Security International.

———. 2006b. "The Drug War and the U.S.-Mexico Border: The State of Affairs." *South Atlantic Quarterly* 105(4):864–80.

[PDDH] Procuraduría para la Defensa de los Derechos Humanos. 2007. *Violaciones a los derechos humanos por responsabilidad de la Policía Nacional Civil de El Salvador.* San Salvador: Procuraduría para la Defensa de los Derechos Humanos.

[PDHBC] Procuraduría de Derechos Humanos de Baja California. 2004. *Recomendación 09/2004.* Tijuana: Procuraduría de Derechos Humanos de Baja California.

———. 2006. *Recomendación 05/2006.* Tijuana: Procuraduría de Derechos Humanos de Baja California.

———. 2007. *Recomendación 04/2007.* Tijuana: Procuraduría de Derechos Humanos de Baja California.

———. 2008. *Recomendación 07/2008.* Tijuana: Procuraduría de Derechos Humanos de Baja California.

Pérez Correa, Catalina. 2008. "Front Desk Justice: Inside and Outside Criminal Procedure in Mexico City." *Mexican Law Review* 1(1):3–32.

Pérez, Luis Alonso. 2009. "Policías en el limbo." *Zeta* 1838: June 19–25.

Peruzzotti, Enrique, and Catalina Smulovitz, eds. 2006. *Enforcing the Rule of Law: Social Accountability in the New Latin American Democracies.* Pittsburgh: University of Pittsburgh Press.

Ponce, José. 2008. "Alerta a los hermosillenses presencia de Policía Federal." *El Imparcial,* June 20.

Pressman, Jeffrey L., and Aaron Wildavsky. 1979. *Implementation: How Great Expectations in Washington Are Dashed in Oakland.* Berkeley: University of California Press.

Presidencia de la República. 2011. Base de datos de estados y municipios sobre homicidios presuntamente relacionados a la delincuencia organizada en el periodo diciembre 2006 a diciembre 2010. Mexico City. Presidencia de la República.

Ramírez, Ana Cecilia. 2008a: "Año de la esperanza." *Frontera,* January 1.

———. 2008b. "Unen fuerzas para revertir criminalidad." *Frontera,* January 1.

———. 2008c. "Van y vienen policías con autos 'chuecos.'" *Frontera,* May 19.

———. 2009. "Dejan Policía 67 agentes en 40 días." *Frontera,* January 12.

———. 2010. "Le agradecen su labor." *Frontera,* December 6.

Ramos, Jorge. 2010. "Corte alerta de riesgos por la reforma penal." *El Universal,* August 12.

Ramos García, José María. 2006. *Inseguridad Pública en México: Una propuesta de gestión de política estratégica en gobiernos locales.* Mexico City: Miguel Ángel Porrúa.

Ravelo, Ricardo 2006. *Los Capos: Las narco-rutas de México*. Mexico City: DeBosillo.
———. 2010. "'La Barbie': Retrato de un criminal." Accessed July 10. *Proceso*. http://www.proceso.com.mx/noticias_articulo.php?articulo=42994.

Reames, Benjamin. 2003. "Police Forces in Mexico: A Profile." Working Paper. Reforming the Administration of Justice in Mexico. La Jolla, CA: Center for U.S.-Mexican Studies.

Reforma. 2010. "Rebasa violencia a Ciudad Juárez." *Reforma*, January 10.

Reisig, Michael D., and Roger Parks. 2002. *Satisfaction with Police—What Matters?* Washington, DC: National Institute of Justice.

Reporters Without Borders. 2010. "Trainee becomes 11th journalist to be murdered this year in Mexico." Reporters Without Borders, Sept. 17.

Reyez, José. 2009. La penetracion del narco en la milicia. *Revista Contralinea*. Accessed May 14: http://www.contralinea.com.mx/c19/html/sociedad/narco_en_milicia.html.

Riding, Alan. 1980. "Region in Mexico Is Pacified by Army." *New York Times*, March 2.

Riva Palacio, Raymundo. 1997. "A Culture of Collusion: The Ties That Bind the Press and the PRI." In *A Culture of Collusion: An Inside Look at the Mexican Press*, edited by William A. Orme. Miami, FL: North South Center Press.

Rodriguez, Victoria E. 1997. *Decentralization in Mexico: From Reforma Municipal to Solidaridad to Nuevo Federalismo*. Boulder, CO: Westview Press.

Rose-Ackerman, Susan. 1999. *Corruption and Government: Causes, Consequences, and Reform*. New York: Cambridge University Press.

Ruíz Harrell, Rafael. 2007. "Estadísticas oficiales vs. percepción ciudadana de la inseguridad: El subregistro delictivo." *Salud Pública de México* 49:143.

Sabatier, Paul A. 1993. "Policy Change over a Decade or More." In *Policy Change and Learning: The Advocacy Coalition Approach*, edited by Paul A. Sabatier and Hank C. Jenkins-Smith. Boulder, CO: Westview Press.

Sabet, Daniel M. 2008. *Nonprofits and Their Networks: Cleaning the Waters Along Mexico's Northern Border*. Tucson: University of Arizona Press.
———. 2009. Two Steps Forward: Lessons from Chihuahua. In *Police and Public Security in Mexico*, edited by Robert A. Donnelly and David A. Shirk. San Diego, CA: University Readers;
———. 2010. "Police Reform in Mexico: Advances and Persistent Obstacles." In *Shared Responsibility: U.S.-Mexico Policy Options for Confronting Organized Crime*, edited by Eric L. Olson, David A. Shirk, and Andrew Selee. Washington, DC: Woodrow Wilson Center.

Sabet, Daniel M., and Eric Olson. Forthcoming. "El Régimen Disciplinario en la Policía Federal." Mexico City: Secretaría de Seguridad Pública.

Salgado, Juan. 2009. "Buenas prácticas en prevención del delito y seguridad ciudadana en México." Presented at the Seminario Internacional de Seguridad y Convivencia Ciudadana. Chihuahua: March 19.

Salinas, Daniel. 2008a. "Detecta filtro 200 'aviadores' en la Policía." *Frontera*, February 9.

———. 2008b. "Imponen 'malandros' su ley en Zona Norte." *Frontera*, March 6.

Salinas, Daniel, and Fausto Ovalle. 2008. "'Es la guerra': 6 Muertos." *Frontera*, January 16.

Sampson, Robert J., and Dawn Jeglum Bartusch. 1998. "Legal Cynicism and (Subcultural?) Tolerance of Deviance: The Neighborhood Context of Racial Differences." *Law & Society Review* 32(4):777–804.

Sánchez, Stephanie. 2009. Juárez Violence: Drug-War Brutality Persists Despite Presence of Military. *El Paso Times*, November 11.

Sandoval Ulloa, José G. 2000. *Introducción al Estudio del Sistema Nacional de Seguridad Pública*. Mexico City.

[SCJN] Suprema Corte de Justicia de la Nación. 1999. *Semanario Judicial de la Federación y su Gaceta*. Novena época, t. X, septiembre de 1999, tesis P./J. 95/99, pg. 709.

[SEDENA] Secretaría de la Defensa Nacional. 2009. *Tercer Informe de Labores*. Mexico City: Secretaría de la Defensa Nacional.

[SESNSP] Secretariado Ejecutivo del Sistema Nacional de Seguridad Pública. 2010. *Servicio Profesional Como Proyecto de Vida*. Unpublished document. Secretariado Ejecutivo del Sistema Nacional de Seguridad Pública.

[SEGOB], Secretaría de Gobernación. 2005. *Conociendo a los ciudadanos mexicanos: Principales resultados: Tercera encuesta nacional sobre cultura política y prácticas ciudadanos*. Mexico City: Secretaría de Gobernación.

Segovia, Rafael. 1975. *La Politizacion del Nino Mexicano*. Mexico City: El Colegio de Mexico.

Selee, Andrew. 2010. *Democracy Close to Home? Decentralization, Democratization, and Informal Power in Mexico*. University Park, PA: Penn State University Press.

Seligson, Mitchell A. 2002. "The Impact of Corruption on Regime Legitimacy: A Comparative Study of Four Latin American Countries." *The Journal of Politics* 64(2):408–33.

Shah, Anwar. 2003. "Fiscal Decentralization in Transition Economies and Developing Countries." In *Federalism in a Changing World*, edited by Raoul Blindenbacker and Arnold Koller. Ithaca, NY: McGill-Queens University Press.

Sherman, Lawrence. 1974. *Police Corruption: A Sociological Perspective*. Garden City, NJ: Doubleday.

Sherman, Lawrence W. 1978. *Scandal and Reform: Controlling Police Corruption*. Berkeley: University of California Press.

Shirk, David A. 2010. "Justice Reform in Mexico: Change and Challenges in the Judicial Sector." In *Shared Responsibility: U.S.-Mexico Policy Options for Confronting Organized Crime*, edited by Eric L. Olson, David A. Shirk, and Andrew Selee. Washington, DC: Woodrow Wilson International Center.

Silva, Mario Héctor. 2010. "Abatirán crimen en Juárez con plan social." *El Universal*, February 11.

Sliva Forné, Carlos. 2009. "Policía y encuentros con la ciudadanía en Ciudad Nezahualcóyotl." PhD diss., El Colegio de México.

Sloat, Warren. 2002. *A Battle for the Soul of New York: Tammany Hall, Police Corruption, Vice, and Reverend Charles Parkhurst's Crusade Against Them, 1892–1895.* New York: Cooper Square Press.

[SNSP] Sistema Nacional de Seguridad Pública. 2010a. *Acuerdo Nacional por la Seguridad, la Justicia y la Legalidad: Informe de avances 2010.* Sistema Nacional de Seguridad Pública, October 19.

———. 2010b. "Posibles hechos delictivos denunciados en los fueros federales y común, 1997–2010." Mexico City: Sistema Nacional De Seguridad Pública.

[SSP] Secretaría de Seguridad Pública. 2009a. *Tercer Informe de Labores.* Mexico City: Secetaría de Seguridad Pública.

———. 2009b. "Sistema Integral de Desarrollo Policial." 2009. Mexico City: Secretaría de Seguridad Pública.

Stigler, George. 1971. "The Economic Theory of Regulation." *Bell Journal of Economics* 2:3–21.

Suárez de Garay, María Eugenia. 2005. "Armados, enrejados, desconfiados . . . Tres breves lecturas sobre la cultura policial mexicana." *Política y Sociedad* 43(2):87–102.

———. 2009. "Mexican Law Enforcement Culture." In *Police and Public Security in Mexico,* edited by Robert A. Donnelly and David A. Shirk. San Diego, CA: University Readers.

Sunshine, Jason, and Tom R. Tyler. 2003. "The Role of Procedural Justice and Legitimacy in Shaping Public Support for Policing." *Law and Society Review* 37: 513–48.

Tamez Guajardo, Macedonio. 2008. "Reflexiones sobre la corrupción entre policías, ministerios públicos y jueces mexicanos." *Milenio,* August 9.

Tapia, Jonathan. 2009a. "Policías se corrompen por miedo y unas monedas." *El Universal,* June 10.

———. 2009b. "Policías desquician calles de Monterrey." *El Universal,* June 9.

Tello, Nelia, and Carlos Garza. 2000. "La cultura de la legalidad, antidote de la inseguridad." *Este País* 116.

Thelen, Kathleen. 1999. "Historical Institutionalism in Comparative Perspective." *Annual Review of Political Science.* Vol. 2: 369–404.

Tilly, Charles. 1978. *From Mobilization to Revolution.* Reading, MA: Addison-Wesley.

[TM] Transparencia Mexicana. 2007. *Índice Nacional de Corrupción y Buen Gobierno: Informe Ejecutivo.* Mexico City: Transparencia Mexicana.

———. 2011. *Índice Nacional de Corrupción y Buen Gobierno: Informe Ejecutivo.* Mexico City: Transparencia Mexicana.

Treisman, Daniel. 2000. "The Causes of Corruption: A Cross-National Study." *Journal of Public Economies* 76(3):399–457.

Tulchin, Joseph S., and Heather A. Golding. "Introduction." In *Crime and Violence in Latin America: Citizen Security, Democracy, and the State,* edited by Hugo Frühling and Joseph S. Tulchin. Washington, DC: Woodrow Wilson Center Press.

Tyler, Tom R. 1990. *Why People Obey the Law.* New Haven, CT: Yale University Press.

———. 2004. "Enhancing Police Legitimacy." *Annals of the American Academy of Political and Social Sciences* 593:84–99.

Uildriks, Neils. 2010. *Mexico's Unrule of Law: Implementing Human Rights in Police and Judicial Reform Under Democratization.* Lanham, MD: Lexington Books.

Ungar, Mark. 2002. *Elusive Reform: Democracy and the Rule of Law in Latin America.* Boulder, CO: Lynne Rienner.

———. 2011. *Policing Democracy: Overcoming Obstacles to Citizen Security in Latin America.* Washington, DC: Woodrow Wilson Center Press.

[UNODC] United Nations Office on Drugs and Crime. 2002. *Results of a Pilot Survey of Forty Selected Organized Criminal Groups in Sixteen Countries.* http://www.unodc.org/pdf/crime/publications/Pilot_survey.pdf.

Valdez Gutiérrez, Rodolfo. 2008. *Primer Informe de Gobierno.* Mexicali: Ayuntamiento de Mexicali.

Valencia Carmona, Salvador. 2002. "La defensa constitucional del municipio mexicano." *Anuario Iberoamericana de Justicia Constitucional* 6:517–50.

Valencia Juillerat, Jorge. 1998. *Plan Municipal de Desarrollo (1998–2000).* Hermosillo: H. Ayuntamiento de Hermosillo.

———. 1999. *Segundo Informe de Gobierno.* Hermosillo: H. Ayuntamiento de Hermosillo.

———. 2000. *Tercer Informe de Gobierno.* Hermosillo: H. Ayuntamiento de Hermosillo.

Vanderwood, Paul J. 1992. *Disorder and Progress: Bandits, Police, and Mexican Development.* Wilmington, DE: Scholarly Resources.

Varenik, Robert O. 2005. *Sistema policial de rendición de cuentas.* Mexico City: Instituto para la Seguridad y la Democracia A.C.

———. 2008. "Responsabilización interna de los policías: Un aspecto básico de la responsabilización y supervisión de los policías." In *Responsabilidad Policial en Democracia: Una propuesta para América Latina,* edited by Ernesto López Portillo Vargas and Hugo Frühling E. México: Instituto para la Seguridad y la Democracia, AC Centros de Estudios en Seguridad Ciudadana.

Veledíaz, Juan. 2009. "Homicidios Violentos, los que nadie investiga." *El Universal,* February 23.

Verduzco, Gustavo. 2003. *Organizaciones no lucrativas: Visión de su trayectoria en México.* Mexico City: El Colegio de México.

Verduzco, Gustavo, Regina List, and Lester M. Salamon. 1999. "Mexico." In *Global Civil Society: Dimensions of the Nonprofit Sector,* edited by Lester M. Salamon et al. Baltimore, MD: Center for Civil Society Studies.

Walker, Samuel. 2000. *Police Accountability: The Role of Citizen Oversight.* East Windsor, CT: Wadsworth.

Ward, Heather M. 2006. "Police Reform in Latin America: Brazil Argentina, and Chile. 2006." In *Toward a Society under Law: Citizens and their Police in Latin America,* edited by Joseph S. Tulchin and Meg Ruthenburg. Washington DC: Woodrow Wilson Center Press.

Ward, Peter, and Victoria E. Rodriguez. 1999. *New Federalism and State Government in Mexico: Bringing the States Back In.* Austin: LBJ School of Public Affairs at the University of Texas.

Weiner, Tim. 2002. "Mexico Holds 41, Including Tijuana Police Chief, in Crackdown." *New York Times,* April 12.

Weldon, Jeffrey. 1999. "Political Sources of *Presidencialismo* in Mexico. In *Presidentialism and Democracy in Latin America*, edited by Scott Mainwaring and Mathew Soberg Shugart. New York: Cambridge University Press.

Weyland, Kurt. 1996. *Democracy Without Equity: Failures of Reform in Brazil*. Pittsburgh: University of Pittsburgh Press.

———. 2008. "Toward a New Theory of Institutional Change." *World Politics* 60:281–314.

White, Michael D., and Gipsy Escobar. 2008. "Making Good Cops in the Twenty-First Century: Emerging Issues for Effective Recruitment, Selection, and Training of Police in the United States and Abroad." *International Review of Law, Computers, and Technology* 22(1–2):119–34.

Wilson, James Q. 1980. *The Politics of Regulation*. New York: Basic Books.

Wilson, James Q., and R. J. Hernstein. 1985. *Crime and Human Nature*. New York: Simon & Schuster.

Yáñez Romero, José Arturo. 2009. "Drug Trafficking Related Violence in Mexico: Organization and Expansion." *Voices of Mexico* 84:83–88.

Zaverucha, Jorge. 2000. "Fragile Democracy and the Militarization of Public Safety in Brazil." *Latin American Perspectives* 27(3):8–31.

Zepeda Lecuona, Guillermo. 2009. "Mexican Police and the Criminal Justice System." In *Police and Public Security in Mexico*, edited by Robert A. Donnelly and David A. Shirk. San Diego, CA: University Readers.

Zeta. 2008. "Balacera: La verdad oculta" *Zeta* 1779, May 2–8.

———. 2009a "Ejecuciones Baja California por año." *Zeta* 1814, December 31, 2008–January 8, 2009.

———. 2009b "Cierre violento." *Zeta* 1814: December 31, 2008–January 8, 2009.

———. 2009c. "Policías y mafiosos, los secuestradores." *Zeta* 1817: January 23–29.

———. 2009d. "Las operaciones de los Zambada en BC." *Zeta* 1825: March 20–26.

———. 2009e. "Los acusan de repartir dinero del narco." *Zeta* 1826: March 27–April 2.

———. 2009f. "CAF amenaza a Leyzaola." *Zeta* 1831, May 1–7.

———. 2009g. "Asesinos de policías siguen libres." *Zeta* 1841, July 10–16.

———. 2009h. "Asesinados por no aceptar teléfono." *Zeta* 1834, May 22–28.

———. 2009i. "Militares apócrifos: Iban por Leyzaola." *Zeta* 1858, November 6–12.

Index